# History of the Ancient Indian Rituals

# HISTORY OF THE ANCIENT INDIAN RITUALS

Navneet Dugar

2008

CYBER TECH PUBLICATIONS
4264/3, Ansari Road, Daryaganj, New Delhi-110002 (India)
Ph.: 011-23244078. Fax: 011-23280028
E-Mail: cyberpublicationsdelhi@yahoo.com

# HISTORY OF THE ANCIENT INDIAN RITUALS

**Navneet Dugar**



First Edition 2008



*Published by :*

**G.S. Rawat** for **Cyber Tech Publications**
4264/3, Ansari Road, Daryaganj, New Delhi-110002 (India)
Ph.: 011-23244078. Fax: 011-23280028
E-Mail: cyberpublicationsdelhi@yahoo.com

*Printed at :* **Amit Enterprises**, Maujpur, Delhi, (9810878184)

# Preface

The Hindus have Varna System. It is not at all caste-equivalent. It simply indicates a social division based on Gunas There exists all over the world one sort of division or the other in a society, which is so inevitable for social growth and prosperity. Each individual is possessed of a particular ability by nature. One may well perform a physical labour, another may be more of a thinker and some may be artistic some inclined to technology, music. Medicine, trade, industry or any other material or spiritual activity. The Lord speaking on action and inaction in Geeta (IV-13) says,'the four Varnas have been created by Him according to differentiation of Gunas and Karmas.' These Varnas are 1-Brahman; 2-Kshatriya; 3-Vaishya; and 4-Sudra.

# Contents

# 1

# OUR RITUALS CAN BRING OUT LOST ORIGINS

## On the Eve of RSA Asvamedha Yajna

*Yajna, Mahayajna, Asvamedha Yajna:* The mahayajnas used to be performed to purify the social life. But, when the need for complete renovation of the nation (Rashtra) and that of the environment was felt, there was a tradition of Asvamedha yajnas at the universal level. In ancient times, simple yajnas used to play an important role in inner refinement and self-purification.

Thus, the yajnas have been classified into three categories; viz, yajna, mahayajna and Asvamedha yajna. The magnitude of their results also increases in the same order. The importance of yajna has been described in detail in Srimad Bhagwat Purana. Several such events have been described in this scripture, which acquaint us fully with the enormous power of yajna. According to this Purana, the universe was created with the help of yajna. This phenomenon has been described as follows.

In an answer to a query, Brahmaji describes the form of yajna as follows:

> *"Yadasya nabhyam caturhortram ca sattam"*
>
> *—Bhagwat, Skandha 2, Addhyaya 6, slokas 22,23,24.*

*Meaning:* "When I was born from the navel of the all-pervading Brahma, I did not see any articles for oblation except the body of the Purush (the male God). Therefore, I created the animals, vegetables, Kusa (a sacred grass), the sacred land where gods can perform yajna and the time, which is full of virtues (meaning the time in which the virtues are worshipped). Then I created all the ingredients of yajna, herbs, milk fats, sweetmeats, metals like gold, clay (earth), water, four Vedas (Rig, Yaju, Sama and Atharva), four Brahmans, and such procedures too by which the yajna may be performed." There is description in the Brahma Purana (Purva Bhag, Addhyaya 1, sloka 5,6,7) that in the beginning of the Kalpa, a very sacred mahayajna was performed for one thousand years.

The organizer of this mahayajna was Brahmaji himself accompanied by His wife Ila. The role of Shamitraka was performed by intelligent and radiant Mrityudev himself. The king Daksha felt very sorry when his yajna was spoiled by her daughter Sati by her self-immolation. After begging pardon from Shiva, he organized Visad yajna as atonement for his sin. Its description is found in slokas 16 to 18 of seventh chapter in the fourth Skandha of Bhagwat; as follows:

Thus Daksha got his sin pardoned, and after consulting Brahmaji, he expanded the work of yajna, beautifully, by taking into account all the aspects, *e.g.* upadhyaya, ritvija, *agni* for yajna, etc. A Purodasa (an oblation made of ground rice and offered in kapalas or vessels) of three kapalas was offered to Lord Vishnu. In order to complete the yajna, offerings were given to virtuous Brahmans to purify the chief stalwarts. When the Adhwaryu took the Havi in his hand and meditated on God after performing havan with pure intelligence along with the Yajman, he sighted the Virat Purush (Lord Vishnu)".

Rishabhdev is considered the incarnation of God. This country has been named as Bharatvarsha in the memory of his son Bharat. The latter made this country a sacred land through the performance of mahayajnas.

Wherever the mahayajnas were performed, Tirthas (holy places) were established. After removing the suffix 'pra' from 'Prayag', what remains is the word 'yag', (which means yajna).

This place has become Tartharaj (the king of Tirthas) because a large number of yajnas have been performed there. The Dasasvamedha Ghat (a bathing place on the bank of the river Ganga) in Kashi (Varanasi) is a proof of the fact that ten major yajnas had been performed there. This is why so much holiness has been attributed to this place. It is mentioned in part 4 of Skand Purana that the king of Kashi, Divodas performed yajan of the Lord Mahayagyeshwar in Kashi city by ten Asvamedha yajnas. From that day, that place became famous as Dasasvamedha Tirtha. Previously, it was known as Rudrasarovar.

The sages asked reverend Sootaji about the place, time, type etc of the first mahayajna. Whatever Sootaji said, in an answer to this question, is described in the second chapter in the first part of "Vayu Purana", as follows:

> *"The creator in the primordial state (i.e. before the actual creation of this universe), performed the sacred yajna for thousands of years with an aim to create this world. In this mahayajna, indeed Tapa (penance) was Yajman and Brahmaji Himself was Brahma of the yajna. In this long and grand yajna of great souls, the 'Nemi' (wheel) of Dharma revolved so much that it shattered and hence that area which was worshipped by the sages and saints, was named as Naimisharanya.*

The fourth sloka in the first chapter in first skandha of Bhagwat says-

> *Naimishe ninishiksetre rshayah saunkadayah*
>
> *Satra swargaya lokaya sahastra samamasat*

*Meaning:* Once upon a time, 88000 sages including Shaunak performed a 10,000 years long mahayajna in the sacred area of Naimisharanya, with a desire to achieve Heaven. It is the sacred effect of these yajnas that this area is supposed to be sacred even today.

A description is found about Ayodhya-that this city was the capital of Suryavanshi (descendants of Sun) king Vaivashwat

Manu, who established himself as a universal monarch. He used to indulge himself always in Mahayajnas and Dana (donations). That is why in his reign no one suffered from the pangs of death, disease and old age, in the city of Ayodhya. The rewards of Asvamedha yajna are far more purifying. In the medieval period, Asvamedha was thought to be the war for the expansion of the empire, whereas it used to be a special mahayajna performed for the benefit of the society and the nation, in the earlier ages.

The pages of Vedas, Upanishads, Darsans and Puranas are filled with the description of the importance of these Asvamedha yajnas. In ancient times, they were performed to achieve ecological balance, to seek the grace of God and to unite the nation. The writer of a scripture says that one gets the same sacred reward by participating in Asvamedha yajna as that achieved by visiting the holy place Gaya, taking a holy dip in rivers Ganga and Yamuna and performing one crore oblations (-Matsya Purana).

*Ima nu kam bhuvana sishadhamendrasca visve ca devah*
*Adityairindrah sagano marudbhirasmabhyam bheshaja karat*
*Yajnam ca nastanvam ca prajam cadityairindrah-*
*Sahasishadhati —Yajur Veda 25-46*

*Meaning: Certainly, the whole world gets joy (by performing Asvamedha yajna). Indra and all the Gods alongwith their Ganas (attendants), accompanied by twelve Adityas and forty nine Marutas make the herbs beneficial. Majestic Indrayajna (for ecological balance) surcharges the bodies of the performers and their children with superior virtues. —Mahidhar Bhashya*

*Sarvan ha vai kaman apnoti*
*Yo Asvamedhen yajate —Shatpatha13/4/1/1*

*Meaning:* Those who perform Asvamedha yajna, all their desires are fulfilled.

*Yajnenasvamedhenayuh kalpatam.*

*One's life span is increased by performing Asvamedha yajna.*
*—Mahidhar Bhashya 22-23*

*Oh dear! The sacred reward of participating in that Asvamedha yajna is matchless, in which the body of Nakul (a mongoose) became golden after it rolled its body in the water left over after eating by ritvijas (priests) who came to conduct the Asvamedha yajna there.*
*—Mahabharata*

*Rashtram va AsvamedhahViryam va asvah*
*—Satapatha Brahmana 13/1/6*

The aim of Asvamedha is to increase the power and strength of the habitants of the nation, and the nations at large.

*The king Vasu performed the Asvamedha. Vrahaspati Upadhyay was its Hota. The three sons of Prajapati, the superior sages Kapil, Katha, Taittari, Kanva, etc. were its rtvikas. This sacred yajna was completed without hurting anyone. "Na tatra pasu ghatoabhuta"-(meaning) no animal was sacrificed therein.*
*—Mahabharata santiparva (3/336)*

The following description is found in chapter 14 of fourth Skandha of Bhagwat Mahapurana. The king Vena had forbidden the performance of yajna etc in his kingdom. He said-"All the gods reside in the king and hence the people should praise and worship me only". In reply to this the sages tried to convince the king Vena thus:

*"Oh king! The entire universe and the gods reside in the yajna. The priests perform yajan of the God who is full of Vedas (knowledge), wealth and devotion, through unique yajnas performed by different methods for your benefit and the prosperity of the people. You are in a position to help in such yajnas. Oh brave man if the people in your kingdom perform yajna, all the gods, who are indeed the different forms of Sri Narayana,*

*will get satisfied and will grant the desired result to all. Therefore, you should not disregard these yajnas".*

When he did not agree even after much persuasion and still remained adamant in his opposition to yajna, the sages cursed him so that king Vena died. After that, his arms were churned which gave birth to king Prithu.

*"Adhadiksat raja tu hayamedha satena sah*

*Brahmavartta manahksetre yatra praci saraswati"*

***Meaning:*** After that Prithu promised to organize one hundred Asvamedha yajnas. These yajnas were performed where the river Saraswati flows towards the west and which is the area of Brahma and Manu, normally called Brahmavarta. It is a sad story that in the medieval period confusion was created about animal sacrifice in these yajnas; partly due to the foreign invasions and partly due to the gradual decline of the true vedic culture. In this context, Pandit Beniramji in his hook "Yagya mimansa" and reverend Satavalekarji have given the correct clarification. The learned Satvalekarji, in his book, writes:

*"The gods of upright thinking and the demon animals of evil tendencies, both exist in the human body. They are shapeless in the human body, but when the evil tendencies, assume the form they become the animals of the visible world.*

That is to say-"It is the evil motives that condemn the human soul to slide back to sub-human (animal) forms. The arrogance results in the shape of hawk. The vulture is the representative of greed. The cunningness leads to birth as a dog. The ignorant souls have to go in the form of owl or donkey. When the animal-like tendencies become universal and assume the powerful shape as that of a horse, the Asvamedha yajnas are organized. The mode of sacrificing these animal-like tendencies is called Asvamedha". The references, about the purity of preparation of Asvamedha yajna that are available in the ancient scriptures also do not enjoin the killing of any creature in these yajnas.

***The Hindu Dharma Kosha States:*** "Three Ishtis (worships) of *Savita* (the Sun) used to be performed daily in the morning, afternoon and evening from the day the horse of Asvamedha used to be sent for global conquest. ***Savita*** used to be worshipped by the name of Satya-prasava in the morning, by the name of Prasavita in the afternoon and by the name of Asavita in the evening. This fact has been described in Ashwalayan shroutsutra (10/6/8), Latyayan shroutsutra (9/9/10) and Katyayan shroutsutra (20/2/6). "This means that Gayatri used to be worshipped for the entire year, following which Asvamedha yajna used to be performed for three days.

> *Gandharvo asya rasanam gribhanat Suradaswam vasvo niratashta.*
> *—Rig Veda 1/163/2*
>
> *-Vasus have created the horse of yajna through the Sun. (It is, therefore, necessary to worship Sun (Gayatri) for the success of Asvamedha).*

It is in this form that one should participate in the Asvamedha yajnas and attain peace and happiness in one's life.

## Dasaratha's Desire for a Child

Ramacandra appeared in the Iksvaku dynasty. He is known as Iksvaku Kuladhana. Kula means "dynasty" and dhana means "property" or "valuable jewel." So he is the jewel of the Iksvaku dynasty. Dasaratha was known as such because he could fight in ten directions simultaneously.

Dasaratha was such a great fighter that sometimes Indra would summon for him when there was a fight with the demons. So Dasaratha would go to the heavenly planets and fight with the demons. And these demons were so expert with maya, they would create darkness, expand into various forms etc. So Dasaratha would fight in ten directions, and when you looked at his ratha, his chariot, it would look as though there were ten kings and ten chariots fighting simultaneously. Dasa means "ten" and ratha means "chariot". That is how he got the name Dasaratha. So Dasaratha was famous for fighting for demigods and righteous kings. And he married Kausalya. From Kausalya, only one daughter was born. She was named Shanti, or "peace." But Dasaratha had no peace, because he only had one daughter, and that daughter would only get married and go to another dynasty. The Vedic system is that when a woman marries, she belongs to the husband's gotra or family line. So if Shanti married to another dynasty, she would belong to it. What about the Iksvaku dynasty?

Dasaratha was so worried. Then he married Sumitra. At least Kausalya had a daughter, but Sumitra had no child. Then Dasaratha was getting old. He gave up the idea of producing dynasties. As he was getting older he saw that some less powerful kings were doing small yajnas, so he did big yajnas. They were trying to get their name known, because once Dasaratha died Kosala would be broken. The kingdom of Kosala started all the way from what they now call the Dalai lama's line. From up in the north, in Tibet, all the way down to the river Godavari in Andhra Pradesh. So this was Kosala, practically it was the whole of India, not the democratic India but the Vedic India. So he was very worried that this kingdom will be broken to pieces and some small-timers will become emperors. Then Vasistha advised him to go to Kaikeya. This kingdom was right on the border of Afghanistan. They now call it the Sind region. Kaikeyi was the only daughter of the king of Kaikeya. The king's name was also Kaikeya. And when Dasaratha came for marriage negotiation, Kaikeya told him, "You have two queens, and they both have no children. Now you will marry my daughter, but what will happen to her if the other wives have children?"

Dasaratha replied, "I don't think they will have children because they have had none up to now. I am also getting old. They're not going to get any child. Only Kaikeyi will get a child." So Kaikeya said, "That's all right, but you must give this in writing." There is a system in the Ksatriya marriage known as kanya-sulka. Sulka means "will". When you accept a virgin in marriage, you must give in writing what properties she will enjoy as your wife if you are a ksatriya. This is kanya-sulka, the "will of dowry." So Dasaratha wrote kanya-sulka. He said, "Whoever is born to Kaikeyi will enjoy my kingdom, even if my other wives produce children later." This kanya-sulka was known to three people. Of course, now we all know it, but at that time only three people knew it. Vasistha knew it, Dasaratha knew it, and Kaikeya knew it. It was kept a secret, because otherwise they would blame Dasaratha, "What is this? He is giving the kingdom to a younger woman." So this kanya-sulka was kept secret.

But at the time of the marriage, due to great attachment, Kaikeya told his daughter this secret, that whoever is your son will rule this kingdom. Kaikeyi kept this at heart. Once Vasistha advised Dasaratha to perform asvamedha-yajna. He was telling him, "If you perform asvamedha-yajna, then all the demigods will personally come to accept the oblations." There are two kinds of offering oblations to the yajna. One is that Agni will take the oblations and offer it to the different destinations. Another is that the devas will personally come in the sacrificial arena. They will stand in the sky holding their hands open, and when you offer in their name in the fire then the harvest will get up from the fire and go into their hands. And they will eat it right there in front of everyone,. These types of sacrifices are considered first-class, because the devas have come in person. So Dasaratha should perform asvamedha, and all the devas will come. And then Dasaratha will tell them, "You have your kingdom only because of my fighting. So why don't you continue my dynasty and give me blessings that I can get some son?" That was the plan. There was a big arrangement for asvamedha-yajna, and wherever Dasaratha's horse went, no-one objected.

Asvamedha-yajna means that you have to select a horse with certain lakshanas or qualities. The ears have to be a certain way, the nose a certain way. There has to be a black part behind the tail. The hooves have to be a certain shape, 35 degrees bent. There is a whole description in karma-khanda. So you have to find out that horse, and after finding it you have to tie a golden leaf on his head. There it will be written, "This horse belongs to King Dasaratha. He will perform asvamedha-yajna, so everyone should donate liberally. And whoever stops this horse will have to meet the army of King Dasaratha." So this horse will go around the whole world, and if any king dares to stop the horse there will be one army which is following about 100 metres behind the horse.

They will have to meet that army. This army would consist of the best fighters in the army, all the generals, and if one can defeat that then more army would be sent. In this way the challenger would have to fight and prove that he is the emperor. So asvamedha-yajna was already started, and then when the yajna was going on, Sumantra (the minister of Dasaratha) came to Dasaratha and said, "I remember one incident when Sanat-kumara came to our assembly, when you were a prince." At that time Dasaratha was not married, and Sanat-kumara was visiting Dasaratha's father, Aja. Sanat-kumara made some predictions. "Maharaja Dasaratha will become very famous throughout the three worlds, and he will perform a putra-kamesti yajna, a sacrifice for getting a son. So in this sacrifice, the yajna-purusha, the personification of fire, will come there and give him some sweet rice. And out of this sweet rice Dasaratha will get the Supreme Lord as his sons." This was predicted by Sanat-kumara.

At that time Dasaratha was just an unmarried prince, a brahmacari. So Sumantra was a very old man and he suddenly remembered this. He came to Dasaratha and said, "You are doing asvamedha for getting a son, but Sanat-kumara told you that you should do putra-kamesti." So then there was confusion over which yajna should be performed. In Treta-yuga everything was yajna. For material benefits, for spiritual realization, for anything tretayam yajato makhaih. Makha means "yajna". Now Dasaratha got confused. So he went to Vasistha's house and prostrated himself before him. "Guru maharaja, we have spent 60% of the treasury, and now we come to know that this is not the proper yajna, that there is another yajna. How am I supposed to do this?" So then Vasistha said, "Oh yes, I remember too now. Sanat-kumara said this.

It is not a very expensive yajna, but the purohit, the priest who performs the yajna must be a very special person. That is the difficulty. That person must have not seen a woman until the time of his marriage. He should not have even known what a woman is. Such a great personality must perform the yajna. Then only can the putra-kamesti be performed with the purnahoti and we will get a son." Then Dasaratha said, "You must tell me where this person is." Vasistha was a walking encyclopedia, because he had been there three lifetimes with the same remembrance. There is no-one in this world who knows better than Vasistha. So Vasistha said, "Yes, there is a person like that."

Dasaratha said, "Who is this person? He has never seen a woman or known what a woman is until marriage? At least he must have known about his mother! What kind of a person is he, that he has never heard of a woman yet he has taken birth?"

## The Queen-Horse Copulation: Ritual of the Asvamedha Yajna

The *asvamedha yajna* was the grand horse sacrifice which Aryan (Hindu) kings conducted to celebrate their supremacy and for the prosperity & fertility of their kingdoms. The queen-horse copulation ritual was sometimes conducted during this sacred rite; the relevant Hindu scriptural quotes are presented below.

I. The sexual ritual of the *asvamedha yajna* quoted from the Vedas (*Satapatha Brahmana*).

II. Lord Rama's mom & co-moms participate in the queen-horse sexual ritual of the *asvamedha* in the Valmiki Ramayana.

### *The Sexual Ritual of the Asvamedha Yajna Quoted from the Vedas*

The priests supervising the *asvamedha*: the efficient (*adhvaryu*), overseer (*brahman*), cantor (*udgatri*) and the invoker (*hotri*). The king's wives which participate in the queen-horse copulation ceremony of the *asvamedha*: the chief wife (*mahishi*), favourite wife, rejected wife and the fourth wife. The *Satapatha Brahmana*, quoted below, offers clear instructions on how the queen-horse copulation ritual of the *asvamedha* is to be conducted; the king's chief wife (the *mahishi*) is to copulate with the carcass of the horse while the priests and all the participants curse each other in degenerate language:

> *"A cloth, an upper cloth, and gold is what they spread out for the horse, and on that they 'quiet' him. When the sacrificial animals have been 'quieted', the (king's) wives come up with water for washing the feet—four wives, and a maiden as the fifth, and four hundred women attendants. When the water for washing the feet is ready, they make the chief queen (Mahishi) lie down next to the horse, and they cover the two of them up with the upper cloth as they say the verse, 'Let the two of us cover ourselves in the world of heaven', for the world of heaven is where they 'quiet' the sacrificial animal. Then they draw out the penis of the horse and place it in the vagina of the chief queen, while she says, 'May the vigorous virile male, the layer of seed, lay the seed'; this she says for sexual intercourse. While they are lying there, the sacrificer insults the horse by saying, 'Lift up her thighs and put it in her rectum.' No one insults (the sacrificer) back, lest there should be someone to act as a rival against the sacrificer.*
>
> *The efficient (Adhvaryu) then insults the maiden: 'Hey, maiden, hey, maiden, the little female bird...' and she insults him back: 'Hey, efficient, hey, efficient, that little bird....' And then the overseer (Brahman) insults the*

*chief queen: 'Hey, chief queen, hey, chief queen, your mother and father climb to the top of a tree....' She has as her attendants a hundred daughters of kings; they insult the overseer in return: 'Hey, overseer, hey, overseer, your mother and your father play in the top of a tree....'*

*Then the cantor (Udgatri) insults the king's favourite wife: 'Hey, favourite, hey, favourite wife, raise her up erect....' She has as her attendants a hundred royal women; they insult the cantor in return: 'Hey, cantor, hey, cantor, raise* him *up erect....' Then the invoker (Hotri) insults the rejected wife: 'Hey, rejected wife, hey, rejected wife, when inside her tight crack....' She has as her attendants a hundred daughters of bards and village headmen; they insult the invoker in return: 'Hey, invoker, hey, invoker, when the gods see that miserable penis....'*

*Then the carver (Kshatri) insults the fourth wife: 'Hey, fourth wife, hey, fourth wife, when the deer eats the barley, (the farmer) does not hope to nourish the animal....' She has as her attendants a hundred daughters of carvers and charioteers; they insult the carver in return: 'Hey, carver, hey, carver, when the deer eats the barley, (the farmer) does not hope to nourish the animal....' These insulting speeches are for all kinds of attainment, for through the horse sacrifice all desires are achieved.*

*Thinking, 'With all kinds of speech we will achieve all kinds of desires', they make the chief queen get up. Then the women walk back the way they came, and the others utter at the end a sweet-smelling verse, the verse that begins, 'I praise Dadhikravan.' For the life-span and the gods go out of those who speak impure speech in the sacrifice. Thus they purify their speech to keep the gods from going out of the sacrifice."*
*—Satapatha Brahmana*

### *Queen-horse Sexual Ritual of the Asvamedha in the Valmiki Ramayana*

To ensure the birth of sons, King Dasaratha conducted both the *asvamedha* and the *putrakamesti yajnas.* The following quote from the *Valmiki Ramayana* details the first of the two sacrifices that King Dasaratha conducted—the *asvamedha yajna,* in particular the queen-horse sexual portion of the sacrifice. Although all three of King Dasaratha's wives were united with the carcass of the horse, Rama's mom Kausalya was the one who had the honour of spending a whole night with the dead animal's genitals plugged in her vagina:

> *"The prescribed victims—snakes, birds, the horse, and aquatic animals—were bound at the place of immolation; each was dedicated to a specific divinity as is set forth in the ritual texts. The priests then bound them all to the posts in the manner set forth in the ritual texts. Three hundred beasts in addition to Dasaratha's jewel of a horse were bound there to the sacrificial posts. Kausalya walked reverently all around the horse and then with the greatest joy cut it with three knives. Her mind unwavering in her desire for righteousness, Kausalya passed one night with the horse.*
>
> *The priests—the hotr, the adhvaryu, and the udgatr—saw to it that the second and the juniormost of the king's wives, as well as his chief queen, were united with the horse. Then the officiating priest, who was extremely adept and held his senses in check, removed the fat of the horse and cooked it in the manner prescribed in the ritual texts. At the proper time and in accordance with the ritual prescriptions, the lord of men then sniffed the fragrance of the smoking fat, thereby freeing himself from sin. Then, acting in unison, the sixteen brahman officiating priests threw the limbs of the horse into the fire, in accordance with the ritual injunctions. In other sacrifices, the oblation is offered upon branches of the*

> *plaksa tree, but in the Horse Sacrifice alone the apportionment of the victim is made on a bed of reeds. The Horse Sacrifice is known as the Three-Day Rite; for both the kalpasutra and the brahmanas refer to the Horse Sacrifice as a rite lasting for three days."*
> *—Ramayana*

## The Universe as a Sacrificial Horse

The commencement of the Brihadaranyaka Upanishad is a description of a symbolic placement of the parts of the individual in the cosmic quarters, with the spiritual intention of an undivided meditation, where the subject commingles with the object. The peculiar technique, adopted here in this Upanishad, is ritualistic as it is characteristic of the Brahmanas in the Vedas, and this technique is supposed to be adopted in the case of every individual character in its correlation with the universe. Here the individual concerned is the horse of the Asvamedha Sacrifice, which is the object of consecration and while, exoterically considered, it is one of the items in the Asvamedha Yajna, and it becomes a part of an external act, in the Upanishad it becomes a piece of contemplation, which is the avowed purpose of the Upanishad to convert every act into a mode of contemplation, to transform every object into the Universal Subject. This is the aim of the Upanishad finally; and for this purpose various methods are prescribed. One method is, here, in this Brihadaranyaka Upanishad, at its beginning, the transformation of the ritual technique into an inward contemplation of the Spirit.

> ***Aum:*** *usa va asvasya medhyasya sirah, suryas caksuh, vatah pranah, vyattam agnir vaisvanarah; samvatsara atmasvasya medhyasya, dyauh pristham, antariksam udaram, prithivi pajasyam, disah parsve, avantaradisah parsavah, ritavongani, masas cardhamasas ca parvani, ahoratrani pratisthah, naksatrany asthini, nabho mamsani; uvadhyam sikatah, sindhavo gudah, yakric ca klomanas ca parvatah, osadhayas ca vanaspatayas*

*ca lomani, udyan purvardhah nimlocan jaghanardhah, yad vijrimbhate tad vidyotate, yad vidhunute tat stanayati, yan mehati tad varsati; vag evasya vak.*

## Verses with Diacritical Marks

This is the first Mantra which is written in prose, the style of the Brahmana portion of the Vedas. Usa va asvasya medhyasya sirah: The dawn is the head of this sacred horse. The idea is that every part of the essential item in the sacrifice is to be identified, correspondingly, part by part, with the sections of the universe outside. In worship, especially that performed in temples, we have also a similar technique adopted, which is known as the Nyasa method-the placement. Nyasa means placement. The parts of the body of the worshipper are correspondingly placed in the parts of the body of the deity, so that the distinction between the worshipper and the deity is abolished.

The two become one. Such a Nyasa is done here. The head of the sacrificial horse must be contemplated as the dawn. Here, the dawn does not necessarily mean a particular time of the eve of the rise of the sun at any particular place, but the eastern part, mostly conceivable by the mind, as the world, as it can be visualised by us to the extent possible. Now, if it is not possible to conceive it in this manner, it can be taken literally as the eastern part of the world where we are living. The dawn is the head of the consecrated horse. The dawn, the beginning of the day, is the head, because the head is the beginning of the body. That is the similarity. The day begins with the dawn, and the body begins with the head. This is the similarity conceived here.

The eyes may be compared to the sun. The similarity is very obvious, because the sun is the eye of the day through which perception is made possible; and the eyes, of course, in the body, are the means of every kind of visual perception.

The Cosmic Wind, the Air that pervades, is the Prana within. We should identify the Prana within the horse with the

Air that is outside, because the two are essentially the same, one working in the world outside and another working within the body of the individual, here, the horse.

The mouth is the Agni Vaisvanara. In some Upanishads, the Aitareya particularly, we have another cosmological description where we are told that from the Cosmic Virat, Fire broke out through the mouth. And the organ of speech is supposed to be presided over, in every case, by the principle of Fire. So the mouth of the individual horse, here, may be identified with the cosmic fire which is Vaisvanara. Vaisvanara is a word which has two or three meanings. It is a fire principle which is hiddenly present in all things, the principle of fire which manifests itself as the visible fire outside, which, again, is sometimes identified with the Cosmic Being. Vaisva-Nara means the Cosmic-Man, and the derivative of this word is Vaisvanara. The Vaisvanara is the Cosmic Person who represents the energy of all things, manifested outwardly as the fire principle, energy secondarily manifest, again, as the power of speech. And so, the mouth is to be identified with the Vaisvanara, the principle of Divine Fire.

The body is the entire process of the year. The Time process is the body, because the body has many limbs, many parts; and likewise, time can be segmented into parts-past, present, future; and if it is concretised further, it becomes capable of division into years, months, days, nights, etc. The comparison is that, as the time has divisible parts, so the body also has divisible parts. The two are identified.

The Sky is the back, as it were. The comparison is that it is on the top, above the body.

The Atmosphere is the belly, because it is hollow, as it were.

The Earth is the hoofs, on which the animal is placed.

The sides are the quarters of the heavens.

The sides of the body, consisting of the bones, may be compared to the intermediary quarters, which are between the main quarters.

The seasons are the limbs of the body. Even as the Samvatsara, or the year, is constituted of various seasons, the body is constituted of various limbs.

The divisions of the year, namely the month, the half-month, the bright half and the dark half of the month, etc., are the parts of the entire physical body, just as the year may be supposed to be placed on the parts consisting of the months, days, etc.

The day and night are the essence of the calculation of Time, and, therefore, the year may be supposed to be rooted in the calculation or conception of day and night. Thus is also the body rooted, or placed, or supported by the feet. So, the day and night are said to be the feet of the horse.

The constellations in the sky may be compared to the whitish bones which are spread out, as it were, in all parts of the body.

The clouds are the flesh of the whole body.

The sand that you can see anywhere, physically, in the world, may be compared to the half-digestcd food that is in a seed condition in the stomach.

The rivers are the veins and the arteries.

The spleen and the liver are the mountains, as it were, which are something like an elevation in the body within.

The trees and the plants and the shrubs may be compared to the hairs of the body.

The sun, rising, is the earlier, fore part of the body.

The hind part of the body may be compared to the sun that is about to set.

The horse's yawning is something like the lightening.

The shaking of the members of the body is like the thunder in the rainy season.

Its making water is like the rainfall.

The sound that it makes, neighing, is the principle of speech.

This description of the Cosmos as Horse is entirely symbolic, and highly complicated to conceive, because the purpose of the Upanishad is to bring out the psychological element that is present in the comparison that is made between the physical counterparts of the body of the horse, and the body of the universe outside. The difference between the horse conceived here, or to make a wider comparison, the case of any individual, for the matter of that, the distinction between the body of an individual, whether of an animal or a human being, and the world outside, is psychological. If it were not psychological and is really physical, an identification would be impossible. That one person is different from another person, is a psychological division. It is not physical. We have had occasion to discuss this subject earlier in some of our discourses.

I shall give you a small example of how physical division does not exist. It is only imaginary. The bodies of people are constituted of the five elements-earth, water, fire, air and ether. Your body, my body and everybody's body is constituted of only these things, nothing else-earth, water, fire, air, ether. If the body of one individual, 'A', is substantially the same as the body of another individual, 'B', because of its being formed of the same five elements, what is the reason for the distinction or the difference that we make between one body and another body? It is that which exists between the two bodies. The space is the cause. But space is a part of the very constitution of the body itself. So, how does this become an element of distinction? That which we regard as spatial, and, perhaps, the only reason for the distinction that we usually make between one body and another, is an element essentially present in the constitution of the body itself. So to say that space is the distinctive mark of division between one body and another is logically not tenable. It is a peculiar thinking of the minds of people that makes it impossible for them to feel the coextensive nature of bodies, as if they are connected at the bottom, like the waters of the ocean. Inasmuch as physical distinctions are not tenable ultimately, the distinctions are to be regarded as purely mental, or psychological; and therefore, a mental act can abolish the mental distinction that has been thus created.

The entire psychology of meditation is nothing but a setting right of errors in thought; and the details of these methods we shall be considering as we proceed further. So, to come to the point, this distinction between the individual unit and the Universal Substance is to be abolished for the purpose of the removal of the sorrow of the individual. Meditation is the technique of the removal of sorrow in the sense that sorrow is caused by the segregation of the individual from the world outside. For this purpose, one enters into the technique of meditation. Now, here, the context being sacrifice, we are given a method which is ritualistic in its nature, and thus the ritualistic horse of the Asvamedha Sacrifice becomes an object of contemplation, literally, liturgically as an animal in the sacrifice, but psychologically and spiritually, as an element like any other element in creation as a whole. The subject is continued in the next Mantra.

> *ahar va asvam purastan mahima nvajayata. tasya purve samudre yonih, ratrir enam pascan mahima nvajayata, tasyapare samudre yonih, etau va asvam mahimanav abhitah sambabhuvatuh hayo bhutva devan avahat, vaji gandharvan, arvasuran, asvo manusyan; samudra evasya bandhuh, samudro yonih.*

Again, this is a ritualistic peculiarity of the Brahmana, concerned with the Asvamedha Sacrifice. Mahima is a term used to designate certain sacrificial vessels, gold and silver, placed in the performance of the sacrifice. The daytime may be compared, says the Upanishad, to the golden cup that is placed in the front of the horse.

The eastern ocean, by which what is intended is the farthest eastern limit of the conceivable world, is the base. The world ends with the ocean. That is how we have to think, because we cannot think more than that. What can a child think? If you ask a baby to think of the world, it will think only up to the ocean. Beyond that, no thought is possible. But this is only a beginning of the method of extending the thought to further and further limits, until we reach the limit of the psychological horizon. The idea is that the eastern ocean is to be regarded as the limit, the farthest possible for the mind in contemplating the horizon of the universe. That is the limit of the horse.

Similarly, the rear part may be compared to the night, and the western ocean, which is the other side of conceivable limit. Thus, the horse is enveloped, encircled by the ritualistic elements, which means to say, in this process of contemplation, the parts of the world are contemplated as associated with the world which is, here, the object of contemplation. Just as the parts in a sacrifice are associated with the element in the sacrifice which is the horse, the parts of the world or the universe are to be conceived as associated with it as parts arc associated with the whole.

Here is a very difficult passage whose meaning is very obscure. But evidently what its meaning is, is this, that there is a gradual ascent and descent of the degree in the concept of the horse, or rather, the concept of the universe. When you think of the universe as an object of contemplation, you think of it in various degrees-the gross, the subtle and the causal. And the commentators, especially Acharya shankara, and others, tell us that the horse mentioned here is the Prajapati, or the Creator of the cosmos. It is not merely the animal in the sacrifice. That is how we have to think in meditation. So, as there is a descent from the causal condition to the subtle condition, and from the subtle to the gross, and from the gross to the variegated forms of manifestation in this world, so also is the horse to be contemplated in the various aspects of its functions, and the functions are mentioned here in respect of the ritual of the Asvamedha Sacrifice.

When the horse becomes the vehicle of the celestials, it is called 'Hayo'. When it becomes the vehicle of Gandharvas, demi-gods, above the earth, it is called 'Vaji', a peculiar name ascribed to the horse. When it becomes the vehicle of the demons, it becomes 'Arva'. It becomes the ordinary horse, Asva, when it becomes the vehicle of human beings. The substance of all these things is the ocean. Here, the great commentator, Acharya shankara, tells us the ocean means the Cosmic Soul. It does not mean the ocean which is water. The Universal Soul is the basis of the world, as the horse is the basis of the entire sacrifice. It is the substratum; and every activity-name, form, action-is something like a wave in the ocean. But the wave is the ocean. The wave is in the ocean, or on the ocean, as you may think of it. Likewise, all actions, name and form, rise and subside within the bosom of the universal Soul, so that you may say, just as waves are the ocean, actions are the Universal Soul. So the universe is the ocean, or rather, the Universal Soul is the ocean. That is the deepest and the nearest associate. The greatest friend of man is God. That is what is intended here. And He is the support, ultimate resort and refuge-Samudra evasya bandhuh, samudro yonih

**Yagna, Dana and Gotra**

Every society has passed through a tribal stage at some time or the other. Some societies are still in the tribal stage for instance the Australian aborigines, and the Red Indians living in the preserves or nearer home in India the Nagas and Bhils, etc.,. This stage is normally characterized by a collective way of living where property is under common ownership of the tribes the institution of monogamous family has not yet been accepted and where livelihood depends on tending of cattle, collection of wild fruits and roots and shifting, subsistence agriculture.

**The Tribal Way of Life was of Collective Activity**

This Collective way of life is conducive to the birth of many of the folklore and rituals of later stages of development when the tribal way of life is no more. The origins of these folklore and rituals is normally lost and hence they are looked upon as timeless and having divine sanction. The main reason for their origin being lost is the absence of a written language during the tribal stage when most of the folklore is born. Due to the absence of a written language, ideas had to be passed on from generation to generation by means of oral narration. Although the origin of most rituals is lost to us, the nature of the rituals that we perform today is at times eloquent about their origins.

## Our Rituals can Bring out Lost Origins

A hard look at these rituals can bring out many of their lost origins. The practice of oral transmission of knowledge due to the absence of a literary medium itself becomes a tradition in some cases. In India our traditions of smriti (remembrance) and Shurti (listening) and sloka pathan (oral narration) are instances of this. Even during our prayers and sacrificial invocations (Yagna) we rarely see the officiating priests reading out the prayer (slokas and Mantras).

These are generally recited or chanted. In this chapter we take up a set of traditions which we observe in today's society and try to reconstruct the social ethos in which they could have originated. The issues we take up are the ritual of fire sacrifice (Yagna) our traditional practice of charity Dana), the concept of Gotra which is a consideration while arranging marriages, the institution of monogamous marriage (Dwanda-Vivaha) and the worship of the Mother Goddess.

## Yagna as a Sacrifice

Yagna is a term we normally hear in today's society. It is popularly understood as a fire sacrifice involving the offering of grains, clarified butter, sandalwood etc, to a fire. This fire is ignited in a special fireplace called the Kund, which literally means a "Pot". Yagna is normally performed with the objective of ushering in prosperity or to avoid disaster. For performing a Yagna a minimum number of five priests are required although many more priests may participate. A Yajna is normally accompanied by mass feeding of people, the food being distributed as Prasad (i.e food which has been sanctified by offering it to the Gods). Rituals similar to yagna are performed during marriage, thread ceremony, vaastu shanti (opening ceremony for a house), etc. when a homa or sacred fire is ignited in a kund. It is widely known that Yagna is a very old tradition in the Hindu religion and it is looked upon as a Vedic ritual. In Vedic literature there are innumerable descriptions of a Yagnas being performed. The origin of the Yagna though lost in history, the rituals associated with it today throw light as to its nature.

## Yagna Centres around a Fireplace

Yagna as a ritual centres around a fireplace. Thus, it obviously must have come into being after fire was domesticated. Even the oldest of the Vedas, the Rig Veda describes a society where man had no fire, no protection against wild beasts, uncertainty of prey and hence the spectre of being perished. This environment is poetically expressed in Vedic literature. Prajapati, the creator suffered abortion in the act of creation and was threatened with extinction. But the world was saved when he was given milk and roasted meat. Praiapati, symbolizes the Aryan man in his most primitive stage, who to the Aryans became a personification of their existence, the memory of which was kept alive by Prajapati being deified in the hymns and songs that constitute the Rig Veda.

### *The Fablised Recollection of the Discovery of Fire*

This fableised recollection also narrates the discovery of making fire and the art of domesticating animals. Agni-fire has been referred to as an eater of dead flesh (Kravyad). Fire also served as a formidable weapon against wild animals and other tribes. It also helped during the hunt for capturing prey and as a shield against the oppressive cold winters of the higher latitudes. Society obtained a respite from the threat of extinction and was lifted above the margin of sustenance.

## Satra the Collective Labour

However man individually was powerless in the fight; against nature, hence whatever was collected or hunted had to be done collectively in large groups (Gana). Thus the auxiliary practices of distribution and consumption were also performed collectively. The absence of the institution of the monogamous marriage and family life as we know it today was another factor that ensured collectivity in all facets of life. The collective labour that was undertaken by Vedic Aryans was termed Satra which means a session, implying collectivity. Thus there was no question of division of society into Varnas and Jatis, so prominent in later Hindu society.

### *The Fireplace was the Nucleus of the Tribal Society*

But the domestication of fire provided a gravitating nucleus for the collective life of the tribe (Gana). As to what the tribal Aryans did around this central fireplace can be guessed from the original Yagna rituals which today are kept alive in the Yagnas as performed by Sadhus (*i.e.* ascetics and hermits).

### All Aspects of Primitive Tribal Collective Life

Contemporary writer describes this Yagna ritual as follows: " The Yagna ritual" is a process in which almost all primitive social life has to be recreated. You have to produce fire by friction of two pieces of wood, to build a cottage where no iron is used but only specific wood and grass, to milk cows, make curds, pound corn with stone (not even a stone mill), boil and cook it,..." This description brings out the fine semblance between the original Yagna ritual and the function of cooking for a tribal household.

In the public Yagnas, like the Rajasuya and Ashwamedha Yagna that were sponsored in later ages by kings, many alterations and refinements were introduced but the original primitive features stuck fast. These royal Yagnas involved the coming together of innumerable Brahmins, the consigning to the central fire, generous quantities of sandalwood, camphor, ghee (clarified butter), grains, and even sacrificial animals and birds. All this corresponds to the central fireplace theory as the origin of the Yagna.

## Fire was an Object of Awe and Fear

Fire had, before its domestication been observed by cavemen and savages only as a formidable destructive medium in the gigantic forest fires, volcanic eruptions etc. Hence it had always been looked upon with fear and awe. But after its domestication, fire spelt prosperity for the nomadic people. Hence it could easily become an object of worship. When the nomadic Aryans had progressed towards settled civilized life the fireplace no longer remained the gravitating nucleus of their daily life. But their social memory continued to be ruled by the past reality.

## *This Lingering Social Memory Perpetuated the Practice of having the Central Fire as the Yagna*

This lingering social memory perpetuated the practice of having the central fire, which in the changed circumstances became a ritualised form of worship. The recollection of the extinct past fermented ideas that invocation of the fire would again spell wealth and prosperity as it had after its domestication.

In the Yagna ritual of later days up to our own age, the hymns sung in the Vedic days are recited, the collective social life is reconstructed in a ritualised rnanner with the fond hope that all this would spell prosperity for the performers of the Yagna. This is one instance of a past being kept alive in later ages by crystallizing it into a ritual.

## Padmini Ekadasi

Suta Gosvami said, "Yudhisthira Maharaja said, 'O Janardana, what is the name of the Ekadasi that occurs during the light fortnight of the extra, leap-year month? How does one observe it properly? Please narrate this to me.

"The Supreme Personality of Godhead, Lord Sri Krishna, replied, 'O Pandava, the meritorious Ekadasi that occurs during the light fortnight of the extra month of leap-year is called Padmini. It is very auspicious. The fortunate soul who observes it with great determination and faith will return to My personal abode. This extra-month Ekadasi is as powerful as I am in nullifying sins. Even four-headed Lord Brahma cannot glorify it sufficiently. Long ago Lord Brahma told Narada about this liberating, sin-removing Ekadasi. Lotus-eyed Lord Krishna became very pleased by the inquiry of Yudhisthira and spoke to him the following pleasing words: 'O king, please listen carefully as I narrate to you the process of fasting on Padmini Ekadasi.' which is rarely done even by great sages.

One should begin his fast on Dasami, the day before Ekadasi, by not eating any urad dal, pink dal, chickpeas, spinach, honey, or sea salt,' and also by not dining in the homes of others or off bell-metal plates. These eight things should be avoided. One should eat only once on Dasami, sleep on the ground, and remain celibate. On Ekadasi, the devotee should rise early in the morning but should not brush his teeth. Then he should thoroughly bathe-in a place of pilgrimage, if possible. While chanting sacred hymns from the Vedas, he should smear his body with cow dung mixed with clay, sesame-seed paste, kusa grass, and the powder of amalaki fruits. Then the devotee should take another thorough bath, after which he should chant the following prayers:

O sacred clay, you have been created by Lord Brahma, purified by Kasyapa Muni, and lifted by Lord Krishna in His form as Varaha, the boar incarnation. O clay, please purify my head, eyes, and other limbs. O clay, I offer my obeisances unto you. Kindly purify me so I may worship the Supreme Lord, Hari.

O cow-dung, you possess medicinal and antiseptic qualities because you have come directly from the stomach of our universal mother, the cow. You can purify the entire planet earth. Please accept my humble obeisances and purify me.

O amalaki fruits, please accept my humble obeisances. You have taken your birth from the saliva of Lord Brahma, and thus by your very presence the entire planet is purified. Kindly cleanse and purify my bodily limbs.

O Supreme Lord Vishnu, O God of gods, O master of the universe, O holder of the conch, disc, club, and lotus, please allow me to bathe in all the holy places of pilgrimage.

Reciting these excellent prayers, chanting mantras to Lord Varuna, and meditating on all the places of pilgrimage located on the banks of the Ganges, one should bathe in whatever body of water is at hand. Then, O Yudhisthira, the devotee should rub his body, thus purifying his mouth, hack, chest, arms, and waist as a prelude to worshipping the Supreme Lord, who wears brilliant yellow garments and gives pleasure to all creatures. By so doing, the devotee will destroy all his sins. Afterwards, he should chant the sacred Gayatri mantra, offer oblations to his forefathers, and then enter a Vishnu temple to worship Narayana, the husband of Laksmi-devi.

If possible, the devotee should then fashion murtis of Radha-Krishna or Shiva-Parvati out of gold and offer them nice devotional worship. He should fill a copper or clay pot with pure water mixed with scents, and then he should cover the pot with a cloth lid and a gold or silver lid, in this way preparing an asana upon which the Radha-Krishna or Shiva-Parvati murtis may sit for worship. According to his capacity, the devotee should then worship these murtis with fragrant incense, a bright ghee lamp, and sandalwood paste, along with camphor, musk, kunkuma, and other scents, as well as selected aromatic flowers like white lotuses and other seasonal blooms, and also very nicely prepared foods. On this special Ekadasi the devotee should dance and sing ecstatically before the Deity. He should avoid prajalpa at all costs and should not talk to or touch low-born persons or a woman in her menstrual period.

On this day he should be especially careful to speak the truth and should not criticize anyone before the Deity of Lord Vishnu, the Brahmans, or the spiritual master. Rather, with other devotees he should listen to Vaisnavas read the glories of Lord Vishnu from the Puranas. One should not drink or even touch water to his lips on this Ekadasi, and one who is unable to perform this austerity should drink only water or milk. Otherwise, the fast is considered broken. One should remain awake that night, singing and playing musical instruments for the transcendental pleasure of the Supreme Person.

During the first quarter of the Ekadasi night the devotee should offer some coconut meat to his worshipable murti, during the second part he should offer bel fruit, during the third part an orange, and as the night draws to a close some betel nut. Remaining awake during the first part of Ekadasi night bestows on the devotee the same merit as that gained by performing the Agnistoma-yajna. Staying awake during the second part of the night bestows the same merit as that gained by performing a Vajapeya-yajna. Staying awake during the third part gives one the same merit as that attained by performing an Asvamedha-yajna. And one who remains awake throughout the night receives all of the above-mentioned merit, as well as the grand merit of having performed a Rajasuya-yajna. Thus there is no better fasting day in the year than Padmini Ekadasi. Nothing can compare to it as a giver of merit, whether it be a fire sacrifice, knowledge, education, or austerity. Indeed, whoever observes this sacred Ekadasi fast receives all the merit attained by bathing in all the places of pilgrimage in the world.

After remaining awake throughout the night, the devotee should bathe at sunrise and then worship Me nicely. He should then feed a qualified Brahmana and respectfully give him the murti of Lord Kesava and the pot filled with pure scented water. This gift will guarantee the devotee success in this life and liberation in the hereafter. "'O sinless Yudhisthira, as you have requested, I have described the rules and regulations, as well as the benefits, regarding the Ekadasi that occurs during the light fortnight of the extra, leap-year month. Fasting on this Padmini day bestows merit equal to that gained by fasting on all other Ekadasis. The Ekadasi that occurs during the dark part of the extra month, which is known as Parama Ekadasi, is as powerful at removing sin as this one, Padmini. Now please listen carefully as I narrate to you a fascinating account connected with this sacred day. Pulastya Muni once recited this history to Naradaji.

Pulastya Muni once had occasion to rescue Ravana from the prison of Kartaviryarjuna, and upon hearing of this event, Narada Muni asked his friend, "O greatest of sages, since Ravana defeated all the demigods, including Lord Indra, how could Kartaviryarjuna defeat Ravana, who was so skilled in battle?"

Pulastya Muni replied, "O great Narada, during the Treta-yuga, Kartavirya [Kartaviryarjuna's father] took birth in the Haihaya dynasty. His capital city was Mahismati, and he had one thousand queens, whom he loved very dearly. None of them, however, was able to give him the son he wanted so badly. He performed sacrifices and worshipped the demigods and forefathers, but due to the curse of some sages he was unable to beget a son-and without a son, a king cannot enjoy his kingdom, just as a hungry man can never really enjoy his senses.

King Kartavirya carefully considered his plight and then decided to perform severe austerities to achieve his goal. Thus he donned a loincloth made of bark, grew matted locks, and turned over the reins of his kingdom to his ministers. One of his queens, Padmini-who was born in the Iksvaku dynasty, who was the best of all women, and who was the daughter of King Harishcandra saw the king leaving. She felt that, since she was a chaste wife, her duty was to follow in the footsteps of her beloved husband. Removing all the regal ornaments from her beautiful body and donning but one piece of cloth, she thus followed her husband into the forest.

At last Kartavirya reached the summit of Mount Gandha madam, where he performed severe austerities and penance for ten thousand years, meditating and praying to Lord Gadadhara, who wields a club. But still he did not get a son. Seeing her dear husband waste away to mere skin and bone, Padmini thought of a solution to the problem. She went to the chaste Anasjjyjj. With great reverence, Padmini said, 'O great lady, my dear husband, Kartavirya, has been performing austerities for the last ten thousand years, but Lord Kesava, who alone can remove one's past sins and present difficulties, has not yet become pleased with him. O most fortunate one, please tell me a fast day we can observe and thus please the Supreme Lord with our devotion, so much so that He will bless me with a nice son who will later rule the world as emperor.

Upon hearing the words of Padmini, who was very chaste and deeply devoted to her husband, the great Anasuya replied to her in a very cheerful mood: 'O beautiful, lotus-eyed lady, usually there are twelve months in a year, but after every thirty-two months an extra month is added, and the two Ekadasis that occur during this month are called Padmini Ekadasi and Parama Ekadasi They fall on the Dvadasis of the light and dark part of the month, respectively. You should fast on these days and remain awake throughout the night. If you do so, the Supreme Personality of Godhead, Hari, will bless you with a son.

O Narada, in this way Anasuya, the daughter of the sage Kardama, explained the potency of these special Ekadasis. Hearing this, Padmini faithfully followed the instructions to fulfil her desire for a son. Padmini fasted completely, even from water, and remained awake all night, chanting the glories of God and dancing in ecstasy. Lord Kesava, thus became most pleased with her devotion and appeared before her, riding on the back of the great Garuda. The Lord said, 'O beautiful one, you have greatly pleased Me by fasting on the special Ekadasi of the extra month. Please ask Me for a benediction.'

Hearing these sublime words from the overseer of the entire universe, Padmini offered the Supreme Lord devotional prayers and asked Him for the boon her husband desired. Lord Sri Krishna was moved to reply, 'O gentle lady, I am very happy with you, for there is no month dearer to Me than this, and the Ekadasis that occur during this month are the most dear to Me of all Ekadasis. You have followed Anasuya's instructions perfectly, and therefore I shall do what will please you. You and your husband will have the son you desire.

The Lord, who removes the distress of the world, then spoke to King Kartavirya: 'O king, please ask of Me any boon that will fulfil your heart's desire, for your dear wife has pleased Me greatly.

The king was very happy to hear this. Naturally he asked for the son he had desired for so long: 'O master of the universe, O killer of the Madhu demon, kindly grant me a son who will never be conquered by demigods, human beings, snakes, demons, or hobgoblins, but whom only You can defeat. The Supreme Lord immediately replied, 'So be it! and disappeared.

The king became very pleased with his wife and returned to his palace in her company. Padmini soon became pregnant, and the mightyarmed Kartaviryarjuna appeared as her son. He was the mightiest person in all the three worlds, and thus even tenheaded Ravana could not defeat him in battle. Except for Lord Narayana, who holds a club, a disc, and other symbols in his hands, no one could overcome him. By the merit that resulted from his mother's strict and faithful observance of Padmini Ekadasi, he could defeat even the dreaded Ravana. This is not at all surprising, O Naradaji, for Kartaviryarjuna was the fulfilment of the benediction of the Supreme Personality of Godhead." With these words, Pulastya Muni departed.

The Supreme Lord, Sri Krishna, concluded, 'O sinless Yudhisthira, as you have inquired from me, I have explained to you the power of this special Ekadasi. O best of kings, whoever observes this fast will surely attain to My personal abode. And similarly, if you want all your desires fulfilled, you should do likewise.

Hearing these words from his beloved Kesava, Dharmaraja [Yudhisthira] became filled with joy, and when the time came he faithfully observed Padmini Ekadasi.

Suta Gosvami concluded, "O sage Saunaka, I have explained to you all about this meritorious Ekadasi." Anyone who devotedly fasts on the Ekadasis that occur during the extra, leap-year months, carefully following all the rules, becomes glorious and happily goes back to Godhead. And one who merely hears or reads about these Ekadasis will also obtain great merit and ultimately enter the abode of Lord Hari.

## Karna: I am Myself Alone

Karna, like Bhishma, harbours grievance against his mother and is chained by an outdated concept of loyalty to a benefactor, regardless of the innate merit of the situation and the superordinate goal of lokasangraha. The mainspring of his actions I, however, not even this dharma, but an obsession with himself. For Karna it is social status and recognition that constitute the source of power. Indeed, he is the true counterpart of Bhishma's Egotistical Sublime.

The fact of his inferior birth is a poisonous ulcer eating into his soul and impelling him to acts of incredible prowess, conquering single-handed for Duryodhan all the territories that the four Pandavas had won for Yudhishthira's rajasuya yajna. Once he had even worsted the mighty Jarasandha, who gifted him the town of Malini in appreciation. For the same reason he took the vow of never refusing a mendicant, and thereby knowingly deprived himself of his invulnerability (when Indra took his god-made armour) and his benefactor Duryodhan of sure victory.

Thus, as in the case of Bhishma, it is inflexible determination to stick to one's word, whatever the consequences, which leads to doom. In both their cases, their own self is prized above all else [in the case of Karna, even above his much vaunted loyalty to Duryodhan and his goal of slaying Arjuna]. Although Karna does not emerge victorious in his encounters with Arjuna and even with the Gandharvas when Duryodhan is captured. Yet he alone saves the Kaurava host from annihilation at the hands of Ghatotkacha. It is of him that Yudhishthira is the most apprehensive. Krishna sets much store by Karna, Knowing that if he stands aside Duryodhan would not dare go to war.

On more than one occasion Krishna tries to persuade Karna to join the Pandavas, the last being just before the battle when Karna, Achilles like, had withdrawn from the battle because of Bhishma's insult. Even Bhishma regarded him as a great warrior ad deliberately insulted him to take advantage of his hypersensitive self-image and keep him from fighting his brothers. Bhishma provides a valuable psychological insight into Karna's character when he informs him that because of his birth against the law of nature-supra-human and mortal intercourse not sanctified by marital rites-he developed an unhealthy envy of nobility of character which was accentuated by his keeping company with a mean individual like Duryodhan.

But, it is this warrior who publicly terms Draupadi a harlot, asks that she be stripped, and joins six others to attack the teenaged Abhimanyu jointly, against all canons of fair battle. It is Karna who seals the fate of this mighty teenager by cutting his bowstring from behind. Unfortunately, Vyasa does not tell us of the inner workings of Karna's mind and heart. In lending a hand in killing his rival's son did he feel he was in some way avenging his many defeats at Arjuna's hands? In calling Draupadi a whore about whom it is of no concerns whether she is clothed or naked, was he taking revenge for having been publicly rejected by her in the svayamvara on account of his caste?

All this shows his confusion over what dharma and power are all about, and it is this confusion about dharma that is flung back at him by Krishna when he entreats Arjuna to wait till has extricated the chariot wheel from the mud, and can take up arms again. Karna, too, is a man divided against himself, yet undoubtedly noble in his silence about his mother's secret and wise in his judgement. For, he tells Krishna not to reveal the secret to Yudhishthira who will invariably offer the kingdom to him and he will inexorably hand it over to Duryodhan. All his tremendous power has throughout been put in the service of adharma because of his profound sense of a lacerated ego. Here is a hero who knows, like Bhishma, that he is on the side of wrong, but is a slave of his word and will not shift to support what he knows to be the right.

His greatness as a man shines radiantly in the fact that while he knows that he is battling his blood brothers, and is promise-bound not to slay them, they are all eager to kill this charioteer's son! His slicing off the skin-armour and flesh earrings is an external symbol of the inner splitting-in-two of his very psyche.

One part of him knows that Duryodhan's plans are evil. This part in Karna is all that is admirable in a human being. It is the "Surya" part of him, shining in an effulgent glory which rivets all attention on him right from the beginning. This it is that catches the eye of Duryodhan who grapples Karna to his breast with hoops of steel. It is this part of him that defeats each of his brothers in turn, except Arjuna, and lets them go unharmed (even with a kiss on the infuriated but helpless Bhima's cheek) although by killing them or by capturing Yudhishthira for Duryodhan [as Drona had planned] he could have ended the war.

However, a miasma of intrigue and evil envelops this sun in Karna. The chariot-wheel of Karna's life is, as it were, entrapped in a quicksand, being sucked under slowly but surely, as he connives in the heinous abuse of state power by Shakuni and Duryodhan, with the blind monarch Dhritarashtra eagerly acquiescing. The helping hand of succour offered by Krishna is rejected on egotistic grounds alone. As Krishna points out:

> *"The world is doomed because you do not accept my advice.*
>
> *When the world's doom nears, my friend,*
>
> *wrong appears right, wrong gets embedded in the heart and stays there."*

All that Karna is concerned about is that his reputation must remain unsullied at all costs and he must find out who is better: Arjuna or himself. Karna has waded in too far by now to return. Perhaps death is his only salvation.

Here we have the classic fox of local politics, the Great Indian Saviour, the Great Betrayer Basdeo Panday!. A man so obsessed with himself that he will willingly sacrifice every Indian to the slaughterhouse just so he can retain his position. Like Karna, he knows what he does is WRONG but blinded by his own lust for power/position, he sacrifices the very people that has faith in him. A man speaks out against the oligarchy yet the moment he attains Prime Ministership joins that very oligarchy.

## Krishna: Power Used to Change the Polity

Krishna presents a total contrast. He has no hesitation in surmounting loyalty to kith and kin in slaying his maternal uncle Kamsa who has become a tyrant and his cousin Shishupala who has allied himself to the imperialistic ambitions of Jarasandha. Free from greed for personal aggrandizement, Krishna refuses to become the ruler of the Yadavas, and puts old Ugrasena back on the throne. The opposite of Jarasandha in his goal, Krishna would be no samrat, for his status is that of svarat, he removes the tyrants and aggrandisers of public wealth. Finally, the killing of Jarasandha restores independence to nearly a hundred chieftains and frees the Yadava clans and indeed the country as a whole, of the spectre of the all—constricting Magadhan python. Krishna's use of power is precisely what should have engaged Bhishma: protect the virtuous and destroy the wicked, paritranaya sadhunam vinashayaca dushkritam.

Krishna respects Bhishma, but prefers to stay with Vidura, for he is aware of the narrow confines of the old dharma which he has made it his mission to demolish. In this task the unknown Pandavas are chosen by him as the instruments for setting up a state founded upon the ancient principle of the raja being the person who ensures the welfare, the happiness, of the people. They are linked to him through their mother Pritha [his paternal aunt] and are free from dysfunctional traditional concepts of dharma because of the very nature of their diverse paternity. He binds them closer to himself by arranging his sister

Subhadra's marriage by Arjuna, and by training their son Abhimanyu to become a great warrior.

He not only builds up the numerous Yadava clans into a confederacy to be reckoned with by the time of the battle of Kurukshetra, which is why both sides vie for their patronage, but also gifts considerable wealth to the Pandavas and guides them into becoming rulers in their own right. He gets them recognized as benevolent, righteous rulers because of their role in the removal of Jarasandha. He ensures that in each conquered kingdom they restore the ruler to his throne, asking for his allegiance only through presence in the rajasuya yajna. After the exile is over, he advises a peace-mission, despite the vociferous protests of his favourite sakhi Draupadi, so that the Pandavas cannot be faulted for having precipitated a war.

Krishna's leadership in the war itself is too well known to need recital. In each case the over-riding concern is that those who use power rightfully for the new dharma of lokasangraha must be victorious. He does not suffer from the limitations of Bhishma or Karna regarding attachment to a vow as a be-all and end-all. Where necessary, he breaks his vow of not taking up arms and rushes to kill Bhishma.

It is again Krishna who dexterously finds a way to prevent Arjuna killing Yudhishthira out of blind adherence to a vow. Knowing that a fresh Karna may overwhelm Arjuna, he avoids a confrontation till Karna is tired, and then browbeats Arjuna into killing him when afoot and unarmed, regardless of what others might say, because with Karna alive the Pandavas cannot win the war. For the same reason, he gets them to pursue a tired-out Duryodhan, denying him time to recuperate.

With unerring instinct he takes the victorious brothers away from their camp, otherwise they would also have been slaughtered by Ashvatthama in his manic frenzy. It is he who saves Bhima from being killed by the Narayana weapon, from losing to Duryodhan in the final duel and being crushed in furious Dhritarashtra's embrace at the end.

Yet, this supreme leader of men failed with his own people. The confederacy he had so laboriously built up destroyed itself. In an internecine strife as tragic and as totally annihilating as the Kurukshetra holocaust. Its seeds lay in the unrestrained indulgence in liquor and the arrogance of wealth that led to flagrant insults to sages. Once again it is unfettered individual liberty that spells doom. We are reminded of Plato's discourse that it is the "democratic man" who is the source of the tyrannical man, for in him all impulses are allowed free indulgence and he considers himself entitled to indulge whichever solicits him most powerfully at the moment instead of being ruled by a superordinate marshalling vision that pursues ends valuable in themselves, namely goodness, beauty and truth. Of these the power impulse is the strongest and establishes a tyranny over the rest.

The intensely human nature of Krishna's own predicament is revealed in an amazing disclosure to Narada:

> *"I live listening to the bitter comments of kinfolk, despite having given them half my wealth. As one anxious to obtain fire keeps rubbing the kindling, similarly my kinsmen are constantly churning and scorching my heart with their harsh words. Sankarshan is mighty but drunk; Gada is delicate and averse to labour; Pradyumna is engrossed with his own beauty. Despite such persons and others among the Andhakas and Vrishnis being on my side, I am helpless passing the days. Ahuka and Akrura are excellent friends of mine, but if I show affection for one, the other becomes furious. Hence, I do not express affection for any. And because of friendship it is very difficult to discard them... whoever has Ahuka and Akrura on his side is miserable beyond compare, and he whose cause they do not espouse is also immeasurably sorrowful...*

The utterly human nature of Krishna's dilemma does not, surely, need any gloss. Krishna himself states

> *"I can express human prowess to the utmost; but I do not have the slightest power to alter what is fated."*

It is the very human-ness of Krishna which is part of the secret lying behind the irresistible fascination he exercises over millions even in the closing years of the twentieth century. Even without going into the Gita, reading of the epic brings out powerfully the remarkable qualities of head, heart and hand which make Krishna pre-eminent among leaders of men. The finest account of this is given by Bhishma himself when he announces why Krishna ought to be honoured above all during the rajasuya yajna:

> *"The sun shames all shining things,*
>
> *So Krishna shames all with his wisdom, strength, and fame.*
>
> *Like the sun shining where there is no sun,*
>
> *like the air blowing where there is no air,*
>
> *Krishna comes among us, illuminates and gladdens..*
>
> *Some of the greatest Kshatriyas have been defeated by*
>
> *Krishna in battle...*
>
> *Which is why we revere Krishna though there are other great kings and elders..*
>
> *O king of Chedi, do not think we are whimsical in Revering Krishna, or that we*
>
> *want benefits from him, or that we think of him as a relative...*
>
> *We revered him first keeping his heroism, success, and glory in mind...*
>
> *There are two reasons for revering Govinda Krishna*
>
> *All the Vedas and Vedangas are known to him, and he has shown boundless prowess.*
>
> *Who else but Keshava can boast as much?*

*Generosity, shrewdness, immersion in shruti, bravery, gentleness,*

*humility, enterprise, intelligence, handsomeness, firmness, joy and success—are Krishna's."*

And yet, what is the end of this supreme human, "Purushottama"? The Empire of Righteousness he has established is a veritable field of ashes, peopled by wailing widows and infants, which Karna had so vividly figured forth in a dream related to Krishna:

*"Powerful Yudhishthira climbed a hill Of human bones,*

*smiled and ate sweet ghee-curd from a golden cup."*

Did Duryodhan have the last word when he told the Pandavas and Krishna, after being felled by a blow below the belt:

*"I have studied the scriptures, given away gifts as prescribed, ruled over the sea-girted earth, placed my foot on the heads of enemies, possessed the greatest wealth, and enjoyed that rare pleasure savoured by the gods which is the envy of other kings, and ultimately won that death in battle which is prayed for by Kshatriyas following dharma. Hence, who can have a better end than mine? Now I leave for heaven with my brothers and friends, while you all stay behind on this earth, the living-dead, with hearts wrung with sorrow."*

Here it is Duryodhan who appears to represent the successful leader! We recall the undying loyalty of Karna and Ashvatthama, and of those hundreds of kings who willingly laid down their lives in his cause. The Pandavas are overshadowed by the radiance of Duryodhan's nobility as he rises to the defence of Karna when his supposedly low birth is laughed at, and his rousing defence of innate worth as the true measure of nobility instead of judging it by one's birth. This is precisely the beauty of Vyasa's epic. There are no easy answers in life. But we must not be swept away by the grandeur of this dying speech. His end itself depicts what happens when power is used for serving egotistic urges. It may bring immediate, illusory success. Ultimately the misuser has to share the ruinous fate of Nahusha and Yayati.

Is there a politician/s that fit this attitude in Trinidad right now?

## Ashvamedha

The Ashvamedha is one of the most important royal rituals of Vedic religion, described in detail in the Yajur Veda (TS 7.1-5, VS 22-25 and the pertaining commentary in the Shatapatha Brahmana). The Rig Veda does have descriptions of horse sacrifice, notably in hymns RV 1.162-163, but does not allude to the full ritual according to the Yajur Veda.

***The Vedic Sacrifice:*** The Ashvamedha could only be conducted by a king (raja). Its object was the acquisition of power and glory, the sovereignty over neighbouring provinces, and general prosperity of the kingdom. The horse to be sacrificed must be a stallion, more than 24, but less than 100 years old. The horse is sprinkled with water, and the Adhvaryu and the sacrificer whisper mantras into its ear. Anyone who should stop the horse is ritually cursed, and a dog is killed symbolic of the punishment for the sinners. The horse is then set loose towards the North-East, to roam around wherever it chooses, for the period of one year (or half a year, according to some commentators). The horse is associated with the Sun, and its yearly course. If the horse wanders into neighbouring provinces hostile to the sacrificer, they must be subjugated. The wandering horse is attended by a hundred young men, sons of princes or high court officials, charged with guarding the horse from all dangers and inconvenience. During the absence of the horse, an uninterrupted series of ceremonies is performed in the sacrificer's home.

After the return of the horse, more ceremonies are performed. The horse is yoked to a gilded chariot, together with three other horses, and RV 1.6.1,2 (YV VSM 23.5,6) is recited. The horse is then driven into water and bathed. After this, it is anointed with ghee by the chief queen and two other royal consorts. The chief queen anoints the fore-quarters, and the others the barrel and the hind-quarters. They also embellish the horse's head, neck, and tail with golden ornaments. The sacrificer offers the horse the remains of the night's oblation of grain.

After this, the horse, a hornless he-goat, a wild ox (go-mrga, Bos gavaeus) are bound to sacrificial stakes near the fire, and seventeen other animals are attached to the horse. A great number of animals, both tame and wild, are tied to other stakes, according to a commentator 609 in total (YV 24 consists of an exact enumeration).

Then the horse is slaughtered (YV VSM 23.15, tr. Griffith)

Steed, from thy body, of thyself, sacrifice and accept thyself.

Thy greatness can be gained by none but thee.

The chief queen ritually calls on the king's fellow wives for pity. The queens walk around the dead horse reciting mantras. The chief queen then has to mimic copulation with the dead horse, while the other queens ritually utter obscenities.

On the next morning, the priests raise the queen from the place where she has spent the night with the horse. With the Dadhikra verse (RV 4.39.6, YV VSM 23.32), a verse used as a purifier after obscene language.

The three queens with a hundred golden, silver and copper needles indicate the lines on the horse's body along which it will be dissected. The horse is dissected, and its flesh roasted. Various parts are offered to a host of deities and personified concepts with cries of svaha "all-hail". The Ashvastuti or Eulogy of the Horse follows (RV 1.162, YV VSM 24.24-45), concluding with:

> *May this Steed bring us all-sustaining riches, wealth in good kine, good horses, manly offspring. Freedom from sin may Aditi vouchsafe us: the Steed with our oblations gain us lordship. A coin created by Samudragupta I to commemorate the Ashvamedha*

*ritual. The tethered horse is depicted on the left; the queen, carrying ritual equipment, is on the right.*

The priests performing the sacrifice were recompensed with a part of the booty won during the wandering of the horse. According to a commentator, the spoils from the east was given to the Hotar, while the Adhvaryu a maiden (a daughter of the sacrificer) and the sacrificer's fourth wife. A historically documented performance of the Ashvamedha is during the reign of Samudragupta I (d. 380), the father of Chandragupta II. Special coins were minted to commemorate the Ashvamedha and the king took on the title of Maharajadhiraja after successful completion of the sacrifice. There were couple of later instances. One was performed by Raja of Kannauj in the 12th century, unsuccessfully, as Prithviraj Chauhan thwarted his attempt and later married his daughter. The last known instance seems to be in 1716 CE,by Jaya Singh II, a prince of Jaipur.

### *Sanskrit Epics*

The Ashvamedha is described in the epics Ramayana (1.10-15) and Mahabharata. In the Mahabharata, the sacrifice is performed by Yudhishtira (Book 14), his brothers guarding the horse as it roamed into neighbouring kingdoms. Arjuna defeats all challengers. The Mahabharata says that the Ashvamedha as performed by Yudhishtira adhered to the letter of the Vedic prescriptions. After the horse was cut into parts, Draupadi lies beside the slain animal (14.89). In the Ramayana, Rama's father Dasharatha performs the Ashvamedha, which is described in the bala kanda (book 1) of the poem. The Ramayana provides far more detail than the Mahabharata. Again it is stated that the ritual was performed in strict compliance with Vedic prescriptions (1.14.10). Dasaratha's chief wife Kausalya circumambulates the horse and ritually pierces its flesh (1.14.33). Then "Queen Kausalya desiring the results of ritual disconcertedly resided one night with that horse that flew away like a bird." [1-14-34]. At the conclusion of the ritual Dasharatha symbolically offers his other wives to the presiding priests, who return them in exchange for expensive gifts (1.14.35).

The ritual is performed again towards the end of the poem, but in very different circumstances. It figures centrally in the uttara kanda (book 7) where it leads to the final major story in the poem. In this narrative, Rama was married to a single wife, Sita, who at the time was not with him, having been excluded from Rama's capital of Ayodhya.

She was therefore represented by a statue for the queen's ceremony. Sita was living in Valmiki's forest ashram with her twin children by Rama, Lava and Kusha, whose birth was unknown to Rama. In its wanderings, the horse, accompanied by an army and the monkey-king Hanuman, enters the forest and encounters Lava, who ignores the warning written on the horse's headplate not to hinder its progress. He tethers the horse, and with Kusha challenges the army, which is unable to defeat the brothers. Recognising Rama's sons, Hanuman sends them to Ayodhya where they are reconciled with their father, who also accepts Sita back at court.

Sita, however, no longer wishes to live, and is absorbed by the earth. It is never stated whether the sacrifice was completed, but after Sita's death Rama is said to have repeatedly performed the Ashvamedha using the golden statue as a substitute for his wife.

Some historians believe that the bala kanda and uttara kanda were latter interpolations to the authentic form of the Ramayana, due to references to Greek, Parthians and Sakas, dating to no earlier than the 2nd century BC.

### *Vedanta and Modern Hinduism*

In Vedantic interpretations, the Ashvamedha is understood as a ritual to get connected to the "inner Sun". In this tradition, it is said that the ashva of the Ashvamedha originally referred to the Sun, and that sacrifices of actual horses represented a degeneration of the spiritual ritual. According to the Brahma-vaivarta Purana (Krishna-janma-khanda 185.180), the Ashvamedha is one of five rites forbidden in the Kali Yuga.

### *Modern Anxieties and Criticism Concerning the Ritual*

The mock bestiality and necrophilia involved in the ritual offended the Dalit reformer and framer of the Indian constitution B. R. Ambedkar and is frequently mentioned in his writings as an example of the perceived degradation of Brahmanical culture. This part of the ritual also caused considerable consternation among the scholars first editing the Yajur Veda. Griffith (1899) omits verses VSM 23.20-31 (the ritual obscenities), protesting that they are "not reproducible even in the semi-obscurity of a learned European language" (alluding to other instances where he renders explicit scenes in Latin rather than English). A. B. Keith's 1914 translation also omits verses.

In modern times some Indian commentators deny that this passage involved a mock sexual ritual, while others argue that the horse sacrifice itself never actually occurred, but was an allegory. Devi Chand's 1964 translation of the Yajur Veda insists (following Swami Dayananda) that the Ashvamedha "does not mean horse sacrifice, but the improvement of land for growing more food."(due to the polysemous meanings of the word 'ashva' as horse as well as fire) The passage above is interpreted as advice to a "learned woman" concerning her duties as a wife. Subhash Kak, citing the Sanskrit grammarian Patanjali (ca. 2nd century BC) and Panini (ca. 4th century BC), says that the diminutive ashvaka may also apply to toy horses.

### Rajasuya Yajna of Yudhishthira

One day, while Krishna and Arjuna were talking under a tree during Krishna's visit with the Pandavas, a Brahmin approached and requested for their help.

"How can we help you?" asked Krishna.

The Brahmin replied, "I am Agni, the fire-god. I am very hungry to eat meat. I am tired of eating only ghee, that is concentrated butter, offered to me by the sages. Help me to eat the animals of the Khandava forest. I tried to accomplish this task by myself several times, but unfortunately, Indra, the god of weather, protects the Khandava forest. As soon as I try to burn the forest, Indra pours rain and I am extinguished. I need your help to stall Indra until I am done consuming the Khandava forest."

Krishna and Arjuna agreed to help Agni. However, they did not have any celestial weapon to fight Indra. They told Agni of their limitations. Then Agni, through his divine powers, produced the celestial weapons that Krishna and Arjuna needed.

When everything was ready, Agni ignited the forest and in no time the entire forest was in flame. Indra was promptly informed and he rushed with his army to protect the Khandava forest. Krishna and Arjuna successfully kept Indra's army at bay. Suddenly Krishna saw a demon running out of the forest and Agni was chasing him. The demon sought Arjuna's asylum. The fire-god turned back and left him with Arjuna. Finally, Agni was satisfied and thanked Krishna and Arjuna.

When Agni left, the demon introduced himself to Krishna and Arjuna. "I am Maya (illusion), the architect of Vishwakarma. I possess a miraculous skill in architecture. Allow me to do something for you in return for saving my life", he said.

Krishna asked Maya to build a palace for King Yudhishthira, which would be the best on the earth. Maya gladly agreed.

In no time, a beautiful palace was built in Indraprastha, the kingdom of the Pandavas. The royal priest suggested that an inauguration be made for the palace before it is occupied. The Pandavas, in consultation with Krishna, decided to perform Rajasuya Yajna for its inauguration. One of the conditions of the Rajasuya Yajna is that the neighbouring kingdoms must accept the supremacy of the performer, the Pandavas. The only one who objected to this was Jarasandha, the ruler of Magadh.

Upon Krishna's advice, Yudhishthira sent the party of Bhima, Arjuna and Krishna to Magadh to meet Jarasandha. Jarasandha had imprisoned many kings and occupied their kingdoms by defeating them on a dual. He was blessed by Shiva and was practically invincible.

The story says that Jarasandha's father was desperate for a son and had prayed to Lord Shiva. Lord Shiva was pleased and gave him a fruit. Shiva said, "Ask your wife to eat the fruit and she will soon have a child," But Jarasandha's father had two wives. He had to be fair to both and so he split the fruit, giving one half to each wife. As a result, each was born with one half of the child. A witch, named Jara, joined these two pieces and thus the son was named Jarasandha. Jarasandha's body had a vertical joint running from top to the lower end of the backbone. The only way he could be killed was to tear him apart and no one was strong enough to do that. However, Krishna knew the secret of killing Jarasandha. He revealed this secret to Bhima.

Jarasandha was informed about the arrival of the party of Krishna, Bhima and Arjuna. As expected, Jarasandha refused to accept the supremacy of the Pandavas. Thus, Krishna asked him to choose one of the Pandavas to settle the matter. Jarasandha knew that he would be no match for Arjuna because of his superior skills in archery. So, he chose Bhima and was confident to defeat him in the dual. They both promised to fight each other until death.

The fight continued for many hours and finally Bhima lifted him up and flung him down with a thud. Then he tore Jarasandha's body into two halves. Jarasandha was dead. All the kings were released from prison. They thanked Krishna and Bhima for saving their lives. They became friends of the Pandavas and accepted their supremacy. Jarasandha's son, Sahadev succeeded the throne of Magadh and became one of the strong allies of the Pandavas.

All kings, including the Kauravas, were invited to the Rajasuya Yajna and the fire worship was completed with great enthusiasm. All the dignitaries honoured Krishna. Bhishma, the grandfather, spoke very highly of him and declared him as the Godhead in a human body.

The only one who was not happy of Krishna's presence was Sishupal, Krishna's cousin. He was jealous of Krishna. Sishupal's mother knew of her son's shortcomings and Krishna's power. So, she made Krishna promise that he will not take any action against her son until Sishupal insulted Krishna more than one hundred times. Sishupal publicly insulted Krishna at the ceremony in spite of Bhishma's request to stop. Krishna stayed calm until the insults exceeded one hundred times. Then Krishna cut his head off with his chakra (disc).

Following the great ceremony, all the guests left with a great appreciation of the Pandavas. But Duryodhan and his maternal uncle Shakuni extended their stay as special royal guests in order to enjoy the grandeur of the beautiful palace of Yudhishthira. The palace was full of illusionary things. Duryodhan was repeatedly fooled and his appreciation soon turned into sheer jealousy. He said to Shakuni, "Uncle, I cannot bear the prosperity of the Pandavas. I feel like attacking them and take away all their wealth."

"I know a way they can be ripped off and sent to exile" replied Shakuni in his cunning voice.

Duryodhan was getting impatient to know of Shakuni's trick. Shakuni however asked him to wait until they got out of the charming palace. "Who knows, the walls may have ears," Shakuni said with agitation.

# 2

# HINDU DEATH RITUALS AND BELIEFS

In traditional Hindu culture, women are held in the highest regard—far more respected, in truth, than in the West. But this does not imply the kind of equality or participation in public interactions that are common in the West.

The qualities traditionally most admired in a Hindu woman are modesty of manner, shyness and self-effacement. Self-assertive or bold tendencies are regarded with circumspection. Feminine refinements are expressed and protected in many customs, including the following:

1. *Womanly Reserve:* In mixed company especially in the presence of strangers, a Hindu woman will keep modestly in the background and not participate freely in conversation. This, of course, does not apply to situations among family and close associates.
2. *Walking behind One's Husband:* The wife walks a step or two behind her husband, or if walking by his side, a step or two back, always giving him the lead. In the West, the reverse of this is often true.
3. *Serving at Meals:* At meals women follow the custom of serving the men first before enjoying their own meal.
4. *Chaperoning:* It is customary for a woman to always be accompanied when she leaves the home. Living alone, too, is unusual.

5. *Women in Public:* Generally it is improper for women to speak with strangers on the street and especially to strike up a casual conversation. Similarly, drinking alcohol or smoking in public, no matter how innocent, are interpreted as a sign of moral laxity and are not acceptable.

## Guests in the Home

1. *Home Visits:* Close friends can visit one another anytime without being announced or making arrangements first. When they drop in, at least a refreshing drink is always served.
2. *Hosting Guests:* Children generally leave the room, with a smile, when guests enter. The mother remains close by to serve as needs arise. The father, if present, will speak with the guest. If he is not present, the mother and a mature son will fulfil this role; and if no son is present, the mother may act as hostess, but only with the accompaniment of someone close to the family.
3. *Wife Home Alone:* If the lady of the house is in home alone and a male visitor comes to see her husband, it is not proper for her to invite him in, nor for him to expect to enter. Rather, he will leave a message and depart.
4. *Giving Gifts:* Gifts are always given when one visits a home or stays overnight as a guest. The value of the gift varies greatly, depending upon circumstances. It is proper to give a separate gift for the wife and the husband. The wife is given the nicest item.

## Body Language

All Hindus know that "Life is meant to be lived joyously!" All is God, and God is everywhere and in all things. This understanding and appreciation is exemplified in every aspect of Hindu deportment.

1. *Kindly Words and Countenance:* Hindus strive to keep a pleasant expression on their face, a gentle smile and a kind word for everyone they meet through the day. They know in their heart of hearts that God is everywhere and that all in the universe is perfect at every point in time. This knowledge gives them strength and courage to face their daily karmas positively and graciously.
2. *Refined Gestures:* Hindus know that every movement of the body, the face, hands, eyes, mouth, head, etc., has a meaning. Youth are taught to be sensitive to the thoughts and feelings of others in their body language.
3. *Eyes:* Eyes are also a primary means of communicating, and the meanings are fairly straightforward. They usually indicate degrees of interest in what the speaker is saying. Smiling with your eyes as well as your mouth conveys sincerity. There are three levels of smiling (and infinite shades and degrees in between). Having the eyes open only slightly indicates mild interest. Eyes more open and a bigger smile indicates more interest and enthusiasm. Having the eyes open wide with a big smile or nod, possibly accompanied by some verbal expression, indicates greater interest or great happiness.

## Hindu Women and Religion

In ancient India, women occupied a very important position, In fact, a superior position, to men. "Sakti" a feminine term means "power" and "strength". All male power comes from the feminine. Literary evidence suggests that kings and towns were destroyed because the rulers troubled a single woman.

For example, Valmiki Ramayana teaches us that Ravana and his entire kingdom were wiped out because he abducted Sita. Veda Vyasa's Mahabharata teaches us that all the Kauravas were killed because they humiliated Draupadi in public. Elango Adigal's Sillapathigaram teaches us Madurai, the capital of the

Pandyas was burnt because Pandyan Nedunchezhiyan mistakenly did harm to Kannaki.

In Vedic times women and men were equal in many aspects. Women participated in the public sacrifices alongside men. One script mentions a female rishi Visvara. Some Vedic hymns, are attributed to women such as Apala, the daughter of Atri, Ghosa, the daughter of Kaksivant or Indrani, the wife of Indra.

Apparently in early Vedic times women also received the sacred thread and could study the Vedas. The Haritasmriti mentions a class of women called brahmavadinis who remained unmarried and spent their lives in study and ritual. Panini's distinction between acharya (a preceptor) and acharyani (a lady teacher or a preceptor's wife), and upadhyaya (a preceptor) and upadhyayani (a lady teacher or a preceptor's wife) indicates that women at that time could not only be students but also the teachers of sacred Vedas.

There were several noteworthy women scholars of the past such as Kathi, Kalapi, and Bahvici. The Upanishads refer to several women philosophers, who disputed with their male colleagues such as Vacaknavi, who challenged Yajnavalkya.

The Rig Veda also refers to women engaged in warfare. One queen Bispala is mentioned, and even as late a witness as Megasthanese (fifth century B.C.) mentions heavily armed women guards protecting Chandragupta's palace.

Hindu religion has been occasionally criticised as encouraging inequality between men and women, towards the detriment of Hindu women. This presumption is inaccurate.

In the Vedic period, we come across female scholars like Ghosha, Lopamudra, Romasha and Indrani. In the Upanishad period, names of women philosophers like Sulabha, Maitreyi, Gargi are encountered.

In religious matters, Hindus have elevated women to the level of divinity. One of the things most misconstrued about India and Hinduism is that it's a male dominated society and religion and the truth is that it is not so.

It is a religion that has attributed the words for the strength and power to feminine. "Sakti" means "power" and "strength". All male power comes from the feminine. The Trimurti (Brahma, Vishnu, Shiva) are all-powerless without their female counterparts.

Devi is the Great Goddess.

This echoes Devi-Mahatmiyam prayer:

> *By you this universe is borne, by you this world is created;*
> *By you it is protected,*
> *By you it is consumed at the end,*
> *O Devi! You are the Supreme Knowledge, as well as intellect and contemplation...*

Women were held in higher respect in India than in other ancient countries, and the Epics and old literature of India assign a higher position to them than the epics and literature of other religions.

Hindu women enjoyed rights of property from the Vedic Age, took a share in social and religious rites, and were sometimes distinguished by their learning. There was no seclusion of women in India in ancient times.

Professor H. H. Wilson says: "And it may be confidently asserted that in no nation of antiquity were women held in so much esteem as amongst the Hindus."

In Ancient India, however, Hindu women not only possessed equality of opportunities with men, but enjoyed certain rights and privileges not claimed by the male sex. The chivalrous treatment of women by Hindus is well known to all who know anything of Hindu society.

Knowledge, intelligence, rhythm and harmony are all essential ingredients for any creative activity. These aspects are personified in Saraswati, the Goddess of Learning, Music and Fine Arts. Without the grace of Saraswati, or Saraswati Kataksham, as it is called, Brahma cannot do a worthwhile job as the Creator. Any maintenance activity needs plenty of resources, mainly fiscal resources. So Lakshmi, the Goddess of Wealth, is an essential companion to Vishnu. Shiva, as Destroyer, derives power and energy from Parvati, or Durga as she is called Sakti. It is only the Hindu tradition, which provides, even at the conceptual level, the picture of the male and female principles working together, hand in hand, as equal partners in the universe. This concept is carried further to its logical climax in the form of Ardhanariswara, formed by the fusion of Shiva and Sakti in one body, each occupying one half of the body, denoting that one is incomplete without the other.

Just the sloka that is commonly recited during daily prayers is enough to show the status of the Goddesses. A sloka on Devi contains the following line: Yaa Brahma Achyuta Sankara Prabhrudibihi Devaissadaa Poojithaa, which means, 'O Devi! Brahma, Vishnu, Shiva and other Gods' always adore you.

In Hinduism, all power, Sakti, is female. Sakti is the fundamental strength of the feminine that infuses all life. Sakti is the divine feminine power found in everything. She is the Goddess. So that, actually, in India, Kali is the great divinity.

Hindus hold rivers in great reverence. The rivers are female divinities, food and life bestowing mothers. As such, they are prominent among the popular divinities represented in the works of art of the classical period. The most holy of rivers, the best known and most honoured, is the Ganga or Ganges. She is personified as Goddess Ganga. The river rises from an ice bed, 13,800 feet above the sea level in the Garhwal Himalayas. The river Saraswati is regarded as the mother god.

One of the most important of all Vedic hymns, the Devisukta, is addressed to Vak (speech, revelation), the goddess who is described as the instrument that makes ritual efficacious: "I am the queen, the gatherer-up of treasures..." It is not unimportant, that Earth (prithivi) is considered female, and the goddess who bears the mountains and who brings forth food that feed all.

Education for girls was regarded as quite important. While Bramhavadani girls were taught Vedic wisdom, girls of the

Ksatriya girls were taught the use of the bow and arrow. Patanjali mentions the spear bearers (saktikis). Megasthanese speaks of Chandragupta's bodyguard of Amazonian women. Kautilya mentions women archers (striganaih dhanvibhih).

Similarly, Kautilya in his Arthasastra, which is also taken to be a document of Mauryan history, refers to women soldiers armed with bows and arrows. Buddhism kept up the traditions of Brahmanical religion in according to womanhood an honoured place in social life. Women were made eligible for admission to what was known as the Bhikshuni-Sangha, the Order of Nuns, which opened to them avenues of culture and social service and ample opportunities for public life.

In Gurukulas, the ancient Universities of India, boys and girls were educated together. Atreyi studied under Valmiki along with Lava and Kusa, the sons of Rama. Fine arts like music, dancing and painting was especially encouraged in the case of girls.

Girls had Upanayana performed for them and carried out the Sandhya rites. A young daughter who has observed brahmacharya should be married to a bridegroom who is learned like her. (Yajur Veda VIII.1). Seclusion of women was unknown in the Vedic times.

The Atharva Veda refers to daughters remaining with their parents until the end of their lives. A part of the ancestral property is given to them as dowry, which becomes their own property, and is called stridhana in later writings. "Home is not what is made of wood and stone; but where a wife is, there is the home." (Sanskrit: Na grham kasthapasanair dayita yatra tad grham-Nitimanjari, 68)

It is significant to note that only Hindus worship God in the form of Divine Mother. In Hinduism the deities for knowledge, learning and material wealth are female and not male. The past social inconsistencies and injustices that did not arise from Hindu scriptures, but from humans who failed to correctly incorporate the teachings of the scriptures, such as the Upanishads and the Bhagavad Gita, into their social philosophy.

This concept of the spiritual equality of souls naturally influenced the status of women on an individual and social level.

Secularists make the predictable allegation that Hinduism as represented by Manu is anti-woman. Actually on reading this text one would realise that neither dowry (dahe) nor self-immolation of widows (sati) figure in it.

> *"Where women are honoured there the gods are pleased; but where they are not honoured no sacred rite yields rewards," declares Manusmriti (III.56) a text on social conduct.*
>
> *"Women must be honoured and adorned by their fathers, brothers, husbands and brothers-in-law, who desire their own welfare." (Manusmriti III, 55)*
>
> *"Where the female relations live in grief, the family soon wholly perishes; but that family where they are not unhappy ever prospers." (Manusmriti III, 57).*
>
> *"The houses, on which female relations, not being duly honoured, pronounce a curse, perish completely as if destroyed by magic." (Manusmriti III, 58)*
>
> *"Hence men, who seek their own welfare, should always honour women on holidays and festivals with gifts of ornaments, clothes, and dainty food."*
>
> *In an old Shakti hymn it is said-Striyah devah, Striyah pranah "Women are Devas, women are life itself."*
>
> *"If a husband dies, a wife may marry another husband.*
>
> *"If a husband deserts his wife, she may marry another." (Manu, chapter IX, verse 77).*
>
> *"A woman's body," says Manu the law-giver, "must not be struck hard, even with a flower, because it is sacred." It is for this reason that the Hindus do not allow capital punishment for women.*

In the Vedas, she is invited into the family 'as a river enters the sea' and 'to rule there along with her husband, as a queen, over the other members of the family.

The idea of equality was most forcibly expressed in the Rig Veda (Book 5, hymn 61. verse 8). The commentator explains this passage thus: "The wife and husband, being the equal halves of one substance, are equal in every respect; therefore both should join and take equal parts in all work, religious and secular." No other Scripture of the world have ever given to the woman such equality with the man as the Vedas of the Hindus.

A Hindu woman whose name was Romasha revealed the 126th hymn of the first book of the Rig Veda; the 179 hymn of the same book was by Lopamudra, another inspired Hindu woman. There are a dozen names of woman revealers of the Vedic wisdom, such as Visvavara, Shashvati, Gargi, Maitreyi, Apala, Ghosha, and Aditi, who instructed Indra, one of the Devas, in the higher knowledge of Brahman, the Universal Spirit. Every one of them lived the ideal life of spirituality, being untouched by the things of the world. They are called in Sanskrit Brahmavadinis, the speakers and revealers of Brahman.

When Sankaracharya, the great commentator of the Vedanta, was discussing philosophy with another philosopher, a Hindu lady, well versed in all the Scriptures, was requested to act as a judge.

It is the special injunction of the Vedas that no married man shall perform any religious rite, ceremony, or sacrifice without being joined in by his wife; the wife is considered a partaker and partner in the spiritual life of her husband; she is called, in Sanskrit, Sahadharmini, "spiritual helpmate."

In the whole religious history of the world a second Sita will not be found. Her life was unique. She is worshipped as an incarnation of God. India is the only country where prevails a belief that God incarnates in the form of a woman as well as in that of a man.

In the Mahabharata we read the account of Sulabha, the great woman Yogini, who came to the court of King Janaka and showed wonderful powers and wisdom, which she had acquired through the practice of Yoga. This shows that women were allowed to practice Yoga.

As in religion, Hindu woman of ancient times enjoyed equal rights and privileges with men, so in secular matters she had equal share and equal power with them. From the Vedic age women in India have had the same right as men and they could go to the courts of justice, plead their own cases, and ask for the protection of the law.

Those who have read the famous Hindu drama called Shakuntala know that Shakuntala pleaded her own case and claimed her rights in the court of King Dushyanata. Similar instance are mentioned in the 10th book of the Rig Veda. As early as 2000 B.C. Hindu women were allowed to go to the battlefields to fight against enemies. Her husband in search of robbers sent Sarama, one of the most powerful women of her day. She discovered their hiding place and then destroyed them.

Regarding this as the highest dharma of all four castes, husbands, though weak, must strive to protect their wives. His own offspring, character, family, self, and dharma does one protect when he protects his wife scrupulously. The husband should engage his wife in dharma, the collection and expenditure of his wealth, in cooking food for the family, and in looking after the necessities of the household.

A father protects his daughter in childhood, a husband protects his wife in youth, and the sons protect their mother in old age. The father who does not give away his daughter in marriage at the proper time is censurable; censurable is the husband who does not approach his wife in due season; and after the husband is dead, the son, verily is censurable, who does not protect his mother. Even against the slightest provocations should women be particularly guarded; for unguarded they would bring grief to both the families.

Motherhood is considered the greatest glory of Hindu women. The Taittiriya Upanishad teaches, "Matridevo bhava"- "Let your mother be the god to you."

Hindu tradition recognises mother and motherhood as even superior to heaven. The epic Mahabharata says, "While a father is superior to ten learned priests well-versed in the Vedas, a mother is superior to ten such fathers, or the entire world."

Hinduism offers some intriguing and unique examples of strong women in the form of Goddesses. Two thousand years ago Saint Trivalvular observed: "What does a man lack if his wife is worthy? And what does he possess if she is lacking worth?" There is more respect in the Hinduism for women and for their role in society.

In many philosophical texts God is referred to a Tat, meaning it and that God is beyond gender. And, one would find a comparable Goddess for each God. Further, we know for a fact that ancient India was permissive; women could have multiple husbands, widows could remarry, divorce was permitted for incompatibility or when estranged.

The names of Gargi and Maitreyi are too well known as great scholars of Vedic scriptures. We have statements like, "This hymn must be recited by the wife," in the Sroutasutras, which clearly endorse the eligibility of women to the study of the Vedas. The Ramayana describes the performance of Sandhya and Havana by Kausalya and Sita. The wife was a regular participant in the sacrificial offerings of the husband. (Rig Veda I-122-2; 131-3; III-53-4-6; X-86-10 etc.). Gobhila Gruhya Sutras state that the wife should be educated to be able to take part in sacrifices.

Woman in the role of wife occupies a position of pre-eminence in ancient Hindu tradition. The Hindus from the Vedic times believed in dual worship Shiva with Sakti, Vishnu with Lakshmi, Rama with Sita, and so on.

In this dual worship, the names of Radha and Sita get precedence over the names of their companions Krishna and Rama. This happens to be true of Goddess Saraswati and her husband Lord Brahma.

Lord Shiva appears united in a single body with Sakti, his spouse; he at the right side and she at the left, in a manifestation known as Ardhanariswara, the half-man, half-woman incarnation of God. Each of the three principal Gods Brahma the Creator, Vishnu the Protector and Shiva the Destroyer in the Hindu pantheon, is accompanied by a Sakti, which is both his female double and his power of manifestation.

The Rig Veda too places woman on a high pedestal of sublimity: Yatr nariyastu poojayante ramante tatr devah, where woman is worshipped, Gods preside there.

Women must be honoured and adorned by their father, brothers, husbands, and brother-in-law who desire great good fortune. Where women, verily are honoured, there the gods rejoice; where, however, they are not honoured, there all sacred rites prove fruitless. Where the female relations live in grief, that family soon perishes completely; where, however, they do not suffer from any grievance that family always prospers.

Women, who once enjoyed an honoured position and are found in the Upanishads conversing freely with men contributing an active role in the society. Young girls led free lives and had a decisive voice in the selection of their husbands. On festive occasions and at tournaments (samana) girls appeared in all their gaiety. In certain Hindu castes the line of inheritance is from mother to (eldest) daughter, and marriage is a "visiting" relationship. Naturally, women were more independent and free in every respect.

Ladies did not lead a secluded life like that of their descendants in later times. Several hymns of the Rig Veda were composed by female Rishis (sages). Young ladies of the time had a voice in their marriage. "The woman who is of gentle birth and of graceful form," so runs a verse in the Rig Veda, "selects among many of her loved one as her husband."

Numerous case of Svayamvara, that is, of ladies selecting their own husbands, is mentioned in the Mahabharata and other works. There is sufficient evidence to show, that widow marriage was allowed, and that the Sati was unknown in the Vedic period.

"Rise up woman," so runs a text of the Rig Veda (X, 18.8) "thou art lying by one whose life is gone, come to the world of the living, away from thy husband, and become the wife of him who holds thy hand and is willing to marry thee."

Every hymn of the Rig-Veda is attributed to a rishi. Though the majority of these hymns were the work of male Rishis, the Rig-Veda contains hymns that were revealed by women seers also. The latter were called rishikas and brahmavadinis.

The brahmavadinis were products of educational discipline of brahmacarya, for which women were also eligible. The Rig-Veda (V, 7, 9) refers to young maidens completing their education as brahmacharinis and then gaining husbands... Rv. iii (55, 16) mentions unmarried learned and young daughters who should be married to learned bridegrooms.

It is, therefore, no wonder that the wife enjoyed with her husband full religious rights and regularly participated in religious ceremonies with him. In fact, the performance of such ceremonies would be invalid without the wife joining her husband as his full partner. Some grammatical passages show that women had other careers open to them apart from a mere literary career.

Some incidents of sati and rash of "dowry murders" have made headlines not only in India, but all around the world, and have focused attention to women's issues in India. In the wake of the discussion it emerged that Indian women's problems are not only problems of Hindu women or problems caused by traditional Hinduism. Media paints India as a dangerous place. But if statistics can be trusted, a study by Hindus against the Abuse of Women presented at the Second International Conference on Bride Burning and Dowry Deaths in India puts USA in the lead of familial femicide. The study says excessive need for control and greed may be the underlying causes, not cultural or religious factors.

The commotion about the sati was just one expression of the colonial mind-set of the ruling class. At one time, most such efforts were closely associated with attempts to justify the British rule in India. The Westernised who controlled the media, either directly or indirectly made news exhibiting themselves as the protectors of Sati and dowry, a cultural projection of a new form of internal colonialism.

Self-burning of widows was not sanctioned by the Vedic religion, but was due to other causes. Some say that, when the Muslim conquered India, they treated the widows of the soldiers so brutally that the women preferred death, and voluntarily sought it.

It is often said that the "British government" has suppressed Sati; but the truth is, that the initiatives in this direction was taken by the noble Hindu, Raja Ram Mohan Roy, who was, however, obliged to secure the aid of the British Government in enforcing the ideas, because India was a subject nation.

The educated classed among the Hindus had strongly protested against this inhuman custom, but as it could not be done without the official help, appeal was made to the then Viceroy, Lord Bentinck, a law against Sati was then passed.

In Hinduism four Vedas, Bhagvad Gita and the two puranas Ramayana and Mahabharata are considered to be the supreme. All others are just commentaries, explanatory notes or stories written by individuals. As commentaries written on the Constitution of India cannot override the articles of the Constitution of India, similarly, commentaries or explanations on Vedas by individuals cannot supersede richas of Vedas or the Ramayana or Gita.

In the Ramayana, everyone knows that after the death of King Dasharatha, his wives were never asked to step into the pyre of Dasharatha. Rather, they lived in family with full honour and Rama always bowed his head before his widowed mothers with full respect. In the Mahabharata, Kunti, mother of the Pandavas did not commit sati. Thus, there is no command in the Ramayana, Mahabharata or in Gita to commit sati.

## A Woman and the Moon

The Earth's one natural satellite, the Moon, is more than one quarter the size of Earth itself (3,474 kms diameter). Because of its smaller size, the Moon's gravity is one-sixth of the Earth's gravity.

While there are only two basic types of regions on the Moon's surface, there are many interesting surface features such as craters, mountain ranges, riles, and lava plains.

The structure of the Moon's interior is more difficult to study. The Moon's top layer is a rocky solid, perhaps 800 km thick. Beneath this layer is a partially molten zone. Although it is not known for certain, many lunar geologists believe the Moon may have a small iron core, even though the Moon has no magnetic field. By studying the Moon's surface and interior, geologists can learn about the Moon's geological history and its formation.

The footprints left by Apollo astronauts will last for centuries because there is no wind on the Moon. The Moon does not possess any atmosphere, so there is no weather as we are used to on Earth. Because there is no atmosphere to trap heat, the temperatures on the Moon are extreme, ranging from 100°C at noon to-173°C at night.

### *How Do the Phases Get their Names?*

When the Moon appears smaller than a quarter, we call it a crescent. When the Moon appears larger than a quarter, we call it gibbous. When the moon is getting bigger (phases new to full) it is waxing. When it is getting smaller (phases Full to New) it is waning.

The Moon, with its emotional sensitivity, has traditionally been viewed as feminine. The Sun, with its charisma and force, has been seen as masculine.

The moon is the celestial body which is the most visible in the nightly sky. The moon dominates the nightly sky and can be seen far more clearly than any other planet or star.

The phases of the moon are one of humankind's best and most ancient means of measuring time. "Moon," "menses," and "month" all share the same root, meaning to measure.

The most visible symbol of feminine energy in the solar system is the Moon. Because it reflects the light from the sun, the pale orbit in the night sky has come to represent a woman's reflective nature, her internalised response to the world.

Earth's moon has been personified as female and has been perceived as a symbol of the feminine principle since time immemorial. An increasing number of contemporary people are beginning to appreciate the profound truth and the high spiritual validity of this universal perception as they rediscover and reimplement ancient spiritual traditions which honour women and embody distinctly feminine spiritual values.

The coincidence of the menstrual cycle with that of the moon is a physical actuality structuring human life and a curiosity that has been observed with wonder. It is in fact likely that the fundamental notion of life-structuring relationship between the heavenly world and that of man was derived from this realisation, both in experience and in thought, of the force of the lunar cycle.

The Lunar calendar year is divided into 12 parts, each of which is called a month. But the word month has other meanings. Several kinds of months are measured by the moon's motion. At one point in the moon's path, it is closest to the earth. This point is called the perigee. The time the moon takes to revolve from one perigee to the next is an anomalistic month. This period averages 27 days, 13 hours, 18 minutes, and 33.1 seconds. If the moon were looked at from a distant star it would seem to make a complete revolution around the earth in 27 days, 7 hours, 43 minutes, and 11.5 seconds. This period is a sidereal month. The proper lunar month, which is called the synodical month, is the period between one new moon and the next, an average of 29 days, 12 hours, 44 minutes, and 2.8 seconds.

It is note worthy to point out here that the average menstrual cycle of women is exactly the same as a sidereal month of Moon. The great sage Tirumular has dealt in Thirumanthram about the similarity of the women and the moon. The moon has Four phases. Likewise a woman has also four phases of a manstural cycle.

The influence of the moon on human life is very high. The moon influences the mind and the sensations of every human. The moon also influences the physiology of a woman very much. The birth star, the moon sign and the thithi of a girl's birth have greater influence on the important physiological cycles of a woman. The day of her attaining maturity, the day of her conception and the day of her menopause can be predetermined with these.

The moon takes a raising trend from new moon to full moon and a falling trend from full moon to new moon. The Vedic scriptures term the first trend as the Suklapaksa and the second trend as the Krishnapaksa.

The full moon occurs on the 14th day of the new moon and a lady is prone to conception on the 14th day of her menstrual period.

## A Mini Refresher in Female Physiology

***What is Menstruation:*** Every month each ovary releases an ovum, which reaches the uterus via fallopian tubes. During this period, a soft and spongy lining develops in the uterus known as endometrium, which is the base of fertile ovum and develops as fetus. Unfertile ovum cannot stay there. The endometrium comes out in the form of a red liquid, for 3 to 5 days. This only is known as menstruation.

Every woman's cycle is approximately 28 days long.

The menstrual cycle is regulated by the hormones estrogen and progesterone. It has 4 phases.

***Menstruation:*** The shedding of about three quarters of the endometrial lining of the uterus lasting 4-5 days triggered by a fall in the estrogen and progesterone levels.

***Proliferative Phase:*** Endometrium regenerating. This phase lasts around 10 to 13 days and ends with ovulation. During this time progesterone levels remain stable and low while estrogen increases. When estrogen levels reach first peak it sets off a chain of hormonal responses, stimulating ovulation.

***Secretory Phase:*** Following ovulation the follicle from which the egg is released changes structurally into the corpus luteum and secretes progesterone. Progesterone levels and estrogen levels increase over 10 to 14 days and the endometrium itself is converted to an actively secreting tissue and the glands lining its surface become filled with glycogen. Glycogen is the main carbohydrate stored in cells.

***Pre-menstrual Phase:*** If fertilization does not occur the corpus luteum disappears and with this its influence on hormonal levels. Over the two days prior to menstruation estrogen and progesterone levels drop to their baseline level. Have you ever wondered about the connection between your body's 28 day cycle and the cycle of the moon? Here's the theory.

The Midpoint of the Menstrual Cycle (About Day 14 in a 28-Day Cycle as the case of full moon). The mature ovum bursts from the follicle about midway (approximately 2 weeks before onset of next menstrual period) through the menstrual cycle. This process is known as ovulation. The ovum then travels from the ovary down the fallopian tube, and into the uterus.

As the moon is raising from the new moon to full moon the progesterone levels and estrogen levels increase till the 14th day of the menstrual cycle and the endometrium itself is converted to an actively secreting tissue and the glands lining its surface become filled with glycogen. In a woman who hasn't become pregnant, the level of progesterone peaks about a week after ovulation and then begins to drop along with the estrogen level. The flow of blood to the endometrium decreases, and its upper portion is broken down and shed during menstruation. At the same time, the corpus luteum withers. This marks krishnapaksa, the falling trend of the moon.

The influence of moon on child birth:

- A woman conceived on an Amavasya (new moon day) or Pradamai (the immediate second day from new moon/ or of a full moon day thithis, delivers a spastic/under developed child or mentally unsound child.
- A women who conceives on her Chandraashtama day delivers a child who will be weak, suffers frequent ailments and illness and suffers with memory loss in the young age itself.
- If conceived on the Ashtami or Navami thittis, then the child likely to grow with some arrogance, aggressive tendency and never learns to adjust to the surroundings/ situations.
- If Amavasya day also happens to be the Chandraashtama day for women who conceived on that day, and if Surya Dasa/bhukti too runs then, the child born will, mostly be blind or with defective eye sight.

***Now, for the positive side:*** Human body in itself is a mystery! No one can say for sure that one has fully control and knowledge of one's own body. Yes, now you can simply do this following test and find whether you are aware of this.

Now take a deep breath. Exhale the same slowly. Check with your pointing finger taking it near to your nose, from which nostril the breathed air is coming out. From right or left nostril? or from both side nostrils? If the exhaling is from the left nostril, it is the moon's breath and if the exhaling from the right nostril, it is the sun's breath.

***For Men:*** If the carbon is released through your right nostril then it is a good women. When starting to do some thing new or when moving out of your home for some auspicious functions, check your breath is emitted from your right nostril. If it is from the left nostril or when the flow is from both nostrils then wait for few minutes to continue. The best timing for having sex with your partner is while the emission is from your right side nostril.

***For Women:*** When the emission of carbon is from your left nostril, then it is the best time for you to start your activities.

Also while planning for a child and having sex see that the carbon emission is through your left nostril. If emitted from both nostrils or from the right one then it is considered inauspicious.

***Interesting facts:*** Some other interesting facts about the coincidence of the moon and women are described here under:

The moon is the sub-planet of the earth. While all other planets are rotating the sun, the moon is only rotating the earth. Consider the nature of women assuming the sun is the husband of the moon. The earth is the parent of the moon. This evidences the fact that a woman's heart is always centering around her parents wherever she is.

A moon becomes shinning and beautiful when it goes nearer to her husband sun. Likewise a women is honoured and respected while she is along with her husband. This is the day of full moon.

A moon becomes dark and unseen when it keeps away from the sun. Likewise a woman looses her glory and respect when she keeps away her husband. This is the day of new moon.

### The Hindu Woman as Wife

Of the ideal woman of the religious orders the West today has very little notion. Teresa and Catherine are now but high-sounding names in history; Beatrice, a true daughter of the Church, is beloved only of the poets; and Joan of Arc, better understood, is rightly felt to be by birth the nun, but by genius the knight. Yet without some deeper sense of kindred with these it will be hard to understand a Hindu marriage, for the Indian bride comes to her husband much as the Western woman might enter a church. Their love is a devotion, to be offered in secret. They know well that they are the strongest influence, each in the other's life, but before the family there can be no assertion of the fact. Their first duty is to see that the claims of others are duly met, for the ideal is that a wife shall, if that be possible, love her husband's people as she never loved her own; that the new parents shall be more to her than the old; that she can bring no gift into their home so fair as a full and abundant daughterhood and a confirmation of their supreme place in their son's love. Both husband and wife must set their faces towards the welfare of the family. This, and not that they should love each the other before all created beings, is the primal intention of marriage.

Yet for the woman supreme love also is a duty. Only to the man his mother must stand always first. In some sense, therefore, the relation is not mutual. And this is in full accordance with the national sentiment, which stigmatises affection that asks for equal return as "shop keeping." When her husband is present or before honoured guests the young wife may not obtrude herself on the attention of her elders. She sits silent, with veil down, plying a fan or doing some little service for the new mother.

But through the work of the day she is a trusted helpmeet, and the relation is often very sweet. Nothing is so easy to distinguish as the educational impress of the good mother-in-law. Dignity, with gaiety and freedom, is its great feature. The good breeding of the Hindu woman is so perfect that it is not noticed till one comes across the exception—some spoilt child, perhaps, who, as heiress or beauty has been too much indulged; and her self-assertiveness and want of restraint, though the same behaviour might seem decorous enough in an English girl of her age, will serve as some measure for the real value of the common standard.

It is not merely in her quietness and modesty, however, that the daughter-in-law betrays good training. She has what remains with her throughout life—a savour faire that nothing can disturb. I have never known this broken; and I saw an extraordinary instance of it when a friend, the shyest of orthodox women, consented to have her photograph taken for one who begged it with urgency. She stipulated, naturally, that it should be done by a woman. But this was found to be impossible. "Then let it he an Englishman," she said with a sigh, evidently shrinking painfully from the idea of a man, yet feeling that the greater the race-distance the less would be the impropriety. The morning came, and the Englishman arrived, but in the Indian gentle-woman who faced him there was no trace of self-consciousness or fear. A superb indifference carried her through the ordeal, and would have been a sufficient protection in some real difficulty.

All the sons of a Hindu household bring their wives home to their mother's care, and she, having married her own daughters into other women's families, takes these in their place. There is thus a constant bubbling of young life about the elderly woman, and her own position becomes a mixture of the mother-suzerain and lady abbess. She is well aware of the gossip and laughter of the girls amongst themselves, though they become so demure at her entrance. Whispering goes on in corners and merriment waxes high even in her presence, but she ignores it discreetly, and devotes her attention to persons of her own age. In the early summer mornings she smiles indulgently to find that one and another slipped away last night from her proper sleeping-place and betook her to the roof, half for the coolness and half for the mysterious joys of girls' mid-night gossip.

The relationship, however, is as far from familiarity as that of any kind and trusted prioress with her novices. The element of banter and freedom has another outlet, in the grandmother or whatever aged woman may take that place in the community house. Just as at home the little one had coaxed and appealed against the decisions of father or mother to the ever-ready granddame, so, now that she is a bride, she finds some old woman in her husband's home who has given up her cares into younger hands and is ready to forego all responsibility in the sweetness of becoming a confidante. One can imagine the rest. There must be many a difficulty, many a perplexity, in the new surroundings, but to them all old age can find some parallel. Looking back into her own memories, the grandmother tells of the questions that troubled her when she also was a bride, of the mistakes that she made, and the solutions that offered.

Young and old take counsel together, and there is even the possibility that when a mother-in-law is unsympathetic, her own mother-in-law may intervene on behalf of a grandson's wife. Before the grandmother, therefore, there is none of that weight of reverence which can never be lightened in the mother's presence. Even the veil need not be dropped. The familiar "thou" take the place of the stately "you," and there is no respect shown by frigid reserve.

Long ago, when a child's solemn betrothal often took place at seven or eight years of age, it was to gratify the old people's desire to have more children about them that the tiny maidens were brought into the house. It was on the grandmother's lap that the little ones were made acquainted; it was she and her husband who watched anxiously to see that they took to each other; and it was they again who petted and comforted the minute grand-daughter-in-law in her hours of home sickness. Marriage has grown later nowadays, in answer amongst other things to the pressure of an increasing poverty, and it does not happen so often that an old man is seen in the bazaar buying consoling gifts for the baby brides at home. But the same instinct still obtains, of making the new home a place of choice, when between her twelfth and fourteenth year—the girl's age at her first and second marriages—the young couple visits alternately in each other's families.

The Hindu theory is that a long vista of common memory adds sweetness even to the marriage tie, and whether we think this true or not, we have all known happy marriages on such a basis. But about the mutual sentiment of old and young there can be no theory, because there is no possibility of doubt. In all countries in the world it is recognised as amongst the happiest things in life. The reminiscence of Aruba, one of the heroes of the great War-Epic, gives us the Indian explanation of this fact. "I climbed on his knee," he says, speaking of the aged knight Bhishma, head of his house, "all hot and dusty from my play, and flinging my arms about his neck, I called him 'Father.'" "Nay, my child," he replied, as he held me to his breast, "not thy father but thy father's father!" With each generation, that is to say, the tie has deepened and intensified.

In all cases where one or two hundred persons live under the same roof, a complex etiquette grows up, by which gradations of rank and deference is rigidly defined. Under the Hindu system this fund of observation has so accumulated that it amounts now to an accomplished culture—a completed criticism of life—rich in quaint and delightful suggestions for humanity everywhere. We may not know why a mother's relatives are apt to be dearer than a father's, but the statement will be approved as soon as made. It has not occurred to us that our relations to an elder sister and a younger are not the same: in India there is a different word for each, for whole worlds of sweetness lie a world apart in one name and the other to the Hindu mind. Yet a cousin is constantly called brother or sister, the one relation being merged entirely in the other. The mere use of a language with this degree of definiteness implies an emotional training of extraordinary kind. It is, of course, best suited to natres of great richness of feeling.

In these, sentiment is developed in proportion to expression, and the same attitude that makes every one in the village "Aunt" or "Uncle" to the children, produces an ultimate sense of kinship to the world. This is perhaps the commonest characteristic of Hindu men and women; shy at first, and passive to slight stimulus, as are all great forces, when once a relationship is established, they believe in it absolutely, blindly; are ready to go to the uttermost in its name; and forget entirely all distance of birth or difference of association. The weak point in the system appears when it has to deal with the harder, more arid class of natures. In these there is less inner response to the outer claim, expressions of difference, therefore, become less sincere and more abject?

This is but a poor preparation for the open air of the modern world, where seniority, sanctity, and rank have all to be more or less ignored, and man stands face to face with man, free and equal so far as the innate manhood of each can carry.

But such persons—though, naturally enough, they cluster round the powerful foreigner as moths about a lamp—are the failures of Hinduism, not its types, and they are very few. In a perfected education, Western ideals of equality and struggle would present themselves to these for their choosing, while far away in Europe, maybe, hearts born too sensitive for their more rudimentary emotional surroundings would be thankful in turn to find life made richer by Indian conceptions of human relationship.

In a community like that of the Hindu home—as in all clan-systems—the characteristic virtue of every member must be a loyal recognition of common duties and dangers. And this is so. The wife who refused to share her husband's obligation to a widowed sister and her children was never known in India. Times of stress draw all parts of the vast group together; none of the blood can cry in vain for protection and support: even a "village-connection" (*i.e.*, one who is kin by association only) finds refuge in his hour of need. This great nexus of responsibility takes the place of workhouse, hospital, orphanage, and the rest. Here the lucky and the unlucky are brought up side by side. For to the ripe and mellow genius of the East it has been always clear that the defenseless and unfortunate require a home, not a barrack.

Into this complex destiny the bride enters finally, about her fourteenth year. Till now she has been a happy child, running about in freedom, feet shod and head bare, eating and drinking what she would. Till now, life has been full of indulgences—for her own parents, with the shadow of this early separation hanging over them, have seen no reason for a severity that must bring in its train an undying regret. From the moment of her betrothal, however, the girl's experience gradually changes. Just as the young nun, if she runs to find her thimble, will be sent back to bring it "more religiously," so about the newly married girl there grows a subtle atmosphere of recollectedness. The hair is parted, no longer childishly brushed back; and at the parting—showing just beyond the border of the veil with which her head now is always covered—appears a touch of vermilion, put there this morning as she dressed in token that she wished long life to her husband; much as one might, in taking up a fan, blow a kiss from its edge to some absent beloved one.

The young wife's feet are unshod, and the gold wedding bracelet on the left wrist, and a few ornaments appropriate to her new dignity, supply the only hint of girlish vanity. But she has more jewels. These that she wears daily are of plain gold, more or less richly worked, but on her wedding night she wore the siti, or three-lined coronal, set with gems, and arms and neck were gay with flashing stones. All these were her dower, given by her father to be her personal property, and not even her husband can touch them without her consent, though he will add to them occasionally at festive moments.

She will wear them all now and again, on great occasions, but meanwhile the silver anklets and the golden necklet and a few bangles are enough for daily use. The girl knows her right to her own ornaments quite well, and the world will never hear how often the wife or the mother has hastened to give up the whole of this little resource in order that son or husband might weather a storm or receive an education. The one thing from which she will never part, however, unless widowhood lays its icy hand upon her life, is that ring of iron covered with gold and worn on the left wrist, which is the sign of the indissoluble bond of her marriage—her wedding-ring in fact.

With all the shyness of the religious novice comes the girl to her new home. Its very form, with its pillared courtyards, is that of a cloister. The constant dropping of the veil in the presence of a man, or before a senior, is the token of a real retirement, the sacrament of an actual seclusion, within which all the voices of the world lose distinctness and individuality, becoming but faint echoes of that which alone can call the soul and compel the eager feet. For India has no fear of too much worship. To her, all that exists is but a mighty curtain of appearances, tremulous now and again with breaths from the unseen that it conceals. At any point, a pinprick may pierce the great illusion, and the seeker become aware of the Infinite

Reality beyond. And who so fitted to be the window of the Eternal Presence as that husband, who is at once most adored and loved of all created beings?

For there is a deep and general understanding of the fact that only in its own illumination, or its own feeling, can the soul find its highest individuation. To learn how she can offer most becomes thus the aim of the young wife's striving. All her dreams are of the saints—women mighty in renunciation: Sita, whose love found its richest expression in the life-long farewell that made her husband the ideal king; Sati, who died rather than hear a word against Shiva, even from her own father; and Uma, realising that her love was given in vain, yet pursuing the more eagerly the chosen path. "Be like Savitri," was her father's blessing, as he bade her the bridal farewell, and Savitri—the Alcestris of Indian story—was that maiden who followed even Death till she won back her husband's life. Thus wifehood is thought great in proportion to its giving, not to its receiving. It would never occur to any one, in writing fiction, or delineating actual character, to praise a woman's charms, as we praise Sarah Jennings', on the score that she retained her husband's affection during her whole life.

A good man, says the Hindu, does not fail his wife, but, apart from this, coquetry and vanity, however pleasing in their form, could never dignify marriage. Lifelong intimacy, to be beautiful, must boast deeper foundations—the wife's love, daring all and asking for no return; the mother's gentleness, that never changes; the friend's unswerving generosity. To the grave Oriental there is something indecorous in the discussion of the subject on any but this highest basis. And yet Persia, the France of Asia, must have been a perpetual influence towards romanticism in Hindu life. There is said to be no love poetry in the world so impassioned as the Persian. The famous verse:

> *Four eyes met. There were changes in two souls.*
>
> *And now I cannot remember whether he is a man and I a woman,*
>
> *Or he a woman and I a man. All I know is,*

*There were two: Love came, and there is one...*

We must believe completely representative of its spirit. The Persian language, however, has only touched India through the Court of Delhi and through letters. It has been the possession of the Indo-Mohammedan and of any man here and there who took the time and trouble to master its literature; but the world of Hindu womanhood has remained probably as remote from it as though it belonged to another planet.

This is not true to the same extent of the romantic aspect of Christianity. The letters taught in English schools result very much in novel-reading, and an indigenous school of fiction has grown up, in the form of books and magazines, which is likely to modify popular ideas on this subject profoundly. Meanwhile, and for long to come, it remains true that according to Hindu notions, the eyes of bride and bridegroom are to be directed towards the welfare of the family and not of themselves, as the basis of society: it is the great springs of helpfulness and service, rather than those of mutual love and romantic happiness that marriage is expected to unloose. Selfish wives and jealous husbands there must be, as among all peoples. But it is a fact, nevertheless, that here the absolute stainlessness of the wife is considered but preliminary to the further virtue demanded of her, the sustaining of the honour of her husband's house.

With this clue it becomes easy to understand even what the West considers to be the anomalies of Hindu custom—the laws regarding rare cases of polygamy and adoption. For it is legally provided that if a woman remain childless her husband may after seven years, and with her permission, take a second wife, in the hope of gaining a son to succeed to his place.

On the European basis of individualism, the permission would probably be impossible to obtain; but with the Eastern sense of family obligation, this has not always been so, and I have myself met the son of such a marriage whose story was of peculiar interest. The elder wife had insisted that the time was come for the alternative to be tried, and had herself chosen the speaker's mother as the most beautiful girl she could find, for the husband.

The marriage once over, she made every effort to make it a success, and welcomed the new wife as a younger sister. Not only this, but when the son was born, such was her tenderness that he was twelve years old before he knew that she was not his mother. After her death, however, the younger wife became head of the house. Amongst the children to be fed, there were degrees of kindred, certain adopted orphans, two or three cousins, and himself. He was the eldest of all, and protested loudly that he came in last and his cousins only second, for his mother's attentions. "Nay, my child," she answered, with a Hindu woman's sweetness and good sense, "if I desired to neglect thee, I could not do it. Is it not right, then, first to serve those who have no protection against me?"

The family life which such a story discloses is singularly noble, and it is not necessary to suppose that polygamy entailed such generosities oftener than we find monogamy do amongst ourselves. In any case, the same tide that brings in individualism has swept away this custom; and whereas it never was common it is now practically obsolete, except for princes and great nobles, and even amongst these classes there are signs of a radical change of custom.

"Where women are honoured, there the gods are pleased: where they are dishonoured, religious acts become of no avail." "In whatever family the husband is contented with his wife, and the wife with her husband, in that house will good fortune assuredly abide." Few books offer such delights to their readers as that known as the "Laws of Manu."

It is in no sense a collection of Acts of Parliament, for the one attitude throughout is that of the witness, and the hastiest perusal shows that it represents the growth of custom during ages, and is in no sense the work of a single hand. This is indeed its first and most striking beauty. As must be, of course, it often happens that the superstition of a habit is stated as gravely as its original intent, but rarely so as to obscure that first significance, or leave it difficult of restoration, and from cover to cover the book throbs with the passion for justice, and the appreciation of fine shades of courtesy and taste, clothed in calm and judicial form. Especially of this type are those dicta on the rights of women, which are household words in Indian homes.

We all know the reaction of the written word on life. Fact once formulated as scripture acquires new emphasis, a certain occult significance seems to attach to it, and the words, "it is written" become terrible enough to affright the devil himself. In this way the fear of a feminine curse has become a superstition in India, and I have seen even a low-class mob fall back at the command of a single woman who opposed them. For is it not written in the book of the law that "the house which is cursed by a woman perishes utterly, as if destroyed by a sacrifice for the death of an enemy?"—strange and graphic old phrase, pregnant of woe!

It is evident then that the laws of Manu are rather the unconscious expression of the spirit of the people than a declaration of the ideals towards which they strive. And for this reason they would afford the most reliable foundation for a healthy criticism of Indian custom. The conception of domestic happiness which they reveal is very complete, and no one who has seen the light on an Indian woman's face when it turns to her husband—as I have seen it in all parts of the country—can doubt that conception is often realised in life. For if the characteristic emotion of the wife may be described as passionate reverence that of the Hindu husband is certainly a measureless protection.

If we may presume to analyse things as sacred as the great mutual trusts of life, it would seem that tenderness is the ruling note of the man's relation. Turning as he does to the memory of his own mother for the ideal perfection, there is again something of motherhood in what he brings to his wife. As a child might do, she cooks for him, and serves him, sitting before him as he eats to fan away the flies. As a disciple might, she prostrates herself before him, touching his feet with her head before receiving his blessing. It is not equality. No. But who talks of a vulgar equality, asks the Hindu wife, when she may have instead the unspeakable blessedness of offering worship?

And on the man's side, how is this received? Entirely without personal vanity. The idea that adoration is the soul's opportunity has sunk deep into the life of the people. And the husband can recognize his wife's right to realise her highest through him without ever forgetting that it is her power to love, not his worthiness of love that is being displayed. Indeed, is not life everywhere of one tint in this regard? Does anything stir our reverence like an affection that we feel beyond our merit?

It is often glibly said that this habit of being served spoils the Indian man and renders him careless of the comfort of others. I have never found this to be so. It is true that Indian men do not rise when a woman enters, and remain standing till she is seated. Nor do they hasten to open the door through which she is about to pass. But then it is not according to the etiquette of their country to do these things. With regard to the last point, indeed, their idea is that man should precede woman, maintaining the tradition of the path-breaker in the jungle; and one of the most touching incidents in the national epic of heroic love is Sita's request to go first along the forest paths, in order to sweep the thorns from her husband's path with the end of her veil. Needless to say, such a paradox is not permitted.

Thus, honour for the weaker is expressed in one way in England and quite otherwise in Hindustan, but the heart of conduct is the same in both countries. The courtesy of husbands to their wives is quite unfailing amongst Hindus. "Thou shalt not strike a woman, even with a flower," is the proverb. His wife's desire for companionship on a journey is the first claim on a man. And it is very touching to notice how, as years go on, he leans more and more to the habit of addressing her as "O thou, mother of our son!" and presenting her to new corners as "my children's mother," thus reflecting upon her his worship of motherhood.

In early manhood he trusts to her advice to moderate the folly of his own rasher inclinations; in old age he becomes, as everywhere in the world, more entirely the eldest of her bairns, and she more and more the real head and centre of the home. But always she remains as she was at the beginning, Lakshmi, her husband's Goddess of Fortune. In those first days he ate from no hand but his mother's or hers; and one of her devotions was the fast, not broken till he had eaten and their talk was over, though her evening meal might in this way be delayed till long past mid-night. Now, with the responsibilities of her household upon her, she feeds a whole multitude before she takes her own turn, and still the mutual pact of soul and soul has not been broken by the strife of "rights." These two have all these years been each other's refuge against the world. And not once have they felt so separated as to offer thanks, or speak, either of the other, by name, as if head and hand could be different individuals!

On that first bridal evening, the little bride was borne before her young husband, and they were told that the moment was auspicious for their first shy look. Then the old Vedic fire was called to witness their rites of union; the girl flung the garland of flowers about the neck of her bridegroom, in exquisite symbolism of the bond that was to hold them; and finally they took seven steps together, hand in hand, while the priest chanted appropriate texts for each stage of life. Such was their wedding. Since then, the rights of one have been the rights of the other; joys, griefs, and duties have been held in common. Till now, if the bride of that distant night be entirely fortunate, the prayer of her childhood is fulfilled to her in the end of her days, that prayer that said:

*From the arms of husband and sons,*
*When the Ganges is full of water,*
*May I pass to the feet of the Lord?*

It has seemed to me in watching Hindu couples that they were singular in the frequent attainment of a perfect intimacy. To what is this due? Is it the early association, or the fact that courtship comes after marriage, not before? Or is it the intense discipline of absolute reserve in the presence of others? The people themselves, where their attention is called to it, attribute the fact to child-marriage. I remember asking a friend of my own, a man of wealth and cultivation, orthodox and childless, "If you could put away personal considerations, and speak only from the outside, which you think better in the abstract, our marriage-system or yours?"

He paused, and answered slowly, "I think—ours; for I cannot conceive that two people could grow into each other, as my wife and I have done, under any other."

Amongst the luxuries of the West I have sometimes thought that the deepening of the human tie was proportionate to simplicity of surroundings. A people to whom all complexity of externals is impossible must live by thought and feeling, or perish in the wilderness.

But whatever be the truth on this point, I have seen clearly and constantly that the master-note by which the Hindu woman's life can be understood in the West is that of the religious life. This is so, even with the wife. Cloistered and veiled, she devotes herself to one name, one thought, yet is never known to betray the fact, even as the nun steals away in secret to kneel before the Blessed Sacrament.

The ideal that she, like the nun, pursues, is that of a vision which merges the finite in the infinite, making strong to mock at separation, or even at change. And the point to be reached in practice is that where the whole world is made beautiful by the presence in it of the beloved, where the hungry are fed, and the needy relieved, out of a joyful recognition that they wear a common humanity with his; and where, above all, the sense of unrest and dissatisfaction is gone for ever, in the overflowing fullness of a love that asks no return except the power of more abundant loving.

# 3

# SPECIAL STUDY OF HINDU RELIGION

## Introduction

The small island of Mauritius off the coast of South Africa (near Madagascar) is 54 per cent Hindu. Britain and the United States have significant, but relatively small, Hindu populations. Hinduism is found in nearly every corner of the globe. Hindus are estimated at 500,000,000 worldwide. According to the CIA, the largest concentration of Hindus are in India (81 per cent of population) and Nepal (86 per cent). Countries with the fewest Hindus include Thailand (95 per cent Buddhist), Malaysia, Singapore, Oman, Yemen, Pakistan (mainly Islamic). Nepal is the only state in the world that is officially Hindu. A large number of Hindus also reside in South America and the Caribbean, including in the countries of Guyana, Suriname, Trinidad and Tobago.

## Hindu Philosophy

The philosophy is rational aspect of the faith, in any culture or Religion. It is an integral part of Hindu religious beliefs and culture in India. It is a rational inquiry into the nature of truth or reality, giving clear solutions to many problems of life and human behaviour. It shows the ways to get rid of the pain and sufferings, to get happiness and peace of mind and to attain liberation and eternal bliss. Theology is considered important in most world religions. Philosophy is often agnostic and it is not part of the religious study. Hindus consider philosophy as an integral part of their religious experience. In Hindu culture, theology is well mixed in all aspects of life through its mythology, art, music and dance and they all carry a moral. Hindu Philosophy is not merely a speculation or guess work of a solution for human problems and doubts, but an organised doctrine based on the mystical experience of the Sages and Seers.

Hindu Philosophy gives a clear understanding to the questions of cycle of life and death, the nature of Soul, the Universe and its creator and reasons for joy and sufferings, happiness and sorrow, health and disease and the ultimate understanding of man's relationship with God. It also explains his duties during this birth as well as about his past and his future. It investigates and inquires the Truth and allows us to think and reason in our search for a solution. Even though the Agamas and Vedas appear to be professing different doctrines, they both are written on the same philosophy but for different population group.

The Agamas give us the Theological aspect of our practice with prayers to God in various manifestations. The Vedas give us all the rituals and also the philosophy of our religious practice. All of them are based on the principle that the Soul is a part of the Divine spirit and is covered by the sheaths of "Upadhis" as an effect of ones Karma. It goes through endless rebirth according to ones Karma to purify itself. Every one should follow his Dharma and perform their duties or Karma without attachment, as an offering to God to receive eternal salvation and liberation as Moksha.

***The Divine Laws that Holds True for Ever:*** The teachings of Hindu philosophy are given to us in the Upanishads which are the wealth of our knowledge. The ethics and tenets are obtained from them through the Six Darsanas and various later schools of philosophers. The glory of Hindu philosophy is seen in the teachings of Hindu dharma, the theory of karma and rebirth, the six darsanas, and the four yogas or spiritual disciplines. They not only create the questions in our mind to think but also give us the answers to the problems. Dharma means "that which holds" the people of this world and the whole creation. It is the eternal Divine law of God. That which brings well being to man and supports the world with prosperity is dharma. It is the absolute Truth and laws of righteous living. The four Vedas are the authority of Dharma. The truth about dharma can not be realised through any other knowledge and one's own reasoning through any analysis alone can not be that authority.

***Ancient sets of Rules that Holds and Changes with Time:*** Purushartha are the four kinds of human aspirations, which are dharma, artha, kaama and Moksha. Among these, dharma is the foremost and is the gateway to Moksha or immortality and eternal bliss. Practice of proper Dharma gives an experience of peace, joy, strength and tranquillity within ones-self and life becomes thoroughly disciplined. It is classified as [i] Samanya dharma or the general and Universal Dharma and [ii] Visesha dharma or specific personal dharma. Samanya dharma includes contentment, forgiveness, self-restraint, spiritual knowledge, absence of anger, non-greediness, non-stealing, truthfulness, purity, non-violence, control of senses and desire, discrimination between right and wrong and between real and unreal. Visesha or specific dharma includes duties due to one's birth, age and family and duties to society and family, due to one's career and job and spiritual life. They also include the specific dharmas for the four ashramas and four varnas. These are the regular duties including the rituals and services to the family, community, ancestors and God that every one is expected to perform. We have separate Dharma for each of the four Yugas or time periods.

***Varying Rules of Duty for Different Times:*** The Vedas give different rules of Dharma for people of different age groups, different family traits and different periods of time. The ashrama dharma gives the standards of living for different age groups of individuals. The varna dharma is one that is most misinterpreted and misused. If properly interpreted and understood, it is the most efficient sociological system of the nation. It is indeed a splendid theory with a flawless rule.

But, the defect came from somewhere else. Various dharma sasthras, or smrithis, written by Rishis like Manu, Parasara, and Yaagnavalkya, have varied for different periods of time according to varying social and emotional surroundings of the Hindu society [Yuga-Dharma]. The Hindus often follow the teachings of various Dharma sasthras for the philosophical guidance for daily living.

***An Unencompassed Light, Transcendent and Immanent:*** The Divine is both in us and out of us. God is neither completely transcendent nor completely immanent. He is divine darkness as well as 'unencompassed light.' The philosophers with their passion for unity emphasise the immanent aspect, that there is no barrier dividing man from the real. Those who emphasise the Transcendence of the Supreme to the human insist on the specifically religious consciousness, of communion with a higher than ourselves with whom it is impossible for the individual to get assimilated.

There cannot be a fundamental contradiction between the philosophical idea of God as an all-embracing spirit and the devotional idea of a personal God who arouses in us the specifically religious emotion. The personal conception develops the aspect of spiritual experience in which it may be regarded as fulfilling the human needs. God is represented as possessing the qualities we lack. Justice, love and holiness are the highest qualities we know and we imagine God as possessing them, though these qualities exist in God in a different sense from their existence in us. The difference between the Supreme as spirit and Supreme as person is one of stand point and not of essence, between God as He is and as he seems to us.

***Panjchakshara Mantra:*** While there are plenty of mantras available, there are a few that are chanted with high esteem by the shaivas. Definitely those are highly powerful ones that can lead the chanter on the great path to mukti (liberation). pranava, panjchakashra, gayatri to name a few. For shaivites the Holy Five Syllables (panhichakshara) with or without combined with the pranava is the ultimate mantra.

***Holy Five Syllables-Panjchakshara Mantra:*** Panjchakshara as popularly known is the holy five syllables (literally holy five letters) that is the supreme mantra of all devotees of Lord Shiva. As the name suggests it is made up of five syllables. This great mantra is namah Sivaya (namah Sivaya). The five syllables in this mantra are na-mah-si-va-ya.

***The Core of the Vedas:*** The Holy Five Syllables nåmah Sivaya is the heart of vedas. It is the core of the very famous chapter of vedas that stands in the middle of the vedas-the shata rudrIyam or rudra suktam. This great mantra of veda samhita while hailing the God as the Lord of everything of the worlds, salutes the God as namah Sivaya cha Sivataraya cha.

***Meaning of the Panjchakshara Mantra:*** The meaning of this matchless mantra is abound. The puranas and the philosophical texts talk in a very detailed and elabourate manner its meaning and significance and hail its ultimateness. Here only a simple meaning is presented to start with.

The word Shiva means auspiciousness and perfection. It refers to the God Who is Perfect without any kind of dependency on anything external to make It complete. Naturally because of this self-perfection, It is completely blissful and ever auspicious. (All other auspicious things are in one way or the other dependent on the external circumstances, etc.) The prefix namaH is the mantra of salutation. The mantra namah Sivaya salutationally invoke the Perfect God Shiva.

***Various Panjchaksharas:*** Panjchakshara has five syllables, so is Lord Shiva with five faces. Depending upon which letter the panjchakshara is starting with, the panjchakshara gets the name of a face of the God. Namah sivaya is the sadyojata panjchakshara and Sivayanamah is the aghora panjchakshara or the aghora mantra. Similarly the other panjchaksharas also get the names.

As the panjchakshara namah Sivaya is at the centre of vedas, it is referred as Vedic way panjchakshara. Sivayanamah is the panjchakshara is used very much in the Agamic worship of the Lord. So it is referred as the agamic way panjchakshara.

***Ways of Chanting the Panjchakshari:*** While many mantras have restrictions as to when and how it can be chanted, etc., there is no such restriction to the panjchakshara mantra. The great prodigy sambandhar says in thevaram, "When you sleep as well as when you do not sleep, think of the Holy Five Syllables with heartful of devotion! This is the mantra that terribly kicked out the death when chanted (by markandeya) with sincerity."

Whoever you are, whenever be the time, whatever be the situation chant the Holy Five Syllables. There are no restrictions of colour, creed, caste, gender or any other restrictions. All it requires is sincerity.

This mantra could be chanted as it is as panjchakshara or could be chanted along with the pranava (Aum) as shadakshara mantra (om namah sivaya). In fact it is to be noted that pranava itself is panjchakshara mantra (akara, ukara, Makara, bindhu, natham).

***Benefit of Chanting the Mantra:*** The thoughts make the person. The one who has the positive thoughts is happier and the one full of worries is the sad one. The thoughts not only have effect at that moment but they definitely make impression on the personality of the individual, which could have a very long lasting impact. In this background while the good thoughts itself would be making things better, what needs to be said about the super-powered mantras that are rich in meaning as well as energy!

Given the fact that "we tend to become what we keep thinking about", when one chants the sacred panjchakshara that hails the God as Perfection and auspicious, it would take one towards that Blissful Perfection. It takes to the union with the Supreme God. What else can be more rewarding ! Even the worst sinner would get corrected and get to the glorious states if chants this mantra piously.

***Widespread Glory of Panjchaksara in Scriptures:*** The importance and glory of this mantra is stressed across the shaiva scriptures, as the most important mantra the devotee has to keep like own soul. Listing them would be highly arduous task given the importance this mantra gets in the scriptures.

Learning the various scriptures and chanting thousands of stotras (praise) of God, is all given secondary importance to chanting this great mantra. The authentic scriptures very clearly state that for the one who chants this mantra, even if none of the other scriptures are known or even any other worship of God is undertaken, that person would definitely gets eligible for the immense grace of the Supreme Lord Shiva. For this the chanting of the Holy Five Syllables has been prescribed as a definite requirement for the devotee. While the rudraksha and Holy Ash are the ornament externally for the devotee the internal ornament is the panjchakshara mantra.

The supreme mantra very simple to chant and comes with no restrictions attached in order for everybody to chant and get benefited. With no inertia in mind chant and keep chanting as much as possible namah Sivaya.

***Pranava Mantra (AUM)-Simple Explanation:*** The mantra that is held very sacred by all Hindus is the mantra Om also called pranava mantra. This mantra is part of every worship. This mantra is hailed in scriptures of various languages. Vedas—the holy scripture—is chanted always after chanting this mantra and always concluded with this mantra. Each of the hailing in the archanai that is performed for the divine is preceded by this mantra Om.

Pranava is the primal sound that existed before the creation and the sound that stays after the parlay. This is the natharupa-the Form of sound, of the Supreme Luminance. This mantra om refer to none other than God. The great yogis meditate in this mantra as the path to Eternal Bliss of the Formless Nameless God! The pranava has five parts. They are akara, ukara, makara, bindhu, natham. (aum). Consequently this is also one of the glorious panjchakshara mantra.

The scriptures that explain the glory of this pranava mantra are quite many. However the significant one is from the skandha purana. It is a well known puranic event that skandha described the real meaning of the pranava mantra to God Shiva. In the above mentioned episode of skandha purana the sage vamadeva seeks the boon from Lord Skandha to tell him too that description. Lord Skandha who was pleased with the devotion of sage vamadeva told him that great secret.

***Aum:*** Tirumular says that the one letter, A, represents the universe. The two letters A and U are Shiva and Sakti, the latter being the all-powerful manifest energy of Shiva. The three letters, A, U, and M are Shiva, Sakti and Light, the last being Jnana or knowledge. The letter M is also Maya. Tirumular calls AUM as one-letter mantra, representing Tandava, the Divine Dance of Shiva. Tandava is derived from Tandu, a dancer and servant of Shiva. Any act performed by Shiva is a dance. The dances are named according to his acts (creation, maintenance, destruction, veiling and Grace), places (Chidambaram, etc.), and competition (Urdhva), 25 Lilas (acts of play). The most celebrated dance is the 'Tandava' in Chidambaram.

***Symbols of Hinduism:*** In Hinduism much importance is given to the symbols than most other religions. The Hindu symbols range from the mark one puts on the forehead to the idols of the deities that are worshipped by the ardent Hindu devotees. Each one has its own significance. Hinduism at its core maintains that there is one God and many see it in different ways (Ekam sad viprah bahuta vadanti). God is formless and is beyond the limitations of the comprehension. This is the basis on which many of the great sages meditate on this Supreme Being that is beyond any contours.

So why are so many forms? The God in its natural form being very difficult to comprehend, leave alone loving that God and worshiping with devotion, the simple minds would certainly need a way through which they could worship the boundless

God in a fairly simplified manner. But at the same time it should not contradict the basis that the God is beyond forms in any way.

Hinduism maintains that because of the abundant Grace of the God, It revealed itself in the Holy symbols for the humans and other creatures to worship. These symbols are easy to comprehend for the minds of the normal human beings, but at the same time they are not just the symbols but they are the objects themselves, which means that they symbolically indicate the God, which is beyond the exploration of knowledge.

Hinduism Symbols are the pranava (Aum) which is held in high esteem by all sects of Hindus and the glorious Shiva lingam (meaning symbol of Shiva, the God) that is considered the most sacred symbol of worship for the Shaivites. The intention is that the Formless Supreme could be achieved by simpler means of these formless-forms, the symbols.

In a way these Hindu symbols are abstract representation of the God. These are quite closer to the ideal as they form a bridge between the Formless one and the mind that expects a form. The simpler minds benefit better if the God could be correlated with the day to day lives they interact with. The God certainly is Graceful to the upliftment of the creatures, it took various forms in various occasions blessing either in valorous or joyful or yogic postures.

There are numerous of these forms that Hindus worship in their temples, which are built in a gigantic manner with the patronage of various emperors that stand as the glorious homes of art and architecture. The maheshvara murthams are good examples of such forms of God.

The Hindus wear various marks on their forehead that also have spiritual significance. For example the ash that the Shaivites wear represents the ash that the Supreme Flame-Lord Shiva has smeared on Him always. The same way the shrichurna and the Tilak have their significance and indications. In essence Hindus achieve the Supreme Things, by simple ways following the symbols.

***Pranava /Aum:*** Revered by all religions of Hinduism. This is the primeval sound Om. This mystic sound is so important that there is little worship without this. The archanas done at the Hindu temples include this for each of the mantra chanted. The holy vedas also start with this. This mantra is one of the renowned mantra for meditation. This sound represents the Supreme Divinity.

***Lingam:*** The prime symbol of worship of Shiva. (In fact the name itself means symbol). This is broad in the middle and conical towards the top. This is the form of flame. In Shaivites philosophy the God is formless. Due to the Grace on the souls for the easy comprehension of the Divine and liberation the God appeared in the form of a Flame. This flame is what is worshiped as lingam in stone and other forms that make the worship easier. This is considered more sacred than form worship by Shaivites.

***Holy Ash / Bhasma/ Vibuti:*** The three bands one could see on the foreheads of the gods and goddesses. These three bands are worn by the Shaivites and the other religions in that family. This symbol is called tripundra (three bands). As the God appeared as a Supreme Flame (This need not be confused with agni. Agni becomes one of the aspects of God but not the Supreme itself), in the Shaivites religion, naturally Ash becomes the symbol that indicates the association with that Parma jyoti (Supreme flame).

***Rudraksha:*** Rudra + aksha translates to the eye of rudra. This is a beed from a tree. This is considered to have emanated from the eye of Lord Shiva when He burnt the tripura asuras. This is one of the holy symbols worn by Shaivites along with Holy Ash. This is worn as a single beed or as garlands of beeds.

***Tilaka:*** This is the dot most of the Hindus have at the eye-brow junction. This could be of sandal or red kumkum or a mix of both. This junction is one of the very significant chakra, called in spiritual terms AGYA chakra. This is a very sensitive point. So the tilaka is kept at this point.

***Shri Churna:*** The vertical three lines (or at times single red line) that is worn by the Vaishnavites are called shri churna.

The two outer lines will be in the white colour and the middle one in the red. The red line is normally with kumkum or the red sand at the base of the tulsi plant. This custom has been introduced in the later parts of time by Ramanuja as vaishnavite symbolism. Vaiahvavas not belonging to Ramanuja sampradaya (for example madhvas) do not follow this custom.

***Nandi:*** This is the Holy Bull-the vehicle and the disciple of Lord Shiva. So Nandi is the first Guru Shaivites. On the wall of the Shaivites temples, in the flags, in the message headers and many other articles this emblem could be found. The ancience of this emblem will be very evident from the fact that this emblem has been found in the excavations of Harappa mahenjadaro (the so-called Indus valley civilization sites). According to Shaivites scriptures bull represents the dharma (justice).

***Trishula:*** The tri headed spear (trident)—one of the renowned weapon of Lord Shiva. So this is the second important emblem of Shaivites after nandi. As the Goddess shakthi also holds this trident, this is the symbol that is held high by the devotees of shakthi as well.

***Shanka Chakra:*** The counch called panjchajanya and the disc called sudarshana in the hands of Lord Vishnu are the important symbols of Vaishnavites. These two are printed as emblems in the artifacts associated with Vaishnavas.

***Spear:*** The spear is the renowned weapon of Lord Skanda. So this is a much respected symbol of the devotees of Lord Subramanya.

> *Oh God, Your Feet is beyond the worlds beneath*
> *and Your Crown beyond the universes above!*
> *You are Immeasurable, Unexplorable, and Unimaginable!*
> *But how simple You have come as a Sivalinga in my hand !! —Basavanna*

**Hindu Culture**

Each of the religions of the world has its own culture, with many customs, traditions and refined qualities. The Hindu culture is a culture of love, respect, honouring others and humbling one's own ego so that the inner nature, which is naturally pure and modest, will shine forth. Here we have described some of the important faith and behaviours of Hindu community.

### *Respect and Reverence*

1. *Respect for Elders:* Respect for elders is a keystone of Hindu culture. This genuine acknowledgment of seniority is demonstrated through endearing customs, such as sitting to the left of elders, bringing gifts on special occasions, not sitting while they are standing, not speaking excessively, not yawning or stretching, not putting one's opinions forward strongly, not contradicting or arguing, seeking their advice and blessings, giving them first choice in all matters, even serving their food first.
2. *Name Protocol:* Younger never uses the proper name of their elders. In the Tamil tradition, a younger brother, for example, refers to his brother as annan, or periannan (older brother), not by name. The elder, however, may use the name of the younger. Children are trained to refer to all adults as auntie or uncle. Only people of the same age will address each other by first name. A Hindu wife never speaks the name of her husband. When referring to him she uses terms such as "my husband," "him" or, for example, "Athan, Mama, etc.,".
3. *Touching Feet in Respect:* One touches the feet of holy men and women in recognition of their great humility and inner attainment. A dancer or a musician touches the feet of his or her teacher before and after each lesson. Children prostrate and touch the feet of their mother and father at festivals and at special times, such as birthdays and before departing on a journey.
4. *Darshan (Darshana):* "Vision, sight." Seeing the Divine. Beholding, with inner or outer vision, a temple image,

Deity, holy person or place, with the desire to inwardly contact and receive the grace and blessings of the venerated being or beings.

5. *Dakshina:* It is tradition to provide dakshina, a monetary fee or gift to a priest given at the completion of any rite. Dakshina is also given to gurus as a token of respect for their spiritual blessings..

***Purity:*** Purity and its opposite, pollution, are vitally important in Hindu culture. Purity is of three forms—purity in mind, speech and body, or thought, word and deed. Purity is the pristine and natural state of the soul. Impurity, or pollution, is the obscuring of this state by adulterating experience and beclouding conceptions.

In daily life, the Hindu strives to protect this innate purity by wise living, following the codes of dharma. This includes harnessing the sexual energies, associating with other virtuous Hindu devotees, never using harsh, angered or indecent language, and keeping a clean and healthy physical body. Here are several ways purity is preserved in Hindu culture.

1. *Purity and Food*: Purity is central to food and nutrition, as the nature of one's nourishment deeply affects the entire physical, mental and emotional nature. One cooking food for others would never taste of the dish from a spoon and then put the spoon back in the pot. If food is to be tasted while cooking, a small portion is placed in the right hand. Similarly, one would not touch the lips to a water vessel that is also used by others. Nor would one offer something to another from which one has taken a bite or a sip.
2. *Flower Offerings*: One does not sniff flowers picked for offering to the Deities; even the smell is for the Gods, not for us. Flowers that fall to the ground should not be offered.
3. *Offerings:* Offerings, such as an archana basket, flowers or garlands, are carried with both hands on the right

side of the body, so as to not be breathed on. All items are washed in preparation and, if carried more than a short distance, wrapped or covered.

4. *The Left Hand*: In Hindu culture the left hand is considered impure because it is used (with water) in the place of toilet paper for personal hygiene after answering the call of nature. Handing another person anything with the left hand may be considered a subtle insult.
5. *Shoes:* Shoes are considered impure. The cultured Hindu never wears shoes or sandals inside a temple or shrine, nor in his home or the homes of other Hindus. Carrying shoes in the hands from one part of the premises to another is also avoided. An ultimate insult is to be struck with a shoe.
6. *Caution with Footwear:* It is very important to apologies immediately if one touches someone with his or her shoe or sandal. This is done by touching the right hand to where the foot touched the other person and then touching one's right hand lightly to his own left eye and then the right. This same remedy applies to inadvertently hitting someone with the hand or foot or bumping into him or her.

### *Exchange of Prana*

1. *Giving and Receiving with Both Hands:* Giving and accepting things from one to another, presenting offerings to the Deity, etc., is most properly done with both hands. The reason for this is that with the gift, prana is also given through both hands, thus endowing more energy to the object. The recipient of the gift receives it with both hands along with the prana from the gracious giver. It is known that this exchange of energies is vital for friendship, harmony and the total release of the gift to the recipient. Hindus never accept gifts from strangers or unknown persons.

2. *Hugging and Embracing:* Hugging and embracing is found in Hindu culture; but it is restricted to close relatives, Guru/disciples and associates that too in a private place. In Mahabharata and Ramayana we find this very often. Hugging and Embracing improves pranic energy and this practice is not allowed with strangers.
3. *Not Pointing the Finger:* Pointing with the forefinger of the right hand or shaking the forefinger in emphasis while talking is never done. This is because the right hand possesses a powerful, aggressive pranic force, and an energy that moves the forces of the world. Pointing the index finger channels that force into a single stream. The harshness of this energy would be severely felt in the nerve system of the recipient. More properly, rather than pointing or shaking the index finger to give direction or emphasise a verbal statement, the entire hand is used as a pointer, with the palm up and the thumb held alongside the forefinger.
4. *Shaking Hands:* The traditional way that Hindu men greet one another is with the anjali mudra, then, with palms still held together, extending their hands to one another, in a two-handed handshake, in a deliberate transfer of prana. The hands of one man, usually the less senior, are gently clasped between the other's. Each looks smilingly into the other's face while bowing slightly in humility. This handshake is not firm, but relaxed and gentle.
5. *Not Throwing Things:* Throwing any object on another person is considered extremely improper, even if the persons know each other very well. Cultured Hindus consider this crude and even mildly violent, even if done in efficiency or jest.
6. *Care in Sitting:* It is improper to sit with one's legs outstretched toward a temple, shrine or altar, or even toward another person. This is a grave insult. Crossing one leg over the knee when sitting in a chair should

be avoided, though crossing at the ankles is permitted. One must always try to follow the example of traditional elders. Worshiping, meditating or sitting in the kneeling pose is not acceptable among Hindus.

7. *Doorways:* Conversations are not held inside or through doorways. This is considered inauspicious. Similarly, to exchange or give or lend an object, one steps inside the room first, or the recipient steps out of the room so that both parties are in the same room.

### Modesty

1. *Modesty:* Interaction in public between men and women is much more restrained in Hindu culture than in Western culture. In Hindu culture, for the most part, men socialise with men, and women with women. Men never touch women in public unless the lady is very elderly or infirm.
2. *Displaying Affection:* Married Hindu couples do not hug, hold hands or kiss in public. Even embracing at airports and train stations is considered not wise. Men, however, frequently walk hand in hand.

***The Three Paths to Salvation:*** Knowing that there is diversity in life and no single way of life as prescribed or ordained by God will be followed by everyone, the wise thinkers have put forward three different paths (marga) for achieving salvation. The first is the Jnana marga, mostly for the intellectuals who are able to study and comprehend scriptures. The second is the Bhakti marga, wherein meditation on a personal image of God will lead one to realising the Truth. The third involves social service. Work in the field of uplifting humanity and performance of duty without expecting anything in return is called the karma marga. Renunciation of all worldly possessions and pleasures and continuous meditation is the fourth alternative, which perhaps is beyond the scope of most human beings today.

On the surface Hinduism certainly looks like a confused, directionless religion to an outsider. But the inclusiveness of

Hinduism with its doctrine of tolerance makes it universally appealing. It is not an organised religion and the method of practice is entirely left to the individual, who will take full responsibility of his or her conduct. Superficially, it is a hodgepodge of beliefs and practices, but its core belief of ONE GOD, universal, omniscient and omnipotent has stood the test of time.

***Jagdish Hare:*** In simple words 'Aarti' means Prayer.

Aarti is the most important ritual performed by the masses of India. This prayer is said to have been penned by Pandit Shradha Ram Phillauri in 1888. The entire prayer is an attempt to praise the glory of the inexpressible God and surrendering oneself to Him. The Aarti can be a very soothing experience. Each person, however, will realise for oneself by listening, singing and contemplating upon this simple but divine prayer.

For my western friends and well wishers, I have reproduced the Aarti below, followed by my understanding about it.

*Om Jaye Jagdish Hare*
*Swami Jaye Jagdish Hare*
*Bhagt Jano Ke Sankat*
*Khshan Mein Dur Kare... Om Jaye Jagdish Hare (1)*
*Jo Dhaywe Phal Pave*
*Dukh Vinshe Man Ka*
*Sukh Sampati Ghar Aave*
*Kasht Mite Tan Ka... Om Jaye Jagdish Hare (2)*
*Maat-Pita Tum Mere*
*Sharan Gahun Kiskee*
*Tum Bin Aur Na Duja*
*Aas Karun Jiskee... Om Jaye Jagdish Hare (3)*
*Tum Puran Parmatma*
*Tum Antaryami*
*Par-Brahm Parmeshwar*
*Tum Sabke Swami... Om Jaye Jagdish Hare (4)*
*Tum Karuna Ke Saagar*

*Tum Palankarta*
*Mein Moorakh Khal Kami, Mein Sewak Tum Swami*
*Kripa Karo Bharta... Om Jaye Jagdish Hare (5)*
*Tum Ho Ek Agochar*
*Sabke Pran Pati*
*Kis Vidhi Milun Dayamay*
*Tumko Mein Kumti... Om Jaye Jagdish Hare (6)*
*Deenbandhu Dukh Harta*
*Thakur Tum Mere*
*Apne Hath Badao, Apni Sharan Lagao*
*Dwar Para Tere... Om Jaye Jagdish Hare (7)*
*Vishay Vikaar Mitao*
*Paap Haro Deva*
*Shradha Bhakti Barao*
*Santan Ki Sewa... Om Jaye Jagdish Hare (8)*
*Tan Man Dhan*
*Sab Hai Tera*
*Tera Tujhko Arpan*
*Kya Lage Mera... Om Jaye Jagdish Hare (9)*

This simply worded prayer produces tremendous vibrations and literally compels a person to become quiet and poised. It can be a very relaxing experience.

I have attempted below to present my understanding of the prayer, followed by my humble interpretation.

*Glory be to thy Name (Om)*
*the Sovereign of the Universe*
*With thy Grace the evils of the worshipper vanish instantaneously (1)*

This is the prologue of the Aarti. In it is revealed the power of the word "Om".

Om, is perhaps the only word that phonetically and logically signifies the primordial sound. The great masters and saints have for thousands of years contemplated upon this one Word. It has even been said that all the Vedas dissolve into Gayatri and Gayatri itself dissolves into Om. In the Yoga, experiments have been conducted extensively to assess the impact experienced by an aspirant by simply uttering Om in a particular manner or by chanting repeatedly (Simran). It is not a case of hypnotism or auto-suggestion, but an established fact that one's association with the word Om with understanding helps in attaining transcendence.

One can go on and on....

Om, thus, simply stated is the Word that is unequaled and unrivaled, therefore Supreme. It is perhaps for this reason that almost all Vedic Slokas (verses) begin with the word Om.

Thus establishing Om as the Supreme One, the prologue of the Aarti asserts that all evils of the worshipper get annihilated instantaneously.

*Anyone who Contemplates on thy name is rewarded*

*Mind's misery gets eliminated*

*Bliss and prosperity ascends*

*Body's ailments are cured. (2)*

In this verse the worshipper is being motivated to contemplate on the Name. Reward is offered in the form of mental peace and healthy body, both essential ingredients to lead a harmonious life.

It is my understanding that all our mental chaos and ill-health is projection of our own ego. It is due to the neglect or the lack of understanding of our own unique individuality that we find ourselves dragged into comparisons both subjectively and objectively. This chaotic state can turn into order when we learn to accept ourselves the way we are.

*Thou art my mother and my father*

*To who else should I surrender*

*Except You there is none else*

*That I may aspire for. (3)*

God, the primordial seed, is the Creator. Thus God is both the mother and the father. This being so, I can only beseech You and surrender myself to You. Without God there is nothing, hence my highest aspirations can only be You.

We notice in our daily life that we neglect God and rely upon transient sources for our existence. Resultantly, our lives are chaotic and full of frustrations. However, by realising that God is the sole Cause, one can understand one's true being.

*Thou art the complete One*
*The all-pervading*
*Residing Beyond the cosmic limits*
*Thou art the Sovereign of all. (4)*

In the fourth verse of the Aarti, the worshipper is guided to realise that only God is complete. It is like looking at Him in the form of an infinite canvas, without beginning and without end. The understanding of the emphasis on God being the only 'all-pervading' One guides us to treat all creation in reverence. This acceptance only brings about Love and compassion.

*Thou art the compassionate Ocean*
*Thou the sole provider*
*I am ignorant and trapped by senses*
*I am the servant and thou the Master*
*Please liberate me. (5)*

The fifth verse glorifies and accepts God as an ocean of compassion and the only provider. The worshipper humbly accepts his state of ignorance and his being entrapped in sensory perceptions. A confession of sort is being made by proclaiming God the Master and the worshipper as the servant to invoke a sense of humility. And in the end the seeker seeks fulfilment which is only possible if one is liberated.

*Thou art the unmoving*
*The Lord of all vital force*
*What means shall I adopt to meet you*
*Reveal to me, I earnestly pray. (6)*

The sixth verse deals with metaphysics. It seems to be projecting the underlying principle of the Upanishads. To the ancient Hindu sages, Sun seemed to be the only constant or immutable object cognizable by the naked eye. The Upanishads proclaimed that everything revolves around the Sun. Everything has manifested from the Sun. Thus Sun is the source of all life as known to us.

In this verse, the worshipper is cognising God as the only immutable principle, the source of all creation. This cognition is realisation of the worshipper. This proclamation is what Apostle Peter says in the Corinthians, "All that you see and hear is subject to change". Guru Granth Sahib says, "Jo Dise So Chalaan Har..." Shankara said, "Brahma Satyam, Jagat Mithya"... Verily only God is Truth, all else is perishable. Having realised that only God is immutable, the worshipper now seeks God's grace so as to be able to understand the technique, through which he can literally be able to "see" that Source.

This verse reveals the curiosity of the worshipper and his yearning to realise the Truth.

*Friend of the meek, Annihilator of evils*
*Thou art my Master*
*Grant thy grace and take me into your fold*
*I pray knocking your temple door. (7)*

In the seventh verse again the worshipper, accepting God as the supreme Sovereign, seeks Him and pleads for His grace.

*Annihilate my sensory traps*
*Forgive me of my sins*
*Grant the boon of faith and worship*
*and desire to serve thy creation. (8)*

The eight verse emphasises the yearning of the worshipper to become compassionate and loving so that he can render service to mankind.

We know that when our actions are performed with a view of rendering service, then even our daily chores become an act of worship.

*Body, mind and material wealth*
*All this belongs to you*
*My offerings to you are already yours*
*There is nothing mine. (9)*

Since the worshipper accepts God as his Creator, the physical body thus already belongs to Him. Consequently, the mind, which is but a subtle part of the body, cannot be ours. It too belongs to Him. The acquired material wealth is a result of body's actions and mental plans. Since the body and mind do not belong to us, how can then we claim the material wealth to be our possession?

In this verse, it is a concrete admittance of the fact that body, mind and material possessions are all transient and subject to change.

Whatever the worshipper places on the altar of God is in actuality taken from God's own creation. To thus claim that "I" did this or "I" did that becomes redundant.

The entire Aarti revolves around the supremacy of God and educates the worshipper to realise this and surrender oneself to this Truth.

## Hindu Ethics

Three documents, namely the Upanishads, Bhagvad Gita and Brahma Sutra form the basis of Vedanta (called Prasthana-traya). From these scriptures are drawn Hindu ethics that help in guiding the Hindu through his daily as well as spiritual journey. Though Vedanta currently is the favourite of English-speaking Hindu intellectuals, it was from the wisdom of the Upanishads and Bhagvad Gita that the ancient Hindus set forth their ethics in a practical way, expected to be followed by all Hindus. The Laws of Manu (Dharmashastra or Manuva Shastra) gave details of societal rules and Artha Shastra of Kautilya detailed the politics and economics.

***Ethics of Upanishads:*** Upanishad means 'to sit down near' because they were explained to the students, who sat at the feet of their teachers. In general Upanishads proclaim salvation by knowledge and realisation, rather than by faith and works. Selfish desires are obstacles to the seekers of Truth (the Higher-Self, also called as Brahman). A seeker of true Divinity will attain salvation when he realises the Truth, the all-pervasive Brahman.

The universe came into existence because of a primeval desire of Brahman. Now it is the duty of the humans to restore it to the state of things before creation. This can be done by sacrifice, benevolence, study and even ascetism, which in turn will permit the seeker of truth to attain bliss. Honesty is especially extolled.

He who has not denounced evil will never obtain Brahman. The worldly perceptions of smell, taste, touch, hearing and sight makes one separate from the True Self. When one can transcend these perceptions there is no consciousness of anything other than Self. This is immortality.

There are six great sayings (Mahavakyas) from the Upanishads that give the basic insight into its philosophy. They are as follows with a brief analysis of each:

***Aham Brahmasmi:*** "I am Brahman". Vedic knowledge teaches that our own "Self" is the true Divinity. The Truth is within us, in our own heart. This states the identity of the inner most consciousness of the individual with the supreme Divine.

***Ayam Atma Brahma:*** "The Self is Brahman". This states that not only individual soul is Divine but all beings are identified with the Absolute Truth.

***Tat Tvam Asi:*** "That art thou". Whatever we see or think about, we are That. We are the ultimate Thou and I in all.

***Prajnanam Brahma:*** "Knowledge is Brahman". Supreme intelligence is present inherently within us and is capable of returning us to the Divine. Our understanding of the truth is the truth itself.

***Sarvam Kalvidam Brahma:*** "The whole universe is Brahman". Not only the consciousness in you and I but also the 'principle of being' are all Divine. The entire universe is Divine, which includes our Self.

***So Ham:*** "Here am I". This identifies the Divinity in our self in something that happens naturally like breathing. "So" is inhalation and "Ham" is the natural sound of exhalation.

These are the six statements of the identity of individual consciousness with the Divine reality. They all merge into and derive from the word "Om (Aum)" or the Divine word "I Am All". All of these statements point to the fact that whatever or however we worship, be it an image, book, an idea or even a God, it is the knowledge that the Truth is within ourselves that will ultimately lead to self-realisation. Self is the true Divinity. This is the essence of Upanishads.

***Ethics of Gita:*** Gita is the highest expression of philosophical Hinduism. It is a chapter of the immense Indian epic, the Mahabharata, the saga of the war between the Pandavas and the Kauravas. Arjuna, hero of the Pandavas, is about to confront the army of the Kauravas on the battlefield of Kuruksetra. Among the opposing army are his friends and relatives. Convinced that it would be wrong to kill his own kinsmen, Arjuna is overcome by despair. He lays down his bow and declares that he will not fight. God Vishnu, incarnated as the charioteer Krishna, explains that Arjuna should do his duty (Dharma) and do battle.

The human soul, which is part of the universal soul, is immortal-therefore no one is actually slain. If people perform the duties appropriate to their station, without attachment to success or failure, then they cannot be stained by action. The rest of the poem provides the full philosophy underlying this insight. The essence of karma yoga and of self-abnegation through yoga of renunciation as well as yoga of meditation, mysticism and devotion are discussed in eighteen chapters as conversation between Arjuna and Krishna.

Detached action along with the fruits of this action is consecrated to God and this forms the basis of karma yoga. Bhagavad-Gita teaches the causation and the effects of karma and how to deal with its manifestations. It also teaches that the human being has a free will that permits him to make intelligent choices, which in turn may alter the manifestation of the karma. The ultimate goal of every Hindu is to reduce the bad karma that he may have to carry with him into his next cycle of birth.

The Gita is variously dated between the third century BC. and the fourth century C.E. The reason for uncertainty is that the Gita is not always consistent and may be the work of several hands. A follower of the philosophy expressed in the Upanishads probably wrote one strand, in which Brahman is the highest unity underlying reality. A devotee of the supreme god Vishnu may have added another strand, focused on a more personal deity, later. The Gita may originally have been written as a separate document and later incorporated into the Mahabharata.

God is in all things, and all things are in God. But the visible universe springs from only a fraction of Vishnu's glory. There is also a hidden part of God, which extends beyond the universe.

Nevertheless, the Gita contains probably the most powerful and thoroughgoing expression of pantheism in world scripture. The one God is the pinnacle of all things—the radiant sun of lights, the thought organ of sense organs, the intellect of beings, the ocean of waters, the Himalayas of mountain ranges, the Ganges of rivers. He is also the inherent essence of everything—including evil. He is the gambling of rogues, the courage of the courageous, the rod of disciplinarians, and the statecraft of politicians, the Knowledge of the knowing.

***Hindu Ethics and Conduct:*** Elabouration of the social code is found in the Mahabharata. There are four great aims of human life (purusharthas), namely dharma or righteousness, artha or wealth, kama or enjoyment and moksha or spiritual liberation; the four stages of life, the student or brahmacharya, the householder or grahasthya, the forest-dweller or vanaprastha and the wandering ascetic or sanyasa and the four castes, the priest-teacher or Brahman, the warrior or Kshatriya, the trader or Vaishya and the worker or Sudra.

The Manuva-shastra (codes of Manu) gives details of social rules and practices. Kautilya's Artha-shastra discusses economics and politics. A Hindu finds the ethics of Hinduism in the poems of Bhagavad-Gita. These were written at a time when there was attack on the establishment by reformers in order to maintain the order of the society. Gita teaches that by fulfilling his class function to the best of his ability, with devotion to God and without personal ambition, a man can find salvation, whatever his class. The teachings of the Bhagvad Gita are summed up in the maxim "your business is with deed and not with the result".

Other texts that that give insight into Hindu ethics also shaped the life of a Hindu. There is the Manasollasa written by 12th Century Deccan king Someshvara III Chalukya that illustrates Hindu morals. Hospitality, charity and honesty are extolled. Piety, performance of religious worship and pilgrimage are also important. Eight virtues of the soul were mentioned in the law book of Gautama, namely compassion, patience, contentedness, purity, earnest endeavour, pure thoughts, freedom from greed, and freedom from envy. Tamil texts of Tiukkural and Naladiyar also stress on the moral codes. Earnest kindliness and tolerance to all human relations along with non-violence had real effect on Hindu life. Desire for the well being of all beings and benevolence in the form of almsgiving were encouraged especially when done with no expectation of rewards at least in this life.

The duties also changed according to the ages and classes of people. The ascetic should set his mind on unworldly things but a layman was encouraged to strike a harmony between religion, profession and material pleasures. Similarly students, householders, elderly and the aged had different functions and duties to fulfil.

Especially the orthodox classes also followed taboos like not coming in contact with an untouchable, eating forbidden meat as well as left over food. However the more intelligent teachers realised that mere outward observance was not meritorious as inner goodness. Rules were not rigid and there was always a way to circumvent the most stringent of the rules.

A Hindu is advised to contain and restrain all the emotions that may lead to a sinful existence. Thus he is asked to control such emotions as Kama (lust), Krodha (anger), Mada (ego, pride) and Matsara (jealousy). The moral codes of various texts repeatedly emphasise the importance of being aware of these ordinary but strong human emotions that lead to the disruptions of a harmonious society.

There are nine basic requirements that a Hindu should be aware of and follow. Personal discipline, good conduct, self-inquiry and meditation are important. Here briefly are the nine beliefs of Hinduism:

1. Belief in the divinity of Vedas.
2. The Supreme Being is both immanent and transcendent, thus both a Creator and Un-manifest Reality.
3. The universe is in an endless cycle of creation, preservation and dissolution.
4. One creates his own destiny by his thoughts, deeds and words. This law of cause and effect is called the Karma.
5. Every soul evolves through a series of births and deaths (janma and punar-janma) until all karmas have been resolved. The cycle of many births (samsara) is the opportunity to shed the effects of karma in order to attain liberation (moksha) form the eternal cycle. Not a single soul is deprived of this destiny.
6. Belief in the existence of divine beings in unseen worlds. Temple worship, rituals, sacraments as well as personal devotions create a communion with the devas and God.
7. A master or a guru is essential to follow the right path to know the Transcendent Absolute.
8. All forms of life are sacred and are to be loved and revered. All must follow the practice of 'non-injury' or ahimsa.
9. No one particular religion teaches the 'only pathway' to salvation. All genuine religious paths are facets of

God's Light and Love, deserving tolerance and understanding.

**What is Special in Hinduism**

1. Hindu Religion is the world's oldest faith. It was followed by the ancient civilization of the Indus valley, Ganges valley, Deccan and Kaveri delta, as well as other parts of India all over the Indian peninsula and surrounding areas of Asia. Hinduism, is as much a "way of life" as a religion and affects every aspect of life for Hindus from birth throughout their life. It is followed by the devout Hindu in every aspect of life and activity, and not just in a prayer only.
2. With Hinduism you can have whatever you want. If you want to live a hedonistic lifestyle Hinduism will show you a way to live it without hurting yourself or others.
3. If you want to dedicate your life to worldly successes Hinduism will show you the way to do so within limitations. If all you want to do is your responsible duty to your neighbours, go ahead and do it. If what you want is liberation you can be shown the way.
4. Hinduism is a very philosophically thought out religion that essentially gives an answer for any question that you might have about your life. With each answer Hinduism gives a reason and a possibility of strengthening your understanding of the answer.
5. Hinduism is guided by the teachings of the Vedas, also believed to be the Revealed words by the Divine Powers. The Vedas are said to be older than the creation of the Universe and were given to the Ancient Sages by God as their intuition during their meditation. The Great Seers and Rishis of ancient times recited these Vedas, obtained by their meditative powers, as the teachings of God. These teaching are very ancient and were memorised and recited by generations of Sages, Teachers and their disciples until they were written down as

texts and codified as the Four Vedas by Sage Vyasa. It is further explained by subsequent texts written by Seers and religious leaders based on these Vedas. Hinduism is also guided by these Upa-Vedas, Vedangas, Upanishads, Itihasas and Puranas, which contain the prayers, Philosophy, rituals and mythology, all in one, to suit everyone's cultural and mental development. While the learned person reads about the qualities of the all-powerful Brahman, the illiterate one is taught the same principle by mythological stories and simple forms of prayers to His manifestations.

6. The philosophy of Hinduism, as Divine revelations, is for all times, as old as creation and as modern as tomorrow. The Vedas have given us the rituals in various forms as a ladder to raise our faith and understanding. The Agamas and Puranas give us the incarnations and manifestations of 'God' in popular forms to condition our thoughts to the faith. It allows and accepts varying forms of worship with a tremendous tolerance of other religious faiths and beliefs. Though one may not agree that the other paths are better or perfect, every one is allowed to follow his own path. Often a devotee is urged to study all the paths and variations to fully understand his own faith.

7. This is the most important and valuable speciality of Hinduism that it has not closed itself inside any contours, but is the realistic representation of the limitlessness of knowledge and experience. It is absolutely open minded.

   This is the religion that calls Let the good things come from all the directions of the world (aa no bhadrah kratavo yantu vishvatah). Thus this religion nurtured the good concepts with a neutral mindset. Hinduism is a dharma (discipline) than a religion. Various religions stand over this dharma. In general this is not the religion of just postulations.

8. Very naturally this religion does not force even the acceptance of God to the followers. The Hindus are not threatened that they would be punished for not praying/ believing the God, whereas the major scriptures advice the followers to hold to the God in order to get liberated from the rough road of pleasures and pains! Even those things undergo a very healthy debate. Nothing is unquestionable. The Hindu scriptures instead of defining the way, in which the Hindus should live, in a better way, act as supporting material for the individual to decide the course of life and stand by that.
9. Hinduism, unlike most religions, has no founder and no one scripture. Hindus do not have one "Holy Book" like many other religions, but many texts including the four Vedas along with their Upanishads, called the "Sruti", several Dharma Sastras or Smritis, Itihasas and Puranas including the Mahabharata and the Ramayana. The Bhagavad Gita, or "Song of God", comes as part of Mahabharata, is an essence of the message of the Upanishads and Hindu Philosophy and is considered to be a guide on how we should live as told by Lord Krishna to Arjuna.
10. Hindus believe that as all streams and rivers lead to the same ocean, all genuine religious (spiritual) paths lead to the same goal; worship of every form of "GOD" and celestial forces leads to the same good. So we do not try to convert others to our religion. (Another example-path to top of mountain may differ but the view from the top of the mountain will be the same.)
11. Hindus believe in one God, beyond form, space and time and beyond human comprehension. They believe that God is Transcendent and Immanent at the same time and will create itself according to everyone's desire and needs to protect the pious, to destroy the evil and establish the Divine Rule of Law and Justice.

12. Most Hindus, needing a form on which to concentrate, worship that one God in different forms, worshiping one aspect of that One Divine Supreme Truth.—Hindus see God in masculine as well as in feminine forms and also like a family. At the same time, they all understand the True nature of the Supreme.
13. In the masculine forms, Hindus see that One God as Brahma—the creator, Vishnu—the protector and maintainer, and Shiva as Shiva—Nataraja—the destroyer and recreator.—In the female forms, Hindus see that One God as Sakti or Durga,-provider of energy and power, as Lakshmi,—provider of prosperity and wealth and as Saraswathi,—provider of knowledge and intelligence.
14. These are the major forms of Hindu "Gods" worshipped, which takes the form as created by the supreme God Paramathma for the benefit of the Human creations to easily comprehend Him as He is. Please understand that many of the sects of Hindus following the various forms of philosophy and worship, visualise this same Paramathma—the Supreme God—as Narayana [Vishu], or as Paramasiva [Shiva] and ParaaSakti [Sakti or Durga].
15. Here please note that unlike the other major world religions, Hindus also see the Supreme as Mother, including as Sri Meenakshi, as Visalakshi, as Kamakshi and as many other names of Sakti. He is also seen as Father as in Shiva in various forms in several Hindu Temples—The Temple in which they are worshipped is not just a congregation hall but a palace of the Supreme God [as the Queen or King].
16. Hindu Rituals and Worship take into account the capacities and inclinations of different individuals.—Types of worship include Ritualistic worship (temple or home), offering (directly or through the priest) flowers,

coconut, fruits, incense, flames of oil lamps and camphor, chanting of prayers in Sanskrit (or their mother tongue), etc.

17. Also Hindu religion advocates Worship through service of one's fellow man (charity) and by one's activity;—Worship through the service to fellow human and devotion to the Supreme;—Worship through meditation with physical and mental discipline and through understanding first the inner self then the divine that is everywhere.
18. Hinduism has also defined concept of Yogas. Jnana yoga is for people who are reflective and seek knowledge find their divinity through rationality and spirituality. Bhakti yoga is the path to God through love and devoted service. It insists on God's otherness and teaches love of God through adoration. Karma yoga is the path to God through work. Be productive and strive to work towards high rewards and work unselfishly.Raja yoga is known as the path to reintegration, a way to God through psychophysical experiments. Self-searching could be one way of describing Raja Yoga. Looking inward to discern the humanness from the Godness and bringing them together. It involves meditation and self discipline.

These and many more specialties of Hinduism make it a harmonious and worth religion, which is suitable for any time in present or future, for any land or creed.

## Some Thoughts Hindus Gave the World

*Brahman, the eternal Trimutri, or Three-in-One God: Brahma, the Creator; Vishnu, the Preserver; and Shiva, the Destroyer;*

*Submission to Fate, since man is not outside, but part of Brahman;*

*The Caste System, determined by the laws of Manu;*

*The Law of Karma that from good must come good, and from evil must come evil;*

*Reincarnation, as a chain of rebirths in which each soul, through virtuous living, can rise to a higher state;*

Nirvana, the final stage reached upon the emancipation of the soul from the chain of rebirths; Yogis, the disciplines which enable the individual to control the body and the emotions; and Dharma, the Law of Moral Order, which each individual must find and follow to reach nirvana.

*Vegetarianism (vegan lifestyle)*

*Ahimsa ("no injury", avoidance of all animal products)*

*Yoga exercise*

*Astrology and horoscopes*

*Gurus and swamis (monks and spiritual leaders)*

*Shanty Path (Prayer for Peace)*

*Aum daub shanty antarikshagwam,*
*shanti Prithivi shanti rapah,*
*shanti roshadaya shanti vanapastayah shantir,*
*vishwe devah shantih,*
*brahma shantih*
*sarvagwang shantih*
*shantireva sama shanti redhi.*
*Aum Shantih Shantih Shantih*

***Meaning:***

*May there be peace in Heaven*
*Peace in the Atmosphere*
*Peace across the waters*
*May there be peace on Earth*
*May peace flow from herbs, plants and trees*
*May all the celestial beings pervade peace*
*May peace pervade all quarters*
*May that peace come to me too.*

# 4

# THE LIFE SYSTEMS STUDY OF THE DIFFERENT STAGES

The four stages may be said to represent periods of Preparation, Production, Service and Retirement. There are four stages of life, *viz.* Brahmachari (student), Grihasta (Householder) Vanaprasta (forest dweller or Hermit in semi retirement) Sannyasi (the renounced one in full retirement) and the Dharma of each is different.

> *"People do not have to be taught to want to be happy, to want to be secure or to want the respect and admiration of their friends and associates—though often they need instruction 'how' to secure these things.*
>
> *Deeper Hindu thinking suggests, however, that there is also a natural progression of these values so that one should grow toward more fundamental interests.*
>
> *This movement toward more enduring and satisfying values has been institutionalised in the understanding of the four stages of life known as 'Ashramas".*

**Purusharthas**

Purusha means human being and artha means object or objective. Purusharthas means objectives of man. According to Hindu way of life, a man should strive to achieve four chief objectives (Purusharthas) in his life. They are:

1. Dharma (righteousness),
2. Artha (material wealth),

3. Kama (desire) and
4. Moksha.

Every individual in a society is expected to achieve these four objectives and seek fulfillment in his life before departing from here. The concept of Purusharthas clearly establishes the fact that Hinduism does not advocate a life of self negation and hardship, but a life of balance, achievement and fulfillment.

***Dharma:*** Dharma is a very complicated word, for which there is no equivalent word in any other language, including English. Dharma actually means that which upholds this entire creation. It is a Divine law that is inherent and invisible, but responsible for all existence. Dharma exists in all planes, in all aspects and at all levels of creation.

In the context of human life, dharma consists of all that an individual undertakes in harmony with Divine expectations and his own inner spiritual aspirations, actions that would ensure order and harmony with in himself and in the environment in which he lives. Since this world is deluded, a human being may not know what is right and what is wrong or what is dharma and what is adharma. Hence he should rely upon the scriptures and adhere to the injunctions contained there in. In short, dharma for a human being means developing divine virtues and performing actions that are in harmony with the divine laws.

Dharma is considered to be the first cardinal aim because it is at the root of everything and upholds everything. For example see what happens when a person amasses wealth without observing dharma or indulges in sexual passion against the social norms or established moral values. Any action performed without observing dharma is bound to bring misery and suffering and delay ones salvation. Hinduism therefore considers it rightly as the first cardinal aim of life.

In ancient India dharmasastras (law books) provided guidance to people in their day to day lives and helped them to adhere to dharma. These law books were written for a particular time frame and are no more relevant to the modern world. The best way to know what is dharma and what is adharma, is to follow the religious scriptures such as the Bhagavad Gita and the Upanishads or any other scripture that contains the words of God.

***Artha:*** Artha means wealth. Hinduism recognises the importance of material wealth for the overall happiness and well being of an individual. A house holder requires wealth, because he has to perform many duties to uphold dharma and ensure the welfare and progress of his family and society. A person may have the intention to uphold the dharma, but if he has no money he would not be able to perform his duties and fulfil his dharma.

Hinduism therefore rightly places material wealth as the second most important objective in human life. Lord Vishnu is the best example for any householder who wants to lead a life of luxury and still be on the side of God doing his duties. As the preserver of the universe, Lord Vishnu lives in Vaikunth amid pomp and glory, with the goddess of wealth herself by his side and yet helps the poor and the needy, protects the weak, upholds the dharma and sometimes leaving everything aside rushes to the earth as an incarnation to uphold dharma.

Hinduism advocates austerity, simplicity and detachment, but does not glorify poverty. Hinduism also emphasises the need to observe dharma while amassing the wealth. Poverty has become a grotesque reality in present day Hindu society. Hindus have become so poverty conscious that if a saint or a sage leads a comfortable life, they scoff at him, saying that he is not a true yogi. They have to remind themselves of the simple fact that none of the Hindu gods and goddesses are really poor.

Hinduism believes that both spiritualism and materialism are important for the salvation of human beings. It is unfortunate that Hinduism came to be associated more with spiritualism, probably because of the influence of Buddhism, where as in truth Hinduism does not exclude either of them. As Swami Vivekananda rightly said religion is not for the empty stomachs. Religion is not for those whose main concern from morning till evening is how to make both ends meet. Poverty crushes the spirit of man and renders him an easy prey to wicked forces.

In ancient India Artha Sastras (scriptures on wealth) provided necessary guidance to people on the finer aspects of managing their wealth. Kautilya's Artha Sastra, which is probably a compilation of many independent works, gives us a glimpse of how money matters were handled in ancient India.

***Kama:*** Kama in a wider sense means desire and in a narrow sense, sexual desire. Hinduism prescribes fulfilment of sexual passions for the householders and abstinence from it for the students and ascetics who are engaged in the study of the scriptures and in the pursuit of Brahman.

The Bhagavad Gita informs us that desire is an aspect of delusion and one has to be wary of its various movements and manifestations. The best way to deal with desires is to develop detachment and perform desireless actions without seeking the fruit of ones actions and making an offering of all the actions to God. This way our actions would not bind us to the cycle of births and deaths.

Hinduism permits sexual freedom so long as it is not in conflict with the first aim, *i.e.* dharma. Hindu scriptures emphasise that the purpose of sex is procreation and perpetuation of family and society, while the purpose of dharma is to ensure order in the institution of family and society. A householder has the permission to indulge in sex, but also has the responsibility to pursue it in accordance with the laws of dharma. Marriage is a recognised social institution and marriage with wife for the purpose of producing children is legitimate and in line with the aims of dharma.

One of the important sects of Hinduism is Tantricism. It recognises the importance of sexual freedom in the liberation of soul. The Tantrics accept sex as an important means to experience the blissful nature of God and the best way to experience God in physical form. They also refer to the concept of Purusharthas to justify their doctrines. They believe that sexual energy is divine energy and it can be transformed into spiritual energy through controlled expression of sex.

Just as the Dharmasastras were written for the sake of dharma, and Arthasastras for artha, Kamasastras were composed in ancient India for providing guidance in matters of sex. We have lost many of them because of the extreme secrecy and social disapproval associated with the subject.

***Moksha:*** If dharma guides the life of a human being from below acting as the earth, showing him the way from above like a star studded mysterious sky is Moksha. Dharma constitutes the legs of a Purusha that walk upon the earth; both artha and kama constitute his two limbs active in the middle region; while Moksha constitutes the head that rests in the heaven.

Human life is very precious because of all the beings in all the worlds, only human beings have the best opportunity to realise the Higher self. It is also precious because it is attained after many hundreds and thousands of lives. Rightly, salvation should be its ultimate aim.

Moksha actually means absence of moha or delusion. Delusion is caused by the inter play of the triple gunas. When a person overcomes these gunas, he attains liberation. The gunas can be overcome by detachment, self control, surrender to god and offering ones actions to God.

If dharma is the centre of the wheel of human life, artha and kama are the two spokes and Moksha is its circumference. If dharma is at the centre of human life, beyond Moksha there is no human life, but only a life divine.

The four Purusharthas are also like the four wheels of a chariot called human life. They collectively uphold it and lead it. Each influences the movement of the other three, and in the absence of any one of them, the chariot comes to a halt.

The Four Yogas as Spiritual Discipline to follow the Dharma

> *Karman.yevaadhikaaras the' maa phalesuu kadaachana!*
>
> *Maa karma-phala-hethur bhoor maa the sangosthv-akarmani!!*

*—II-47 !! Chapter II-47*

*Thou hast a right to action or work alone, and never to its fruits;*

*let not the fruit of work be thy motive, let not thy attachment to inaction.*

*yoga-sthah: kuru karmaani sangam thyakthvaa dhananjaya!*

*siddhy-asiddhyoh: samo bhootvaa samathvam yoga uchyate' !!*
*—II-48 !! Chapter II-48*

*Do thy work being steadfast in devotion and abandoning attachment, O Arjuna !*

*and being equal in success and failure. This evenness of mind is called Yoga*

*doore'na hy avaram karma buddh'i-yogaadh dh'ananjaya!*

*buddh'au saranam annnviccha kr.panaah phala-hethavah:!!*
*-II-49 !!Chapter II-49 —Bhagavad Gita*

'O' Arjuna mere action performed with attachment is inferior to action performed with mind poised in evenness. Seek shelter in this state of unperturbed evenness in a desireless mind. Those who work for selfish gains are indeed pitiable.

***The Spiritual Discipline and Teachings Applied for the Practice:*** The Philosophical teachings of Hinduism, like any scientific theory, are of no use to the common man unless it is applied for their daily practice. It has survived the test of time for many thousand years and still remains popular due to the sound principles on which its practice is based. It gives different rules of ethics and conducts for various categories of people.

The Dharma Sastras and Smritis teach us of normal conduct in performing our work. Dharma, Artha, Kama and Moksha are the four Purusharthas that govern out activity. Dharma is the proper rules of one's duty, which literally means "that which holds" the universe and its beings.

They are classified as Samanya Dharma or the general and universal rules and Visesha Dharma or specific personal rules for each individual. They give peace, joy, strength and tranquillity. Artha and Kama are the materialistic desire and passion, that also govern our actions. Unless one seeks the material benefits and pleasures within the scope of Dharma, it will cause grief with greed and lust. Moksha is the relief from pain and suffering and ultimate liberation that is the main reason for all our actions.

***The Four Yogas as Spiritual Discipline :*** As rituals became popular and were being considered as the sole path for the eternal bliss, the soundness of its philosophy and ethics of practice were reestablished by the sages. The four Yogas give us the spiritual discipline of our conduct. Karma Yoga is the correct path of performing work without greed or desire and the action performed without looking for the fruits of benefit or loss. Raja Yoga is the discipline of control of our body and mind. It teaches concentration, meditation, breathing and physical exercise and a state of equanimity of the mind as a natural reaction to all activities. Bhakti Yoga is the spiritual discipline of absolute devotion and love of God. It teaches prayers and surrender to God at all times. It teaches to see and feel God in all people and all actions. Jnana Yoga is the path of obtaining Spiritual knowledge through action, study, meditation and devotion.

***Three Gunas:*** Vedas describe three personality traits, Sathvika, Rajasika and Tamasika. Sathvika Gunas are present in the pious person who follows all teachings of the faith and Dharma. Compassion to all animals, Ahimsa and vegetarianism are advocated as Sathva Guna. The Rajasika Gunas are present in people who enjoyed some amount of worldly pleasures directed by desire and ego, which are Artha and Kama. Tamasika persons have no knowledge of the proper Dharma or they do not care for them. They are driven solely by Artha and Kama which are passion, greed and lust. These Gunas are present in all but one is dominant. The Yogas advocate the ways to follow the superior Sathva Guna and the ways to suppress the undesirable Artha and Kama without the proper Dharma.

Performance of proper Dharma and all the Karma leads to a sense of peace and equanimity of mind and eternal bliss. The individual makeup of a person, his Guna and effects of his Karma determines the rebirth and ultimate liberation. Performance of one's duty without devotion to God is dry and empty. Performance of such duty should be without any attachment to its fruit but as a devotion to God. Hinduism gave us the four Vedas, the three Agamas, the six Dharsanas and the four Yogas.

> *Bhakti Yoga, the attainment of Divinity through worship.*
>
> *Guru Brahmah Gurur Vishnuhuhu Guru Devoo Maheswaraha*
>
> *Guru Sakshath Para Brahma Tasmai Sree Gurave' Namaha*
>
> *Guru is Lord Brahma, Lord Vishnu and Lord Maheswara,*
>
> *Guru is nothing but the Supreme Brahman devoid of attributes.*
>
> *That is the reason why we bow to the Guru.*
>
> *Bhakti Yoga, the methods of worship.*

### *Various forms of Devotion and Sanskara*

Hindu Religious Faith and practice are based on its strong philosophy and the ancient tradition. Most of the followers know about the Vedas and the Vedantha philosophy. Every one understands that there is one God who is worshipped in many forms. Most of them are familiar with the Advaita theory and Vedanta philosophy of oneness of the Divine and the human soul. However, the practice is much more closer to the Dvaita and Visista-advaita theories for the worship of the Divine. The paths of Karma yoga, Raja yoga, Bhakti yoga and Gnana yoga are taught as the spiritual disciplines for the practice. Some feel that Gnana or the path of wisdom is the ultimate while others consider that after performing duties without attachment as in Karma yoga, practicing meditation and controlling thoughts as in Raja yoga and gaining knowledge of Gnana path one will reach the state of ultimate surrender of Bhakti yoga.

Among all the paths of Hinduism, the most common and popular ones have been the ritualistic [Sanskara] path and the Devotional [Bhakti] paths of worship. The ritualistic path involves the practice of sanskaara which are performing the regular rituals for the formless Supreme Divine as prescribed in the Karma kanda and Upasana kanda portions of the Vedas. They are performed every day and for various events in one's life. These are practised and performed mostly by persons knowledgeable in the Vedas and the Hindu philosophy and those initiated to the practice of these rituals.

The Bhakti pathway is much easier to follow for everyone. It teaches a method of love and attachment towards a supreme God through one of His manifestations as in the Agamas and Puranas with devotional prayers and worship to various forms of Deities through poojas and bhajans. This form of Bhakti develops into various levels and degrees as an inner attitude of an attachment and feeling of love towards God, from a blind faith and devotion to God in one form to total surrender to the Supreme.

***Bhakti Yoga-the Devotional Pathway:*** Para-Bhakti is the form of devotion with contemplation on the formless and unmanifested Brahmam. It is the highest form of Bhakti suitable only for few learned people, the Jnana Yogis, who have the true knowledge of God.

Apara-Bhakti or Gauni-Bhakti is the primal level of love and devotion to a manifested Iswara and prayers to one of His forms accepted as Ishta-Devatha or a personal God. There are many levels or grades in this, the most important being Bhaya-Bhakti, Anyaya-Bhakti and Ekantha-Bhakti.

Bhaya-Bhakti is the very external form of worship of a Deity as God. It is the adoration paid to a form of God outside ourselves. It is the most basic form of a faith, based on the unenlightened or Tamasika feeling that God is external to us and dwells in a particular locality like the prayer room or Temple. The pilgrimages, worship of several images of God, symbols and sacred books are examples of this. Most popular religions do not rise above this level.

Anyaya-Bhakti [meaning "not another"] is the exclusive and passionate, or the Rajasika, form of worship of one's Ishta-Devatha in the heart. It is an intense form of monotheism and gives a healthy direction to the spirit of devotion. But, it shall not give rise to bigotry and cruelty towards those who have different concept of God and different methods of approach. Among Hindus, it is well recognised that the gods whom others worship are only different forms of his own Ishta-devatha.

Ekantha-Bhakti is the purest and Sattvika form of devotion. Here, the devotee loves God for His own sake and not for His gifts. He learns to crave for his personal God alone, in prosperity as well as in adversity. He sees the presence of God, as his Ishta-devata, in all places, at all times.

Bhavas as an expression of Devotion and Love:

1. *Santha Bhava:* [means calmness of mind] The mind of the devotee is filled with divine knowledge and is emotionless, always undisturbed, peaceful and tranquil. Only Yogis and Jñanis, like Bhishma, who are highly developed and have had direct experience of God will be able to practice Santha Bhava.
2. *Dasya Bhava:* The devotee considers himself as inferior to God. He takes God to be his Master and looks upon himself as just a humble servant. He considers it is his duty to worship and to love God. Hanuman is an example of Dasya Bhakti.
3. *Sakhya Bhava:* The devotee considers God to be a dear friend, the sole supreme companion, and as his equal

in relation, with pure friendship not degenerating into familiarity. Arjuna is an example of Sakhya Bhaktha.

4. *Vatsalya Bhava:* The devotee considers God as his Child and the themselves as the mother giving and also getting the unconditional love of the Child. Mother Yashoda had Vatsalya Bhakti towards Child Krishna as her own child.
5. *Kantha Bhava:* This is the expression of devotion with a feeling like the one a wife gets and gives towards her husband, as in the case of devotion of Sita or Rukmini towards Sri Rama and Sri Krishna, called Kantha Bhava.
6. *Madhurya Bhava:* This is the highest expression of Divine love. Here, the devotee takes the lord to be his beloved, with deep love, devotion and surrenders himself. When Gopikas like Radha develops Bhakti towards Sri Krishna, it is the romantic love and surrender of the self to the lover, without any sensuality but with pure devotion and surrender, called Madhurya Bhava.

Fundamental Disciplines Needed for Bhakti Yoga:

1. *Abhyasa:* Practice of constantly and continuously remembering God with a steady mind.
2. *Viveka:* Discrimination, the ability to choose between right and wrong.
3. *Vimoka:* Intense longing for God, rejecting everything that hinders our progress.
4. *Sathyam:* Truthfulness, to be always observed as a basic rule of spiritual ethics. We have to live a life of truth, think truth alone, speak truth and listen carefully to their own inner voice called conscience.
5. *Arjavam:* This is straightforwardness or honesty.
6. *Kriya:* Doing good to all beings, as the devotee will God in all forms.

7. *Kalyana:* This is wishing well of others with a loving heart, praying to the Lord for the well being of others, for the peace and welfare of the world.
8. *Dhaya:* Compassion, as God is love, mercy and compassion personified. As we seek to realise Him, we, too, must develop the same qualities.
9. *Ahimsa:* The practice of non-violence, non-injury to all creatures, by way of action, thought or word.
10. *Dhaana:* Abundant and spontaneous charity with a pure heart, for relieving the suffering of the distressed is a potent means of growing spiritually.
11. *Anavasada:* To be cheerful and hopeful is an essential quality of a devotee. One must always have faith and hope.

*manmana bhava madh-bhakto madh-yaaji man namaskuru!*

*mam-e'Vaishyasi sathyam the' prathijane' priyo'sime' !!*

*Bhagavad Gita Chapter XVIII-65*

With your mind engrossed in Me, become My devotee, worship Me and salute Me. I promise you that you will come to Me alone, as you are so dear to Me.

*Etham Vibhoothim Yogam Cha; Mama Yo Ve'tthi Thatthvathah: !*

*So'vikalpena Yogena Yujyate'; Nathra Samsayah !!*
*Bhagavad Gita Chapter X-7.*

He who knows about this manifestation of My divine majesties and my power unites with Me in steady and unfaltering communion. About this there is no doubt.

*Cycles of time as recorded in the Vedas and Upanishads*

*Here are cycles of time as recorded in the Vedas and Upanishads.*

Small Yuga: 2,000 years. The axis of the earth spends 2,000 years in an astrological sign and the moves on to the next sign, going backwards through the signs of the zodiac. Since we are finishing the Pisceaen cycle, we are ready to enter the Aquarian cycle for the next 2,000 years. We commonly refer to entering Aquarius as the "dawning of the age of Aquarius." Complete Cycle of Small Yugas: 24,000 years. This is the amount of time needed for the earth to spend 2,000 years in each sign of the zodiac.

***The Great Cycle:*** In addition to the earth's axis moving in an arc as it travels through the signs of the zodiac, there is another cycle. This is a cycle which involves the revolution of the entire solar system around the Central Sun of the Galaxy. The orbit is elliptical rather than circular. To make the elliptical movement of the solar system around a great central point more understandable, the analogy of "seasons" is used. This is a useful analogy because changes in overall states of consciousness are represented as "seasons" through which the solar system passes on its journey.

When consciousness is in a high state, it is summer. At this time, 90 per cent of the inhabitants of the earth are enlightened. This is called Satya Yuga, or the Age of Truth. When Fall or Spring are in full swing, the numbers of enlightened beings drops to less than 10 per cent. When Winter comes, far less than 1 per cent of the people on earth are enlightened. However, there are trade offs.

First, it is easier to make progress in the "'winter of consciousness." The analogy is often used that if one tries to row one's boat in air, very little progress will be achieved. But when the oars are placed in water, much more rapid progress can be made. This is because compared to air, the resistance of water is much higher enabling the work of the oars to bear fruit. It is the resistance itself which provides a route to rapid progress. Similarly, in spiritual winter our efforts to achieve spiritual growth produce much faster results than they would in any other age of consciousness because of the great general resistance to things spiritual.

There is no disagreement among all the sages, pandits, gurus and swamis that Kali Yuga, the present spiritual winter, affords an opportunity for more rapid spiritual progress than any other age. Further, the medium for rapid growth is almost universally prescribed by these same classes of spiritual teachers as divine sound through the medium of mantra. Here are the various seasons and ages of the universe as measured in human years.

Winter (Kali Yuga): 432,000 years:

The year 2001 is 5,093 years from the beginning of Kali Yuga of the long cycle. For the short cycle, winter is ending with the entrance of the planetary axis into Aquarius, which begins the season of Spring for the shorter, 24,000 year cycle.

*Spring: (Treta Yuga) 1,296,000 years*

*Summer (Satya or Krita Yuga) 1,728,000 years*

*Autumn (Dwapara Yuga) 864,000 years*

*Total Time for One Cycle or Manvantara: 4,320,000,000 years*

*This is called "A Day of Brahma" and is followed by a night of equal length.*

*One complete day and night of Brahma: 8,640,000,000 years*

*360 of these days is called "One Year of Brahma": 3,110,400,000,000 years*

*100 of these years constitute the life of Brahma called a Maha Kalpa: 311,040,000,000,000 years*

At the end of a "Maha Kalpa" or cycle of creation, Shiva manifests his destructive influence and the universe is dissolved. The ancient texts call this the cosmic dissolution. All the levels of the manifest universe disappear. After a great cosmic rest cycle, another creative cycle begins as a new Brahma emerges out of the navel of Narayana and the universe is created anew.

Another item of importance is that one who has achieved the highest level of conscious realisation is said to realise and become one with Brahman. At this point, all individuality as we know it disappears. The individual Jiva, Soul or Atman returns to its source from which it will not return of its own volition. However, for reasons known only to itself, certain souls may return for reasons understood only by Narayana.

**Samskara**

The ultimate goal of every Hindu is to attain Moksha. This can only come through atma-vidya, which is knowing one's self, through thought and introspection. To attain this, the scriptures give some guidelines. The first step is to master eight characteristics. These called atmagunas are:

1. Compassion (daya)
2. Forgiveness or patience (kshanti)
3. Absence of jealousy (anasuya)
4. Cleanliness (sauchyâm)
5. Not feeling mental strain or doing work with effortless ease (anayasa)
6. Auspiciousness (mangala)
7. Non-miserliness (akarpanya)
8. Non-grasping or non-desiring nature (asprha).

Toward cultivation of these characteristics, the Vedas also give guidelines as to the rituals to be performed over one's lifetime. Sixteen such rituals are collectively called Shodasha Samskara. Samskara denotes purification ritual. Starting from the time when the child is in the womb, these sixteen rituals end in the final journey of the body into the afterlife.

They can be divided into those performed during five different stages of life, *i.e.* prenatal, childhood, student, adult life and old age or wisdom years. Forty rituals are discussed but sixteen are still in practice.

1. *Garbhadana Samskara:* Performed by a married couple when conceiving a child. This important samskara raises the act of conception to a sacred occasion, and is powerfully purifying and uplifting for the unborn child.

2. *Pumsavana Samskara:* Usually performed between the second and fourth month of pregnancy. Its purpose is, first, to promote the birth of a male child (for perpetuation of the family line and tradition); second, to insure the good health of the fetus and the proper formation of its organs, regardless of gender.
3. *Simantonoyana Samskara:* In the fourth or fifth month of pregnancy, the mind of the fetus begins to develop. This is when simantonoyana samskara is performed. Its purpose is to protect the fetus—especially its newly forming mind—from all negative influences, and also to stimulate the development of the unborn child's intellect.
4. *Jatakarma Samskara :* It is the ritual performed at the birth of a child. It awakens the child's intellect, gives it strength and promotes long life for the child.
5. *Namakarana Samskara:* On the 11th day after the child's birth, namakarana samskara is performed. In this ceremony, the child receives its name.
6. *Nishkramana Samskara:* The baby's first outing into the world, beyond the confines of the home, is the occasion of nishkramana samskara.
7. *Annaprashana Samskara:* The first feeding of solid food to the baby, usually in the sixth month after birth, is the occasion of Annaprashana samskara.
8. *Karnavedha Samskara:* Usually performed in the sixth or seventh month after birth, consists of the piercing of the baby's ear lobes, so earrings may be worn.
9. *Chudakarana Samskara:* At the end of the first year, or during the third year, the child's hair is shaved—all but a tuft on the top of the head. This ritual shaving of hair, performed with ceremony, prayers and Vedic chanting is for both boys and girls.
10. *Vidyarambha Samskara:* This samskara begins a student's primary education by ceremonially introducing the child to the alphabet.

11. *Upanayana Samskara:* Initiates the formal study of the Vedas. It is one of the most important and esteemed of the samskaras. Upon performance of upanayana, a boy traditionally moves from home to live in the ashram of the Guru.
12. *Samavartana Samskara:* With samavartana samskara the disciple graduates from his Vedic studies and returns from the house of his Guru. Thereafter, the disciple will marry and raise a family, and so enter the stage of householder, grihasthaashrama.
13. *Vivaha Samskara:* The traditional Hindu wedding ceremony. It is considered by many to be the most important of all the samskaras.
14. *Panchamahayajna Samskara:* A married couple performs these five great sacrifices daily. In this samskara, one honours, in turn, the rishis (ancient seers of Truth), the gods, the ancestors, humankind and all created beings.
15. *Vanaprastha Samskara:* According to the Vedic tradition, vanaprastha is the third stage of life, following brahmacharya (Vedic student/disciple) and grihastha (householder). Here, a man leaves behind his life in the world and retires to the forest (with or without his wife), to live an ascetic life devoted to study of the scriptures and to meditation.
16. *Antyeshti Samskara:* The final sacrament, the funeral rites.

***Initiation or Upanayana:*** The initiation ceremony called the Upanayana or the second birth is a very ancient practice. The boy who undergoes the ceremony is said to be twice born or Dvija. He is also now considered an Aryan. The ritual consists of wearing a sacred thread called Yajnopavita with the utterance of the sacred mantra, which goes as follows:

> *"Om yajnopaveetam paramam pavitram prajapateryat sahajam purastaat.*

*Aayushyamagryam pratimuncha shubhram yajnopaveetam balamastu tejah."*

*"The sacred thread is great and pure.*

*It came to existence along with the birth of Brahma.*

*It is as old as He is.*

*May it, which is blessed by celestials, give us long life, strength and radiance."*

The sacred thread is hung over the left shoulder and under the right arm. The cord is not to be removed once placed unless it is defiled by death or birth in the family. The cord was made of three threads, each of nine twisted strands made of cotton, hemp or wool, for Brahman, Kshatriya and Vaishya classes respectively. At this ceremony the boy (called Vatu) is taught the sacred Gayatri Mantra, whispered in his ear by his father and Guru (called Brahmopadesha). Only the higher classes can recite this mantra. It is as follows:

*"Om Bhuh, Om Bhuvah, Om Suvah, Om Maha, Om Janah, Om Tapah, Om Satyam,*

*Om, Tat Savitur vareniam, Bhargo devasya dhimahi, Dhiyo yonah prachodayat."*

*"Om Earth, Om Sky, Om Heaven, Om Middle Region, Om Place of Births,*

*Om Mansion of the Blessed, Om Abode of Truth,*

*Let us think of the lovely splendor of God Savitur (Sun) that he may inspire our minds."*

The Gayatri Mantra can also be translated as "That Eternal God or Creator, Independent Reality, the Worshipful, One who has no Beginning, Light of Wisdom and Truth. That Lord who manifests through the Sun (Savitur), propitiated by the highest Gods; One who bestows wisdom, bliss and everlasting life; we meditate on that Light.

May that Light of God illuminate our intellect." A long time ago, most Kshatriyas and Vaishyas ceased to perform the initiation ceremony in its full form. The term 'twice born (dvija)' came to be applied more and more to the Brahman class.

***Panch Mahayajna:*** Performance of numerous religious duties consists of proper following of one's Dharma. These are the bounden or obligatory karma of a Hindu. There are five great sacrifices (Pancha-mahayajna). These are to be performed thrice daily at sunrise, noon and sunset. They consist of:

- Brahmayajna, the worship of the Brahman the World Spirit, by reciting the Vedas:
- Pitryayajna, the worship of the ancestors, by libations of water and periodical Shraddha
- Devayajna, the worship of the gods, by pouring ghee on the sacred fire.
- Bhutayajna, the worship of all living things, by scattering grains and food for the animals and spirits.
- Purusayajna, the worship of men, by showing hospitality.

Kama was a legitimate branch of human activity and physical love was not disparaged. Though the term generally means desire, the word has definite sexual connotation. The Hindu literature, both religious and secular, is full of sexual allusions and symbolisms.

The temple carvings of the Middle Ages are full of couples in full embrace and sexual positions. Vatsyayana's Kamasutra is the most famous text dedicated to Kama. It is a remarkable work giving detailed instructions of erotic technique and aphrodisiac recipes and charms. There is emphasis on mutual gratification and foreplay. There are at least sixteen types of kisses detailed! In the historical perspective it gives a great insight into the life of Hindu upper class of the times.

It is important to remember the difference between similar sounding words. 'Brahman' is the Universal World Soul mentioned in the Vedas. 'Brahmanas' are the appendices to Upanishad where the sacrificial rituals are carefully delineated. 'Brahman' or 'Brahmana' is the priest class of Hindus, which is one of the four castes.

### Brahmacharya (Celibate)

Brahmacharya means Student, usually between 12 and 24 years of age.The first stage is Brahmacharya. The duty of a student is to study. On initiation into Brahmacharya by means of the Upanayana rites, he becomes a 'Dvija' (a twice born). 'Upanayana' means 'bringing near'-the disciple is brought near the Guru for receiving the initiation of mantras.

For the Brahmachari, celibacy is his forte, discipline is his norm, devotion to his Guru is his duty and concentration in studies is his vocation. In "Gurukula Vasam"(or staying with the preceptor) he learns the nuances and intricate renderings and interpretations of Vedas, Upanishads and Sastras though by means of rote so that when he comes of age the significance of what he learnt would be realised by him in real life situations, which he would be facing in his next Ashrama.

Thus, it is a period of probation, a period of training, in a practical manner without prejudice to the injunctions of Sastras he had so studiously learnt as a Brahmachari. Only when someone consoles we feel relief; only the 'Guru Upadesa' can change our mental attitude. The first lesson of the student is the performance of 'Sandhya Vandanam' at morn, noon and evening, Ablutions, recitation of Gayatri, breath control, sipping and sprinkling of water, pouring libations of water to the Sun-God, etc. were enjoined on the twice-born and they could never be missed.

### Grihastaashrama

Grihasta means House-holder usually between 24 and 48 years of age. The next stage is of the householder. After the 'Gurukula Vasa' he graduates himself into the mundane world, taking a wife to assist him in his performance of Dharmic duties.

All Sastras proclaim the importance of the Grihastaasrama as the fulcrum of all other Ashramas. People in the other three Ashramas heavily lean on the Grihasta for support and sustenance required to carry out their respective duties. The Grihasta earns his livelihood by whatever a vocation befitting his being a member of his group, raising children, supporting his own family, kith and kin besides the persons performing their duties in the other three Ashramas.

The life of a Grihasta is therefore, considered a 'Jivayagna'—a lifelong saga of self sacrifice for the benefit of others in society.

Marriage is not meant as a means to satisfy carnal craving. It is regarded as a means to spiritual glory, a sin qua non for the development of lineage—a necessary link between the dead past and an unborn future that must come alive to be undertaken as a part of spiritual duty with devotion (Shraddha) to perpetuate the family tradition.

According to Bhagavata Purana, a Griha (house) is not a person for one who has controlled his senses, delights in spirit and is eager for knowledge.

Partners who enter in wedlock are not 'paragons of virtue' as they appear in the first flush of enthusiasm. None is perfect and to seek for perfection in the partner is like seeking a mirage in the desert.

Perfect relationship is created by conscious effort and not discovered all of a sudden. The incompatibilities have to be resolved by a continual mutual adjustment and reconciliation by a willing attitude of 'give and take'.

Marriage is marriage and is not a mere love affair which is but an infatuation. Love affair is a relationship just for the pleasure of the person involved and it has no consideration of the families of the persons. When the pleasure wears out, the affair is gone.

But, marriage is a life commitment.If you make a sacrifice, you are not sacrificing to that person. It is a sacrifice to a permanent relationship. Love bears all, endures all. If the relationship has pains, remember that life is a mixture of joys and sorrows.

The practice in India that a husband and wife could continue to remain as husband and wife till death and also celebrate the Golden jubilee of their wedding at the 60th age of the husband is still very common.

Those that end in divorce or separation are misfits for the marriage life who have no understanding of the marriage and its divinity. They fail in 'making it work' and deserve the real pain, indeed the devastating trauma attaching thereto.

The duties of the Grihasta include the performance of 'Panchmahayagna' (five great sacrifices) laid down in Manu Dharma Sastra.

***Deva Yagna:*** (Deity worship) The daily worship and puja to Ganapathi,Kula devata and Ishta devata. Visiting kula devata temple often or atleast once in a year.

***Brahma Yagna:*** (Seer worship) Each day the householder expresses his debt to the the human kind by doing some services to the society. Performing ones own profession/vocation with the standards of ethics itself is a service to the society. Brahma Yagna also includes Guru worship and studying, teaching, repeating and meditating upon the Vedic scriptures.(Vedic rituals)

***Pitru Yagna:*** (Ancestor Worship) Respecting the ancestors, parents of the self and spouse and getting their blessings by making salutations to them by leaning towards their foot. Parentless children should perform Annual Shraddas (Thithi) and observe fasting during new moon days and beginning of months, offer rice balls (pindas) to crows or in holy river.Those persons who do not know the thithi of their parents death should perform thithi on the new moon day of the month "Thai" which usally comes between the second week of January and the second week of February. The thithi given or the fasting observed on thai amavasya constitute a remembrance of ancestors back to the 7th generation.

***Bhuta Yagna:*** Worship of living beings by scattering grains, offering food at the threshold for animals, birds, insects, etc. Loving and watering plants also do constitute bhuta yagna.

*Nara Yagna or Purusha Yagna or Manushya Yagna* (Guest worship) Obligation to love and honour ties of fellowship with humanity by showing hospitality to fellow humans, friends, relatives or even strangers and beggars.

It is to be noted here that a person performing his Panchmahayagna everyday without fail will not be disturbed by kali purusha. Marriage is an integral part of a Grihasta for it is said that no ritual is efficacious without the presence of the wife, the Sahadharmini.

The wife always accompanies the husband in discharging his duties. Marriage is no doubt, primarily for begetting children but it was also required for the proper performance of worship.

Marriage is not only a contract between individuals but a contract between families.

The difference in the family values as between those obtaining in India and in the West would reveal how different are the expectations about marriage in these two cultures.

The first three nights after marriage, the couple are expected to remain continent to impress that marriage is not a license for sexual pleasures but a holy and irrevocable contract not only between the man and wife but also casts the burden of ensuring it to be so, till the very last, on the community comprising of the families of both sides.

The husband is expected to first satisfy the wife's soul and the wife satisfies the husband with her body and gets his soul.

On Abortion, the Sastras are very clearly against it. The foetus is considered to be a living person with consciousness who is required to be protected and reared with care and affection.

Rig Veda even goes to the extent of pleading for mercy on behalf of the foetus.

Atharva Veda characterises the killer of a foetus as brunagni, one of the most heinous sins.

Kaushitaki Upanishad equates it to the killing of one's parents.

Gauthama Dharma Sastra advises such persons as having lost their caste status-considered in those days as equal to capital punishment.

Susrutha Samhita the medical treatise, however, permits abortion on purely medical grounds Mudhagarbha which explains the steps to be taken to save both mother and child in case of emergency and advises that if the foetus is alive, every attempt should be made to remove it from the mother's womb alive. If dead, it may be removed in the normal course. Surgical removal (Caesarian) should not be resorted to if it is likely to harm the mother and / or the child. In extreme cases, it permits inducing miscarriage of the foetus if that were the only means to prevent the loss of the mother. Children were loved to the point of becoming spoilt darlings.

**Vanaprasta Ashrama (The Anchorite)**

Vanaprasta is the third stage of Elder Advisor usually between 48 and 72 years of age. A stage comes when business, family, secular life like the beauties and hopes of youth have exhausted themselves and need to be left behind. The person retires usually from worldly attachments to lead a life of contemplation and meditation alone or with his wife.

What life holds beyond middle age depends in the end not on fancy and imagination but on the realities of the values of life we regard as inviolable. Vanaprasta may be termed as the beginning of a person's real 'adult education' to evaluate his performance thus for as Grihasta and reorder his life in such a way as to discover who he is and what life is all about.

"The time had come for him to probe 'the secret of 'I' with which he has been on such intimate terms all these years yet which remains a stranger, full of inexplicable quirks, baffling surds, irrational impulses."

It is curious to find that many do not wish to venture into this but would like to remain in Grihastashrama even by remarrying if the first spouse predeceases the man.

A playboy of 25 may impress but how could one pose perpetually as the 'prince charming' at 50, 60 or 70 years of age? Look at those who try hard to do this. However hard they might try, they not only fail to receive recognition but also incur the derision of people whom they seek to impress.

***Sannyasa Ashrama (The Renounced):*** Sannyasi is the fourth stage of an Ascetic-Solitaire-usually beyond 72 years of age. This means 'Samyak Nyasa'—'Total detachment' from worldly pleasures including the bare necessities to subsist. This is the last 'Ashrama'. He does not aspire to be recognised as somebody who matters—he wish of the Sannyasi is just to be a 'persona non grata'—one who exists almost without giving any thought to his being-with no desire for name or fame or recognition.

> *"He no more cares whether his body falls or remains than does a cow what becomes a garland that someone has hung around her neck—for the faculties of his mind are now at rest in the holy power, the essence of bliss."*
>
> *"Business, family, secular life, the beauties and hopes of youth and the success of maturity have now been left behind, Eternity alone remains. And, so it is to that—and, not to the tasks and worries of their life, already gone which came and passed like a dream-that the mind is turned."*
>
> *"The Sannyasi has his spiritual eye on goods that men can't give and cares little for anything that men can take away. Therefore, he is beyond the possibility of either seduction or threat."*

***Sannyasa is of Four Kinds:*** 'Vidvat'-born out of real wisdom and is spontaneous 'Vividisha' springing from a yearning for self-realisation through study of the Scriptures and practicing the rigours prescribed Aatura upon one's deathbed when there is no hope in living further, and Markata-embracing Sannyasa as an escape from great misery, disappointment or misfortune that one is not able to face in worldly activities.

No one is encouraged to become a 'Sannyasi' unless one has gone through one's natural impulses through the three previous Ashramas. He who runs away from marriage (Grihastaashrama) is no better than a coward deserting the battle field.

The student's attention is directed inward, preparing for life ahead. In Grihasta and Vanaprasta attention is directed outward-Grihasta supporting the entire society, Vanasprasta sharing his experiences for the good of others. The Sannyasi is again inner directed. Having contributed to society and having received from society what he needed, he prepares himself for the final release.

Sannyasa means renunciation not of life alone but of Kama, Artha and even worldly Dharmas. Sannyasa may be deemed a second phase of Brahmacharya.

The first was a preparation for life; the second a preparation for death. While Brahmacharya and Grihasta show the 'Pravritti Marga (towards the world), Vanaprasta and Sannyasa indicate the 'Nivritti Marga' (away from the world) through introspection and renunciation.

Thus, while 'Varna' is determined by past 'Karma', Ashrama is determined by the stage of maturity displayed by individuals in viewing the goals of life.

"Varnas stress human nature; Ashramas stress human nurture"

And, Lord Krishna advises "One's own duty, though done imperfectly is preferable to the duty of another even if well performed. Even death in doing one's own duty is blissful; doing another's duty is frightful".

So, everyone is advised to do his / her 'Dharma' according to one's Varna and Ashrama—and not to venture doing those outside one's own.

Every person has his Svabhava (natural being) fitting him for his Svadharma (natural function). We cannot change either our natural being or our natural function because nature cannot be forced into a change by our whims and fancies.

A Sadhu was rescuing a scorpion that had fallen into a pond. Every time he lifted it out of water, it stung him but he would not give up until it was saved. One of his disciples asked why he was persistent in saving the scorpion that stung him. The Sadhu replied: "The `Dharma' or nature of scorpion is to sting; the nature or Dharma of a Sadhu is to rescue a being from distress—and in this case sure death by drowning. So long as the scorpion does not give up its Dharma why should I give up mine and give up saving it?" The `Dharma' of fire is to burn, of water is to be cool, of wind is to blow. So, the Dharma of man is to be humane. This story emphasises how one should go on doing one's duty even if obstacles, impediments and difficulties intervene in discharging it.

The Dharma of a student is to study. If the student—neglects his studies he neglects his svadharma; if fire does not burn, it is not fire; When heated by fire (by external influence) water loses its nature (Svadharma) of being cool. When Svadharma is not practiced, there ensues an imbalance in the environment. This understanding and adherence to Svadharma is what distinguishes human beings from other beings.

## Born to Death: Sixteen Hindu Sacraments

Man Making is a science. Like a gardener, parents & teachers work on a person so that the best can flower out from him or her. The whole thrust is to help bring about greater awareness & love in the mind, and canalise the interest & energies into positive fields. The whole 'work' is on the mind alone, and is comparable to the work of a genetic engineer. The only difference is that while a genetic engineer plays & transforms with the basic structure, a teacher works to manifest the basic inherent beauty, freedom & potential which facilitates to carve out a dynamic, creative, intelligent & magnanimous personality.

Interest is a very subjective thing, and has to come out from within. It can never be imposed. Interests are created by impressions & knowledge. That is what ad agencies too do. They create impressions, and this 'works' on the mind of the person to bring about the interest in him in the desired field. Once the interest has been manifested we can just sit back and see the person work for his or her field of interest in a dynamic way. While the experts of the advertisement world are generally seen to use this 'knowledge of impressing minds' for their selfish & commercial ends, the Vedic Masters used this knowledge to help bring out a positive & dynamic personality. While the former conditions the mind to the extent that the very thinking process of their target crowd is conditioned in their favour, but the Rishis saw to it that the very power to think & question daringly, independently & creatively grew. Thus we have all our scriptures in the form of question & answers.

These deliberate & positive impressions which help create a deep & lasting impressions on the mind of a person—so as to generate interest in him about the Truth & Dharma, help bring out a positive personality and free the mind of its negativities are called 'Samskaras'. No one while living in the world remains free of the conditionings of his or her environs & teachings, so the question is not whether we can stop all conditionings but to see to it that a person is looked after like a plant and help his or her potentials bloom.

To a question whether Samskaras are deliberate positive conditionings, well the answer is that, the objective of the entire exercise is to help a person awake to a state which is free from all conditionings, so while impressions are certainly put effectively & deliberately yet they are the very antithesis of what is implied by the word conditionings. This is one of the finest & blessed science, and has been perfected here as an art form too.

Samskaras are the turning points of life and need to be celebrated. Celebrations are very important ingredients of Samskaras. They directly or indirectly involve our respected elders, scholars, near & dear ones. Everyone gets together to convey their best wishes & blessings to the person concerned and thus there is social & religious sanction for the act & ceremony. Samskaras are great, time-tested tools in our traditional systems which help carve out a great personality. Apart from scriptural validation, history also proves to us the great effectiveness of these methods. When Vedic Masters had their way, India was on top of the world. The people of the far off land prayed that they will one day see this great land of plenty, prosperity & righteousness.

In this section we shall present an introduction to these famous sixteen Samskaras of Hindus which cover the entire life span of a person and take him to the door steps to Truth.

1. *Garbhadan:* The first coming together of the husband & wife for bringing about conception.
2. *Pumsvan:* Ceremony performed when the first signs of conception are seen, and is to be performed when someone desires a male child.
3. *Seemantonayan:* A ceremony of parting of the hairs of the expectant mother to keep her spirits high & positive. Special music is arranged for her.
4. *Jatakarma:* After the birth of the child, the child is given a secret name, he is given taste of honey & ghee, mother starts the first breast-feeding after chanting of a mantra.
5. *Nama-karana:* In this ceremony the child is given a formal name. Performed on the 11th day.
6. *Nishkramana:* In this the formal darshan of sun & moon is done for the child.
7. *Annaprashana:* This ceremony is performed, when the child is given solid food (anna) for the first time.
8. *Chudakarana:* Cuda means the 'lock or tuft of hair' kept after the remaining part is shaved off.
9. *Karna-vedha:* Done in 7th or 8th month. Piercing of the ears.
10. *Upanayan and Vedarambha:* The thread ceremony. The child is thereafter authorized to perform all rituals. Studies of Vedas begins with the Guru.
11. *Keshanta:* Hairs are cut, guru dakshina is given
12. *Samavartan:* Returning to the house
13. *Vivaha:* Marriage ceremony

14. *Vanprastha:* As old age approaches, the person retires for a life of tapas & studies.
15. *Sanyas:* Before leaving the body a Hinddu sheds all sense of responsibility & relationships to awake & revel in the timeless truth.
16. *Antyeshthi:* The last rites done after the death.

### *Objects of Samskara*

Samskaras (Sacraments) are rituals and sacrifices. By virtue of their performances the life of the performer receives a higher sanctity. Samskaras cover the entire life of a Hindu from the moment he is conceived in the mother's womb till his death-inclusive of his funeral ceremonies and thereafter, for the smooth passage of his soul to another world.

Just as gold and diamonds that are dug out from the ore need refining and polishing in order to shine in all their splendour, man too needs these Samskaras or purificatory ceremonies in order to shine in his best form physically, psychically and spiritually.

There are several objects of the Samskaras, as can be seen from the Mantras and symbolism used in the ceremonies. These can be broadly divided into two categories; to invoke beneficence from the kindly gods and to keep away or remove hostile or evil powers that beset human life at various stages.

Samskaras aim in the first instance at material gain to the individual. During some ceremonies prayers are offered to gods for health, wealth, children, intellect etc., which contribute to domestic and social felicity. Samskaras mirror self-expression of joys and sorrows, hopes and ambitions, which man exhibits in a dignified way when he celebrates these functions with feasts, presents, decoration, music and also in funeral ceremonies in an appropriate mood.

Samskaras also create an awareness of the attainment of social status and privileges for the individual. The boy who is given the sacred thread acquires the right to study the Vedas;

the married man gains the title to perform the Dharmas mentioned in the Vedas.

Samskaras bring about cultural gains. The ancient lawgivers underscored the introduction of higher religion and sanctity in the lives of those who undergo Samskaras. Some impurity is inherently attached to the prenatal stage of birth and Manu and Yajnavalkya see in the Samskara ceremonies, the removal of those impurities, so that man's body is made fit to become a temple for God to reside. Samskaras are moulders of character.

Sage Angiras poetically refers to the development of personality that the Samskaras endow on its adherents: "Just as a picture is painted with various colours, so the character of the individual is formed by the proper performance of the Samskaras."

Sage Gautama said that Samskaras along with the eight Atmagunas take one to Brahman (Supreme Self) or Moksha.

In short, the whole gamut of Samskaras is designed to channel the entire energies of man towards the creation of a perfect secular as well as spiritual life in himself in a manner that is not only ingenious but essentially practical, dignified and compulsory in the interest of all-round human welfare. To quote Max Muller, the emphasis placed upon these ceremonies by the ancients disclose "the deep-rooted tendency in the heart of man to bring the chief events of human life into contact with a higher power, and to give to our joys and sufferings a deeper significance and a religious sanctification.

### *History and Sources*

The earliest suggestion of Samskaras are found in the Rig-Veda. Hymns now used in the rituals of marriage, conception and funeral are to be found there, besides others that are generally recited during all rituals. In the Yajurv Veda we have references to the tonsure ceremony. This is common to the Shrauta or Yaga ceremonies. The Atharva Veda is a rich source of Mantras relating to several of the Samskaras like marriage, funeral, initiation for Vedic studies etc.

Coming down to the Brahmana period, Gopatha Brahmana contains references to Upanayana or the thread-ceremony. The word Brahmacharya is to be found in Sathapatha Brahmana.

Taittiriya Aranyaka contains Mantras for cremation.

Chandogya Upanishad relates how a Brahmacharin is admitted to the Gurukula (boarding school).

Mention of Gayatri Mantra is made in Brahadaranyaka and other Upanishads.

Taittiriya Upanishad contains the famous convocation address. This Upanishad also contains Mantras used for begetting a learned son and also relating to funeral ceremonies.

It is reasonable to conclude that Samskaras were developed, amplified, codified and given an institutional bias in later years with the development of civilization, catering to the needs of the time for giving stability to the community.

***Sources***

The rituals constituting the Brahmanas received systematic treatment in what are called Kalpa-Sutras. These are exegetical texts of the Vedas. The need for them arose because short manuals were required by the priests as an aid for their daily performance. Among these texts, those that deal with Vedic sacrifices are called Srauta-Sutras and those that deal with domestic rituals are called Grihya-Sutras which, though not valuable as pieces of literature, are yet valuable as "Folk-lore" journals of ancient India. They portray an accurate picture of the social lie, popular customs and usage of ancient India.

Some important Grihya Sutras are listed below: 1.Apastamba 2. Aswalayana 3.Baudhayana 4.Bharadwaja 5.Gobhila 6. Hiranyakesia 7.Jaimineeya 8.Khadira 9.Manava 10.Paraskara 11.Sankhayana 12.Varaha Grihya Sutras. There is another class of texts called Dharmasutras that are an extension of the Grihya Sutras. These texts deal mainly with secular and religious laws relating to the Ashramas. These are again supplemented by what are called Parisishtas or addenda. The Commentaries of which 25 are known; Prayogas, of which

24 are known. There are also a dozen Karikas or specialised treatises on individual Samskaras.

In addition to these are Apta-vakyas or the words of the saints and the wise who observe and follow Sanatan Dharma (Vedic religion). They have the sanctity of Smritis in cases of doubt.

These, then, are the real sources of information about the Samskaras. It can easily be seen from the number of works on the subject, how important the ancients considered the Samskaras.

## Sixteen Main Sacraments

### *Pre-Natal Samskaras*

1. *Garbhadhana:* We can call it the conception ceremony. There are certain Do's and Don'ts during the 'Ritu' period of the woman, which are of great psychological significance. The propitious day and time are fixed astrologically for Garbhadhana and the ritual follows a set pattern. The Mantras uttered in this Samskaras are essentially prayers offered to God to help the bride conceive a good son. The Mantras make use of occasional metaphors of joint action. They can be freely translated thus:

"May we produce strong and long-lived sons as fire is produced by friction; may he be well behaved. I am part of God and I shall produce good sons to liberate my ancestors. May we beget shining, wealthy children. May we donate liberally to the needy and attain moksha. May God make you fit for conception. Let the evil spirit flee from you. Let your child be free from defects like lameness, deafness etc. Be you like the divine Kamadhenu etc."

Procreation is a compulsory duty enjoined on the Hindu to repay his ancestral debt, except when either or both the partners are functionally unfit.

2. *Punsavanam:* This ceremony is performed in the second, third and the fourth month of pregnancy. The meaning and object of this ceremony is to "quicken a male child" in the woman. The Punsavana is performed on a day of male Nakshatra. During this ritual, a few drops of the juice of the Banyan stem are put into the right nostril of the pregnant lady to inhale it, with a prayer for the birth of a son or a worthy child. According to Susruta, the great Ayurvedic writer, the juice of the Banyan tree has all the properties of relieving trouble during pregnancy.

Sanctified thread is tied to the left wrist of the lady by way of protection. The mantras, freely rendered, pray: "May God Isana fulfil our wishes; Dhata bless the world with children and wealth. May He bless this household too with children. May the immortals live in this house. May Agni bless me with sons. May Indra bless me with children. May I have handsome children."

[Note: The following explanations are from the writings of Swami Dayananda Saraswati (The founder of The Arya Samaj). The translation is by Acharya Vaidyanath Shastri].

Placing his hand on the womb of his pregnant wife the husband should pronounce the following Mantra from the Yajur Veda, the meaning of which is given below:

"O soul in the womb! May you have the swiftness of nice-winged swift bird, may there arise in your head the trio of action, contemplation and learning. Gayatri be your eye. Brihat and Rathantara like your sides. Rig Veda your soul, metres your limbs. The hymns of Yajuh are your name. The Vamadevya is your body. The deeds worth doing and shunning are your hind part. The yajnas are like your hooves, the feet. You are a noble soul, the master of noble qualities. Acquire knowledge and attain to happiness in life and beyond."

After this the pregnant lady should live in a disciplined way and lead a life with proper (restricted) diet and confined movements. She should eat a small quantity of the cocculus cordiclius (giloy) Brahmi herb, and dry ginger (Soonth) with milk. She should avoid too much sleep, avoid too much talking, avoid saltish food preparations, avoid sour, pungent, bitter things and avoid purgatives like Termunallia Chebula (Haritaki). She should avoid anger, aversion, greed etc. and should always keep her mind joyful and happy. She should lead a life of good conduct.

3. *Simantonnayana:* The third in the series of prenatal Samskaras, this is performed during the period between the fifth and the eighth months of pregnancy. The specific materials used during this Samskara, that are for the lady only, are, the quill of a porcupine, an ear of ripe paddy and some Udumbara leaves. The deity invoked is Rika, the presiding deity of the full-moon. Their implications are: that the pregnancy should be fruitful; the child should be endowed with sharp and penetrating intellect (like the sharp quill of the porcupine). The child should be beautiful like the full-moon. The gist of the Mantra is: "I beseech the goddess Raka. May she make this ceremony blameless. May my son be endowed with sharp intellect."

Music, especially on the veena, is indicated to be played on this occasion. This increases the mother's suckling power besides conferring other psychological benefits. Ladies are asked to sing: "Be a mother of heroic sons" thus creating a heroic atmosphere. The mother fasts and keeps silent after the ceremony till night time when the stars become visible. At the close of the ceremony she touches a male calf, symbolising a son.

[Note: The following abridged explanations are from the writings of Swami Dayananda Saraswati (The founder of The Arya Samaj). The translation is by Acharya Vaidyanath Shastri].

"I, the husband, call my wife who is as beautiful as the full moon in the night and is possessed of good words of praise for me, I call her to participate in all the functions of the prayers. Let her, the lady of good fortunes, listen to my words and understand them with her spirit. May she perform the functions of progeny in such a good way as she sews the clothes etc. with the needle that does not pierce the fingers when sewing. May she give me a brave son. Whatever is uttered herein is true. The oblation offered is meant for Raka and it is not me."

"O full-moon like beautiful lady, and who is munificent nature, come to me with heart full of joy, and with wealth of praiseworthy advice regarding various physical and spiritual wealth. O lucky one, come to me giving a thousand kinds of fortunes. Whatever is uttered herein is true. The oblation offered is meant for Raka and it is not for me."

"My husband who is potentially vigorous has established the embryo of life in me, who is desirous of a son or vigorous child. May husband be free from all evils and accompany me with noble son."

### *Post-Natal Samskaras*

4. *Jatakarma:* The persons concerned sprinkle water on the woman that is giving birth to a child.

This is the authority from Paraskar Grihya Sutra and thus the same has been written in the Ashvalayana, Gobhiliya and Shaunakiya Grihya Sutra.

At the time when delivery is going to take place, the sprinkling of water on the body of the pregnant woman should be done with the Mantras from the Yajur Veda and from other sources.

The ceremony proper should be performed (unless prevented by death in close family circles) before the umbilical cord of the child is severed. The father looks at the face of the newly born infant and this at once redeems his debt to his ancestors. Thereafter he must immediately bathe in cold water with his clothes on. Actually, he must jump into a river or a lake so as to cause the splashing waters to rise in the air as high as a palm tree. He is then enjoined to perform dana, dharma etc. (charity and other good deeds) as the merits earned by him at that time are of immense benefit. The father then touches the tongue of the infant with a drop of honey touched by a gold ring, uttering Mantras. This action endows the child with Medha or intelligence. Susruta praises honey's properties in this respect.

A name is also given to the child, in secret, lest his enemies should practice black magic on the child with that name. Then the father utters a prayer for long life in the ear of the infant. Other Brahmins (priests) too bless the child with long life by breathing the breath of life upon the infant. The father prays to Mother Earth "May we live a hundred years." By another hymn that says: "Be a stone; be an axe (unto enemies); be the imperishable gold." The father prays that the child be endowed with strength, valour and fame.

After severing the umbilical cord, the child is handed over to the mother to suckle when the husband prays to the water-god to protect the mother too.

[Note: The following abridged explanations (greatly abridged extracts selected at random) are from the writings of Swami Dayananda Saraswati (The founder of The Arya Samaj). The translation is by Acharya Vaidyanath Shastri].

After offering oblations with Mantras the husband should sing Vamadevayagana given at the end of Samanyaprakarana. There after the father of the child should write AUM syllable on the tongue of the child with the pre-prepared golden bar dipped in ghee (clarified butter) and honey mixed properly. Doing so he should whisper 'VEDOASITI' (your confidential name is Veda) in the right ear of the child and then, with the bar of the gold make the child lick a little of the mixed ghee and honey with the following Mantras:

"O child, for you I give this ghee and honey has been produced by God who is the producer of all the wealth of the world. May you be preserved and be protected by learned men and your parents. May you attain long life and live in this world for hundred autumns."

"I establish in you the idea of God who is the giver of life. I establish in you, O child, the idea of God who is all beatitude. I establish in you, O child, the idea of God who is the source of all movements. I establish in you the idea of God who is the life of all, all beatitude and the source of all movements."

"May we attain Divinity, who is the Master of all the assembled masses of the world, who is wondrous and eternal, who is desired and attainable by individual souls and also the wisdom of discrimination."

After giving ghee and honey six times to the child to lick with these above listed Mantras, rice and barley in a very meager quantity should be cleaned and crushed and mixed with water. The liquid thus prepared be strained through a piece of cloth and be kept in a pot. The father of the child or a person concerned place a drop of this liquid in the mouth of the child using the thumb and the last finger taken together, pronouncing the following Mantra:

"This is ghee. This is grain or cereal. This is for life and this is immortality or the nectar of eatables."

[Note: This is the opinion of only Gobhiliya Grihya-Sutra and not of any other authorities]

Thereafter the father of the child should whisper in the right ear of the child the following Mantras:

"O child, may God, the creator of all bless you with firm wisdom. May Saraswati (the goddess of learning), the all knowing goddess bless you with firm wisdom. May the sun and the moon, stationed in space, be the source of firm wisdom for you."

"The fire is the source of life, it gains this power from the wood-fuel. May you attain long life, O child, with that life giving fire."

"Soma, the moon is the source of life. Knowledge and wisdom is the source of life. It gains this power with the Brahmanas, the knower of the Vedas. The enlightened persons are the source of long life. They gain this power through immortality.

He seers (Rishis), possessing penetrative genius, are the source of life. They gain this power by austerity and discipline. The parents, grand-parents etc. are the source of life. They gain this power from grains, cereals and other foods. The Yajna is the source of life. It gains this power through qualified ways of performance. The ocean is the source of life. It gains this power from the rivers. With that life of moon, with that life of knowledge and wisdom, with that life of the learned persons, with that life of the seers, with that life of parents and grand-parents, with that life of yajna, with that life of ocean, O child, may you attain long life, knowledge and wisdom."

These Mantras should again be recites in the left ear of the child.

Thereafter, the father of the child, placing his hand very gently upon the shoulders of the child, should recite more Mantras. Of these one only is reproduced below:

"O child, may you become firm and strong like a rock. May you become like an axe to destroy injustice, may you become as bright as gold with knowledge and action. O child, you are my soul and spirit. May you not be subjected to an immature death. May you live a hundred autumns."

A month before the expected date of delivery, a maternity room (Sutikagriha) is selected on an auspicious day. The room should be in the south-west corner of the house; the ground should be even. The would-be mother enters the room a couple of days before the expected date, after worshipping the elders, family deities and accompanied by auspicious sounds like ringing of bells or music and also accompanied by experienced and pleasant mothers.

They cheer and otherwise prepare the lady for safe delivery by means of approved diet, ointments etc. The room is made comparatively dark, because it is said, the sunlight will be too bright for the new-born babe and for ensuring for it a black retina. When the time arrives, the would be mother is made to lie on her back. Mantras are chanted outside to ward off evil spirits. An elderly person at home unties several knots of a rope suggesting the loosening of muscles tying the child in the womb.

The Turyanti leaves are placed near the lady to ward off evil forces and also to expedite delivery. If the delivery is difficult, the verse from the Atharva Veda meant for it, is chanted. On safe delivery a small fire called Sutika-fire is lighted in the room to purify and protect the child and its mother. Mustard seeds and grains are thrown into the fire to counteract evil forces and evil eyes.

5. *Namakarana Samskara (Naming the child):* This is a simple ceremony in which the child is given a name. According to Asvalayana, the names of boys should have an even number of syllables. A two-syllable name will bring material prosperity and fame and a four syllable name will bring religious fame.

The names of girls should have an odd number of syllables and end in "I" or "aa". They should be easy to pronounce, pleasing to the ear and auspicious. They should not suggest awkward suggestions.

By traditions, names are chosen after the Nakshatras of birth (letters are allocated to the signs of the zodiac). Some people name their children after the ancestors. The practice of naming children after favourite deities began from the Puranic times. The rise of the Bhakti (devotion) movement made this practice generally popular. By naming children after gods, we are deemed to gain several opportunities for uttering God's name whenever we call the child.

The Namakarana Samskar is performed, normally on the tenth or twelfth day after birth. If there are inconveniences then it is taken to the end of the first year.

After preliminaries, the parents give the offerings to gods and feel the breath of the child symbolising the awakening of its consciousness and utters in its ear three times: "Your name is .....". The Brahmins and elders are asked to follow, calling the child by that name and blessing it.

[Note: The following abridged explanations are from the writings of Swami Dayananda Saraswati (The founder of The Arya Samaj). The translation is by Acharya Vaidyanath Shastri].

The parents, Acharya (teacher) etc. give name to the child. It is written in the Gobhiliya 2/8/8-18 and the Shaunaka Grihya Sutra that a meritoriously attractive and pleasant name should be given to the child.

The name should be given to the child on the 11th day leaving 10 days from the day of birth of the child or on 101st day or on the very day of the birth of the child in the beginning of the second year. On the day fixed for giving name to the child, the Yajaman (the father of the child) and the priests of the yajna invite the guests present and commence the ceremony.

After reciting prayers as prescribed in 8 Mantras from Samanya Prakarana, Svastivachana, Shantikarana, and the complete procedure of Samanya Prakarana, four oblations of Aghavarajyabhagahuti; four Vyahriti oblations; eight oblations with eight Mantras beginning with 'Tvanno Agne' from the Samanya prakarana, should be offered.

Thereafter, the mother of the child, bathing the child with clean water, dressing the child with nice clean clothes, coming near the Yajnakunda (sacred fire), passing behind the father of the child, stands on the right side of him (child's father) keeping the head of the child in the north direction. She then places the child into the hands of the child's father and she herself returns from the back side of her husband (the child's father). She should take her seat in the north side keeping her face in the east.

The father of the child, keeping the child's head in the north direction and feet in south direction, should give the child to his wife (the mother of the child). They then follow the procedure that has been mainly prescribed for Namakarana Samskara. A Yajna is performed. Filling the spoon with ghee, the Yajaman (father of the child) should offer one oblation (into the sacred fire) pronouncing this Mantra: "Om Prajapataye Swaha".

Thereafter, four oblations–one oblation with each of the Tithi, Nakshatra, Tithi Devata and Nakshatra-Devta should be offered. These Tithis and Nakshatras are the lunar dates and the stars under which the birth of the child took place.

Thereafter, one oblation with the "Svishtakrit Mantra" from the Samanya Prakarana and four Vyahriti oblations from Samanya prakarana, and thus totaling five oblations in all should be offered.

Then the mother taking the child in her lap sits on a nice seat and the father of the child feels the breaths being exhaled from the nostrils of the child. He then utters a few mantras.

### *Forbidden or Prohibited Names*

The following female names should be avoided.

Names after a constellation such as Rohini, Revati etc. should be avoided.

Names of trees and plants such as Champa, Tulasi, etc.

Names of rivers such as Ganga, Yamuna, Saraswati, etc.

Names formed on the basis of lowering merit like Chandali.

Names of mountains like Vindhyachal, Himalaya, etc.

Names of birds like Kokila, Hansa, etc.

Names of snakes such as Sarpini, Nagin, etc.

Names suggestive of menial servants or other orderlies like Dasi, kinkakari etc.

Names that create an awe or fear like Bheema, Bhayankari, Chandika etc.

The above types of names are prohibited names for female children.

The scriptural authority for the above prohibitions is taken from Manusmriti 3/9. Which reads as follows:

"Let him not marry a maiden named after a constellation, a tree, or a river, nor one bearing the name of a low caste, or of a mountain, nor one named after a bird, a snake, or a slave, nor one whose name inspires terror."

Distinguishing factors merit attention when giving names. For example take the names –Dev or Jaydev. In the case of the child possessing a promising tendency of becoming Brahmana, or the parents desiring to make their child a Brahmana should give him the name such as Devsharma. Similarly, in the case of Kshatriya, Vaisya and Sudra, the names be respectively given to children as Devavarma, Devgupta, and Devdas etc..

If the child is female, the name should be of one or three or five letters like Shree, Hrihi, Yashoda, Sukhada, Saubhagyaprada etc.

6. *Niskramana Samskara*

[Note: The following abridged explanations are from the writings of Swami Dayananda Saraswati (The founder of The Arya Samaj). The translation is by Acharya Vaidyanath Shastri].

The infant is taken out of the house into the climate of fresh air and sunshine.

From the Gobhil Grihyasutra 2.8.1:

"Chaturthemaasi Nishkramanika. Suryamudikshayati Tatchakshuriti.

Also,

"Jananaadyastriteeyo jyoutsnastasya Triteeyaayaam."

The time of Niskramana. Two dates are mentioned.

The first date is the third lunar date of the third full-moon fortnight from the birth date of the child.

The second date is the birth Tithi (date) of the child in the fourth month from the date of birth.

***The Procedure:*** In the morning, after sunrise, the infant is bathed and dressed. The mother of the child brings the child in Yajnashala (place of Sacred Fire Ceremony), approaching from the right side of her husband faces her husband and gives the child into the hands of her husband, keeping the head of the child in the north direction and the child's face and chest facing upwards.

The mother then walks clockwise from behind her husband and takes her seat on the left side of her husband keeping her face eastward.

The same ceremony and the same Mantras are used as for Jatakarma Samskaras.

Thereafter the father of the child gives the child to the mother, keeping the child's head in the north direction and the feet in the south direction. Keeping silence, the husband touches the head of his wife. The child is then taken out in the sun with the following Mantra from the Yajur Veda. This Mantra is recited on behalf of the infant child.

"Om Tatchakshurdevahitam Purustaatshukramuccharat. Pashyema Sharadah Shatam Jeevema Sharadah Shatam Shrunuyaam Shradah Shatam Pra Bravaam Sharadha Shatamadeenaahaa syaama Sharadah Shatam Bhooyashcha Sharadah Shataat."

O Benefactor of devotees! I concentrate on Thy pure energy. Grant me perfect health. May my eyes, ears, tongue and the other organs function in a strong and healthy way for a hundred years. May I not become helpless and dependent during this time. Grant me a hundred years of joyous life free from disease.

After exposing the child to the sun and fresh air, the child is brought back into the Yajnashala where people bless the child with the following sentence:

"Tvam Jeeva Sharadah Shatam Vardhamaanah."

May you be endowed with health and strength and live a life of hundred years.

### *Exposing the Child to the Moonlit Night*

In the night, the mother brings the child approaching the husband from the right side, facing the husband gives the child to her husband, keeping the child's head in the north direction. The mother then walks clockwise walking behind her husband stands on his left side facing the moon. With a little water in her right hand palm a prayer is offered with the following Mantra.

*"Om Yadadashchandramasi Krishnam Prithivyaa Hridayam Shritam*

*Tadaham Vidvaagvam Statpashyanmaaham Pautramagham Rudam."*

The water in the hand is then sprinkled to the ground. The mother then walks anticlockwise from behind her husband and facing him takes the child. Then again walking clockwise from behind her husband stands to the left of her husband keeping the child's head in the north direction and feet in the south direction. This time the father of the child takes a little water in his right hand palm and recites the same Mantra..Then he sprinkles the water to the ground.

Thereafter both husband and wife, in a happy frame of mind, take the child back into the house.

7. *Annaprashana Smaskara:* This is the ceremony for the first feeding of cooked rice. The object of this ceremony is to pray to the gods with Vedic Mantras to bless the child with good digestive powers, good thoughts and talents. It is performed when the child is six months old which is the weaning time. Susruta commends this weaning time as best for both the mother and the child.

Offerings are made to the goddess of speech and vigour. Prayers are offered so that the child's senses have their full gratification and live a happy and contented life. The father feeds a little of the sweet food anointed with gold to the child with Mantras that say he feeds the child with food that may ensure a healthy life to the child and prevent ill-health. Apart from the efficacy or otherwise of this ceremony, its observance creates in all concerned an awareness of the cumulative needs of the child at that age in a scientific and tender manner. Its systematic observance therefore ensures the results expected especially when fortified by Mantras.

[Note: The following abridged explanations are from the writings of Swami Dayananda Saraswati (The founder of The Arya Samaj). The translation is by Acharya Vaidyanath Shastri].

The first feeding of cereal to the child.

When the child is six months old.

The authority for Annaprashana Samskar derives from Ashvalayans Grihyasutra (1.16.1,4,5). Also the authority of Paraskar Grihya Sutra.

The Annaprashana ceremony should be performed at the time when the child gains strength to digest cereal and preparations made from cereals. The first feeding of cereal commences with this ceremony. He who desires his child to be brilliant and famous should feed cooked rice mixed with ghee (clarified butter) or the rice mixed with honey, curd and ghee.The samskar ceremony for the first feeding commences with prayer, followed by Svastivachana, Shanitkarana and complete Samanya Prakarana. It is indicated that this ceremony should be performed (when the child is six months old) on the day on which the child was born.

The rice should be prepared thus: Rice is washed, cleaned, cooked nicely and ghee in proper quantity is mixed in the rice when it is in the cooking process. When this rice has been cooked properly and has become cold, then it should be placed in Homasthali or the tray of Homa. From this Homashali the rice is then given in small containers to the Yajman, to Purohita and Ritvij (Priests), accompanied with chanting of Mantras.

The Yajmana (father of the child) then performs Agnyadhan and Samidadhana. Offers four oblations of Aghavarajyabhagahuti and four oblations of Vyahriti. Thereafter the oblation of the cooked rice that was given to the Yajman and to the priests, should be offered with one Mantras from the Rig Veda and one Mantra from the Yajur Veda.

Thereafter the Yajmana mixes small quantity of curd, honey and ghee. Adds this to the rice that remained after the oblations. This should be fed to the child in minute quantity according to the desire of the child with the following Mantra from the Yajur Veda:

"Om Annapateannasya No Dehyanamivasya Shushminah/

Pra Pra Dataaram Taarisha Oorjvam No Dhehi Dwipade Chatushpade.

"O Lord of plenty (of food)! Vouchsafe us a share of food that invigorates us, and brings no sickness. O Lord, thou art our leader. Grant us nourishment (maintenance) both for bipeds and for quadrupeds."

Thereafter the child is blessed by the mother and father of the child and also by the priests, the elders and the guests. The child is blessed with the sentence:

"Twam Annapatihi Annavo Vardhamano Bhooyaaha" meaning

"O child, May you be endowed by God's grace with Anna (grains or food). May you grow in strength and may you live a long life."

8. *Chudakarma:* This ceremony of the first tonsure is to be performed in the third year of the male child.. Also it initiates the maintenance of a 'Sikha' (tuft of hair on the head) as a religious necessity after that age. According to Susruta, a tuft of hair on the head protects a vital part on the head.

Susruta and Charaka confirm that removing the hair, excess nails etc., contribute to strength, vigour, longevity, purity and beauty of the individual.

An auspicious day is selected for the ceremony. A porcupine quill, Darbha grass, and a dummy razor are the specific materials used by the father for symbolically cutting the child's hair first. The gist of the Mantra used in this particular ceremony is:

"May the child live long beyond a hundred years. May his eye sight remain unimpaired. May he become prosperous and wealthy so that he can feed (and cater to the needs of others) liberally. May his digestion be perfect. Let him become a Varchasvi (prominent)."

[Note: The following abridged explanations are from the writings of Swami Dayananda Saraswati (The founder of The Arya Samaj). The translation is by Acharya Vaidyanath Shastri].

*From Ashvalayana Grihyasutra:*

> *"Triteeye Varshe Chaulam. Uttaratoagne Vreervihiyavamaashatilaanaam prithakpoorna Sharaavaani Nidadhaati."*

*From Paraskara Grihyasutra:*

> *"Samvatsavarikasya Choodaakaranam."*

Gobhiliya Grihyasutra 2.8.10.6 is also of the same opinion.

This ceremony should be performed in the third year or in the 1st year from the date of the child's birth. The dates for this ceremony should be chosen during the northern solstice and during the bright fortnight of the moon's phase.

***The Procedure:*** A hairdresser (Barber) is invited to this ceremony.

Four earthenware pots are brought to the Yajnashala (place of sacred fire Ceremony). They contain rice, barley, Mung and in the fourth Sesumum (Til). These four pots are placed in the north side of the Yajnavedi (Havan Kund).

A Havan Ceremony is performed.

Thereafter, addressing the hairdresser, the following Mantra from the Atharva Veda is recited.

"Om Aayamagantsavita kshurenoshnena vaaya Udakenehi.

Aadityaa Rudraa Vasava Undantu Sa Chetasah Somasya Ragno Vapata Prachetasah."

This barber, who is competent and swift has come with his razor (or a pair of scissors). Using lukewarm water, may the learned man (barber) known as Rudra and Vasu make the hair wet with utmost care and (thereafter) cut the hair like the king of Soma (as the Soma herbs are cut with care).

The father of the child mixes hot and cold water reciting the following Mantra.

"Om Ushnena Vaaya Udakenehi."

Let the hot water be mixed with cold water.

Thereafter, applying to the hair a mixture of the lukewarm water and a little butter or curd to moisten the hair of the child. The following mantra is recited.

*From Atharva Veda:*

"Om Aditihi Shashru Vapatvaapa Undantu Varchasaa

Chikitsu Prajapati Deerghaayutvaaya Chakshase."

Let this unbreakable razor (or scissors) cut the locks (hair on the head), let the waters with their moistening (softening) power soften the hair of the child, May the Lord of creatures (God) remove disease from this child. May this child attain to long life. May this child acquire knowledge.

*From Paraksara Grihyasutra:*

"Om Savitra Prasoota Daivyaa Aapa

Undantu Te Tanu Deerghayutvaaya Varchase."

O Child! Let the mighty celestial waters produced by the sun drench your head. May you attain a long life. May you acquire knowledge.

The father takes a comb in his hand and using the comb, gathers some hair from the right side of the child's head. Taking three blades of the Darbha (kusa) grass, while touching the hair with the grass and slightly pressing the hair against the grass, the following Mantra is recited.

*From Gobhiliya Grihyasutra, 219.14*

"Om Oshadhe Traayasvainam."

Let the herb protect this child.

Then holding the razor in a hand the father recites the following Mantra

*From Gobhiliya Grihyasutra, 219.13 -1.6.4*

"Vishnorda Ashtroasi"

This instrument (razor) is the means in the performance of this Yajna (Samskara) of Chudakarma.

*From the Yajur Veda:*

> *"Om Shivo Namaasi Svadhitiste Pitaa Namaste (Astu) Ma Ma Hrimsihi."*

This instrument (razor) is for auspiciousness. It is made of steel (metal) that is as strong as Vajra (a weapon). Let this razor be fit for cutting the hair. Let it not cause any pain whatsoever.

*From the Yajur Veda:*

*"Om Svadhite Mai Nam hrimsihi"*

Let not this steel razor inflict any harm to this child.

*From Yajur Veda:*

*"Om Nivarttayaam Yaayusheannaadyaaya Prananaaya Raayasposhaaya Sooprajaastvaaya Suviryaaya."*

O Child! I perform this tuft-ceremony so that you can attain to long life, constructive power, strength and wealth, good progeny and vigour.

The father of the child then holds the child's locks in a loop made from the Kusa grass and applies the first cut with the following Mantra.

*From the Atharva Veda:* The meaning of the Mantra is:

"O priest and all the learned guests! This competent barber shaves this child by the same razor (or scissors) that he uses to shave the head of our glorious King and the heads of noble men (men of merit). May this child be prosperous, wealthy and have good progeny."

All the hair cut by the razor or scissors, together with Kusa grass and the leaves of Mimosa (Shami) should be placed in an earthenware container. All lose hair pieces on the floor should be carefully picked up and placed in this container.

The detailed procedure entails the father cutting a little of the hair first from the right side of the child's head. Appropriate Mantras being recited. Then the same sequence is followed for the left side of the head. The third time from the back of the head The fourth time again the father cuts a little hair from the back of the hair.

Thereafter the father of the child blesses the child (with Mantra) by placing his right hand on the head of the child.

Then with the following Mantra, the father gives the razor (and scissors) to the barber.

*From Ashvalayana Grihyasutra, 1.17.15*

*"Om Yatkshurena Marchayata Supeshasaa Vaptaa Vapasi Keshaan Shundhi Shiro Maasyayuhu Pra Moshihi."*

O Barber! You are the cutter of the hair. Cut and shave the head of the child with that swift soft razor. Do not decrease (cut or shorten) the child's life.

The father then tells the barber to sharpen his razor on his sharpening stone. The father then requests the barber to gently drench the child's head with lukewarm water and that he should shave attentively with smooth hand, avoiding any cut from the razor. With these words he leads the barber to the north of the Yajna-Kunda. He sits with the child facing eastward. The barber shaves the child's head.

A little tuft of hair may be left on the head. It is considered more proper to shave all the hair in the first year. A little tuft of hair should be left on the head when Chudakarma Samskara is performed in the third year.

The barber is given the four earthenware containers filled with cereal grains together with clothes, money etc. The barber carries the cut hair together with the Darbha grass, Shami leaves etc. to some remote place *e.g.*, river side or in the woods; there to bury these in the ground. A member of the family or a friend can accompany the barber.

The father then rubs a little butter or curd on the head of the child. The child is then bathed. When the child is dressed, the father sits with the child facing eastward and chants Mahadeva Gana. The guests, before leaving, bless the child saying:

"Om Tvam Jeeva Sharadah Shatam Vardhamaanah."

O Child! May you live a hundred autumns growing in strength and vigour.

9. *Karnavedha:* Piercing the ears in the third or fifth year

*From Katyayana Griyhasutra 1.2*

"Karnavedho Varshe Triteeye Panchame Vaa."

The piercing of the child's ear should be done in the third or the fifth year (from the date of birth.)

An experienced physician who is a specialist and who has studied the treatise of Charaka and of Sushruta is invited to this ceremony.

In the morning, after bathing and getting the child dressed with clothes and ornaments, the mother brings the child to the Yajnashala. A Havan ceremony (Sacred Fire Ceremony) is performed with Mantras from the Samanya Prakarana.

The physician then should pierce the right ear first with the following Mantra:

*From the Yajur Veda: 25.21*

"Om Bhadram Karnebhihi Srunuyaama Devaa Bhadram Pashyemaakshabhiryajatraa Sthirairangai Stushtumam Sastanoobhirvyashemahi Devahitam Yadaayuhu."

O sociable learned persons, may we with our ears listen to what is good, and with our eyes see what is good. With limbs and bodies firm may we, extolling God lead a life conducive to the good of the sages.

He physician should pierce the left ear with the following Mantra:

*From the Yajur Veda 29.40.*

"Vakshyanti Veda ganeeganti Karnam Priyam Sakhaayam Parishasvajaanaa Yoshevaa Shing Kte Vitataadhi Dhanvatrjyaa eeyam samane paarayanti."

This bow string strained on the bow whispers like a woman, and protects us in the combat, as a wife fain to speak, offering advice, embraces her affectionate, praiseworthy husband.

The physician then inserts thin wire like objects in the freshly pierced ears to prevent the holes from closing up. The physician then applies healing ointments to the ears.

10. A. Upanayana and B. Vedarambha

Sacred Thread and Commencing the Study of the Vedas

### *Investiture of Sacred Thread (Janoi)*

The thread giving ceremony is performed in the eighth, eleventh and twelfth years of the male child calculated from the date of conception, for the first three Varnas (Brahman eighth year, Kshatriya eleventh year and Vaisya twelfth year) respectively. Etymologically, the word Upanayana means taking the child to the teacher or to Gayatri Mantra, according to some.

This ceremony gives the child a second birth (Dwija), as it were, where the Guru (teacher) becomes his father and Gayatri becomes his mother. The investiture with the Sacred thread entitles the child to study the Vedas and participate in Vedic functions. In essence, the child commences his journey on the road to spiritual life. This is contrasted with a life of eating, sleeping and procreating, which kinds of life animals also live. The Gurukula (Boarding school) type of education seeks to mould the child for an ideal life.

Gayatri is the most powerful of the Mantras. Initiation into it is described as 'Brahmopadesa'. It leads to the realisation of Brahman (the Supreme Reality). Along with this Mantra the Guru imparts his Shakti (power) too to the child; hence the Guru and the disciple are insulated by means of silken clothes at the time of the initiation.

The materials used in this ceremony are full of mystical significance. The Yajnopavita or the holy Thread consists of three folds, symbolising the three Gunas – Sattwa, Rajas and Tamas. It reminds one of the threefold debt one owes to one's manes (ancestors), Rishis (Seers who realised spiritual wisdom), and gods. The three threads also reminds one of the three letters of Pranava- AUM – as also Brahma, Vishnu and Shiva (Creator, Sustainer and Destroyer).

While investing it, the Acharya (the principal teacher) asks for strength, illumination and long life for the boy. The deerskin attached to the thread signifies spiritual and intellectual preeminence. The Kaupina or undercloth is the garment of immortality. The girdle (Mekhala) shows that the three Vedas (Rig Veda, Sam Veda and Yajur Veda) encircle the boy. Mekhala is "the daughter of Faith and sister of Rishis," protecting his purity and warding off evil. The staff (stick) of palasa wood given to the boy to hold makes him a guardian of the Vedas, and gives him long life, lustre and holiness.

Before initiating the boy into the Gayatri Mantra, the Guru (the spiritual father) pours water in the joined palms of the boy. This is to symbolise purifying him before receiving the Mantra. The boy is asked to see the Sun. He is asked to learn from the Sun unswerving duty and discipline. The boy offers prayers to the Sun for attainment of virtues.

By mounting a stone the boy is asked to develop firmness of resolve and steadfastness in his duties and studies, and develop physical strength and excellent health.

During the performance of the Samskara of Upanayana, certain Vratas or vows are undertaken. These are the vows 1. To uphold vows 2. To attain prominence in the world 3. To engage in creative activities 4. To perform charity 5. To please the gods 6. To please fellow-men 7. To protect subjects or dependants 8. To procreate when married 9. To keep equipoise 10. To serve the elders etc. The invocation of the three entities Pranava, Medha and Sraddha – God, Intelligence and Faith – in this function is the coping stone of the edifice of Brahmacharya or bachelorhood, whose daily chore is regulated by good habits, collectively going by the name Ahnika (Sandhya, Samidadhana Havan etc.). One cannot conceive of a more thoughtful scheme of timetable calculated for the development of character in the young.

[Note: The following abridged explanations are from the writings of Swami Dayananda Saraswati (The founder of The Arya Samaj). The translation is by Acharya Vaidyanath Shastri].

*From Ashvalayana Grihyasutra 1-19-1-6.*

"Ashtame Varshe Brahmanamupanayet (1). Garbhaashtame va (2). Ekaadashe Kshatriyam (3). Dvaadashe Vaishyam (4).

Aashodashaad Braahmanasyaanateetah Kaala (5). Shraadhhaavimshaatkshatriyasya, Aachaturvishaadd-vaisyasya, Ata urdhvam Patitasavitrikaa Bhvanti (6)."

The Brahman, the child of the Brahman, or the child promising to be a Brahman, should be invested with the sacred Thread in the eighth year from the date of birth or from the date of conception. The Kshatriya, the child of Kshatriya, or the child promising to be Kshatriya, should be invested with the Sacred Thread in the eleventh year from the date of birth or from the date of conception. Vaisya, the child of Vaisya or the child promising to be Vaisya, should be invested with the Sacred Thread in the twelfth year from the date of his birth or from the date of conception. Positively the children of Brahmana, Kshatriya and Vaisya should respectively be invested with the Sacred Thread before the years 16th, 22nd and 24th of their age. If they are not invested with the Sacred Thread during these years, then they are regarded or treated as having fallen from their duties.

Similar sayings are found in the Paraskara Grihyasutra etc.

*From Manusmriti:*

"The time for the Savitri (Gayatri) initiation of a Brahmana does not pass until the completion of the sixteenth year (after conception), of a Kshatriya until the completion of the twenty-second year, and of a vaisya until the completion of the twenty-fourth." 2.38.

"After those periods, men of these three castes who have not received the sacrament at the proper time, become Vratyas (outcastes), excluded from the Savitri initiation and despised by the Aryans." 2.39.

"With such men, if they have not been purified according to the rule, let no Brahmana ever, even in times of distress, form a connection either through the Veda or by marriage." 2.40.

The time for the Yajnopavita Samskar.

*From Shatpath Brahmana, 2.13.5.*

"Vasante Braahmanamupanayet. Grishne Raajanyam. Sharadi Vaishyam. Sarvakaalameke."

The child of Brahmana in the spring season. The child of Kshatriya in the summer season and the child of Vaisya in autumn be respectively be invested with Sacred Thread. Or the investiture of Sacred Thread can be performed in all seasons. (Morning time is the best period for the performance of this ceremony.)

### *Limited Fasting*

*"Payovrato Braahmano Yavaagoovrato*

*Raajanya Aamikshaavrato Vaishya."*

For three days (or for at least one day) prior to the day of the ceremony, the child should drink only milk (once a day or more than once a day). The child of a Kshatriya should eat only barley gruel (Yavaag), prepared from crushed barley, boiled in water with sugar to taste. The child of Vaisya should complete his fast by eating only Aamikshaa. This is sometimes called Shrikhanda or Sikhanda. This is prepared from cottage cheese four parts, milk one part, sugar to taste and saffron (Keshar). This preparation is strained through a piece of cloth. The children of the three Varnas, as describes above, should eat only those foods prescribed for them respectively when they feel hungry and should not eat or drink any thing else.

***The Procedure:*** The utensils to be used in the Yajna etc. should be collected and appropriately sorted and cleansed a day before the ceremony. On the day of the ceremony, everything that is needed for the Yajna as mentioned in the Samanya Prakarana should be arranged by the Yajna Kunda. The boy to be invested with the Sacred Thread should have his head shaved, bathed and should dress appropriately. Either the father of the child or the Acharya, having fed the child with sweets, eatables etc. leads him to his seat to the west of the Yajnavedi (Havan Kunda), keeping his face eastward. The father of the child and the priests of the Yajna as mentioned in the Samanya Prakarana, should take their seats in the prescribed manner perform Aachaman (sipping of water) and Angasparsha (touching various limbs with water). (Om Amrito Pastaramasi Swaha etc. and Om Vangme Asyestu etc.)

Thereafter, the Acharya conducting the ceremony should make the child pronounce the following sentence from the child's own mouth.

"May I observe the discipline of celibacy and thus may I be a celibate."

The Acharya then pronounces the following Mantra and gives to the child a garment and a Upavastra to wear.

From Paraskara Grihyasutra, 2.2.7.

"Om yenendraaya brihaspatirvaasah Paryadadhaada-mritam.

Ten Tvaa Paridadhaamyaayushe Deerghaayutvaaya Balaaya Varchase."

O Child! I give this garment to you to wear for your long life, strength and vigour. This is in accordance with the tradition whereby the Acharya gives a strong and durable garment to his disciple.

Thereafter the child holds the Sacred Thread in his hand and sits in front of the Acharya. The Acharya invests the child with the Sacred Thread with the following Mantra and places (makes the child wear) the Sacred Thread on the left shoulder and slung across under the right armpit.

"Yagnopavitam Param Pavitram Prajaapatayeryatsahajam Purastaat.

Aayushyamagr Yam Pratimuncha Shubhram Yajnopavitam Balamastu Tejah.

Yajnopaveetamasi Yagnasya Tvayajyapayaveetenopanaa-hayaami."

This Yajnopavita (Sacred Thread) is very sacrosanct. Prajapati Himself has sanctioned this Sacred Thread. I invest you with this white Yajnopavita (Sacred Thread). This is the main (most important ) article for you. May it bring you strength and vigour.

This sacred Thread is really a Sacred Thread.

I tie you with this for the purpose of performing Yajna.

The Acharya then performs the Yajna (Havan) ceremony with the child seated on the right side of the Acharya. Some of the oblations (ahutis) are to be offered by the child.

Some of the Mantras used during this ceremony:

"Om Agne Vratapate Vratam Charishyami Tatte Prabraveemi Tatchhakeyam.

Tenrdhyaasimidamahamarnritaat Satyam Upaimi Svaaha. Idamagnaye Idanna Mama.

Om Vayo Vratapate Svaaha. Idam Vaayave Idanna Mama.

Om Surya Vratapate Svaaha. Idam Suryaaya Idanna Mama.

Om Chandra Vratapate Svaaha. Idam Chandraaya Idanna Mama.

Om Vrataanaam Vratapate Svaaha. Idamindraaya Vratapataye Idanna Mama."

O Self-refulgent God! Thou art the master of vows. I declare before Thee, I shall observe the vows and disciplines of celibacy. May I be enabled to observe this vow. May I prosper with this vow and attain the highest truth. Whatever has been uttered herein is true. The oblation offered is meant for Agni and it is not for me.

Oblations are offered to all moving god Vayu, All effulgent Surya, all blissful Chandra, the lord of all vows and laws Indra.

The Acharya then sits to the north of the Yajna Kunda keeping his face eastward. The child sits in front of the Acharya keeping his face westward. Looking at the child, the Acharya should recite the following Mantra. The meaning of the Mantra:

O Self-refulgent God! We have received excellent cooperation from this child. Kindly lead us to the company of good men and good teachers. Together with this youth, may we follow the path of knowledge with ease. May this child do whatever is auspicious for him and for all.

Addressing the Acharya, the child says:

O Acharya! I have resolved to observe the disciplines of continence. Kindly admit me and invest me with the Sacred Thread.

The Acharya says:

What is your name?

The child states his name.

The Acharya makes the child hold water in his right hand palm. The Acharya recites Mantras.

The waters are the source of happiness. May the waters be helpful to us in attaining grains and may they help us to retain good eye sight.

Let the pleasant essence of waters be useful to us, like the mothers who, for the well-being of their children, give them their breasts to suckle..

Let the waters enable us to grow cereals and herbaceous plants. Let these be used for the welfare of our progeny.

The Acharya then takes water in his right hand palm and empties this water in the right hand palm of the child, mixing the two waters. This is done while the Acharya chants Mantra.

For our maintenance we accept whatever good food has been provided by God, who is the mighty power and Creator of the world. We also accept the strength and might of all-powerful God who maintains and preserves the existence of all the objects of creation.

The Acharya, chanting Mantra, then makes the child empty the water from his palm into a container.

O Child! I admit you in this life so that you can attain power and prosperity bestowed by God, who is the Creator of the world. I hold your hand in my own with the firmness and strength of the vital breaths called Prana and Apana and with the firmness and strength of Pushan, the all preserving vitality of the body.

The Acharya takes water in his right hand palm and empties it into the child's right hand palm. Holding the child's hand the Acharya chants Mantra.

O Child! Your hand has been grasped by Savitar, the mighty teacher who is the preserver of all knowledge.

The child then empties the water from his palm into the container.

For the third time, the same procedure is followed, the Acharya giving water into the palm of the child.

O Child! Again, the Self-refulgent God is your Acharya. (God is your real teacher).

Thereafter, the Acharya takes the child outside and while standing and facing the sun shows the sun to the child with chanting of Mantras.

O Creator and Lord of the world! This child is the Brahmacharin (student observing celibacy) of Thine. Please protect and preserve him. May he perform his duties well. The Acharya returns to the Yajna Mandap with the child; both seating to the north of the Yajnakund. The child sits facing the Acharya. The Acharya pronounces the following two Mantras.

"Om Yuvaa suvaasaahaa Pariveeta Aagaatsa oo Shreyan Bhavati Jaayamanah" This child (pronounce the name of the child), possessing strong physique, dressed in nice garments, wearing the sacred Thread, and who seated before me, has taken the second birth. May he (successfully study) the Vedas and acquire respect."

"Om Suryaasyaavritamanvaavarttasva Asou."

O Child, You circumambulate yore Acharya who is the sun (source) of knowledge. (As the sun is the source of life so the Acharya is the source of knowledge.)

The child circumambulates the Acharya.

The Acharya then places his right hand upon the right shoulder of the child, covering his hand with a piece of cloth. A Mantra is chanted about the vital airs.

Then the Acharya touches the child's belly, heart, again the right shoulder with various Mantras.

O Child, I appoint you (to study and) attain the knowledge of God and follow God's commands.

The Acharya touches the child's left shoulder, breast, saying Mantras.

Let the learned men of firm intentions and swift intellects, attaining the highest feats of knowledge through their minds and spirits, elevate this student to high status of genius and character.

O disciple! Make one (fine tune) your mind and heart with my mind always, and becoming fully attentive grasp my words with affection and understand the meaning of these words. May God, who is the Master of Vedic speech, unite you with me in thought and action according to your vow from this very day.

And the child replies in the affirmative.

Then the Acharya asks the student: "What is your name?"

The Student says : "Sir, my name is"

Acharya: "Whose Brahmachari are you?"

Student: "Yours, Sir."

The Acharya pronounces the following Mantra.

"Indrasya Brahmah Achaaryyasya, Agnihi Achaaryastvaahamaachaaryastava Asou."

O Child! You are the Brahmachari of Almighty God. The Self-refulgent God is your Acharya. I am your Acharya as God's representative.

*Further Mantras:*

O Child! You are the Brahmachari of Prajapati. You are the Brahmachari of Prana, God who is the all pervading Soul. Prajapati invests you with the Sacred Thread for your happiness. I also urge you to follow the command of Prajapati.

O Child! I urge you to attain the knowledge of Prajapati who is the Lord of all creatures. I urge you to attain the knowledge of the might sun. I urge you to attain the knowledge of liquids and herbs, of the earth and the heavenly regions, of all the physical and spiritual forces. May you be successful in maintaining peace and tranquility among all beings.

Upon the completion of the Upanayana ceremony, if time permits, the Vedarambha (commencing the study of the Vedas) ceremony should preferably take place on the very same day. Otherwise, the Vedarambha ceremony can take place on another day.

The mother, the father, the Acharya and other guests then bless the child together with the following words.

"Om tvam jeeva Sharadah Shatam Vardhamaanah.

Aayushmaan Tejasvee varchasvee Bhooyaaha."

O Child! May you grow in strength and vigour and live a hundred autumns. May you become long lived, brilliant and radiant.

10 B. *Vedarambha:* To observe the disciplines and to commence and undertake the studies of the Vedas and their branches (systems and limbs known as 'Sangopanga')– is called Vedarambha.

***The Procedure:*** In the morning, the student, after bathing and wearing clean clothes, sits to the west of the Yajnavedi (Havankund), keeping his face eastward. The Acharya begins the ceremony with Achaman Mantra (sipping of water) and Angasparsha Mantra (touching various organs with water) followed by Ishwar Upasana (prayer), Svatsivachan, Santikarana.

The Havan ceremony (Sacred fire ceremony) is then commenced. The student participates in the Yajna and offers ahutis (oblations). During the Havan ceremony, before the Purnahuti, Vishesh Mantras (Mantras used for Vedarambha ) are used.

Some of these Mantras are described below.

O famous Acharya! Please make me earn fame in the field of education. O Acharya! Enable me to attain to your status of learning and prominence and a preserver of knowledge, Yajanas etc.

The student then standing on the south side of the Yajnakunda and keeping his face northward, takes a samidha (small wooden stick), dips it in ghee, and offers it in the middle of the fire as oblation with the following Mantra.

I am offering this ahuti (oblation) to add to the burning flame of the Yajna that is mighty in nature and present in all the created beings and objects of the world. As this fire blazes forth with the samidha (wood-fuel), so may I shine with wisdom, knowledge of the Vedas and of Brahman (God) and may I be endowed with vigour, long life, progeny and wealth. Grant long life to my Acharya and to his sons. May I be enriched with high intellectual power. May I not be arrogant to anyone. Grant me prominence, vigour, divine merits and food and grains.

Two further oblations are offered with samidha dipped in ghee.

The student now sits in the west side of the Vedi facing the east. Applying a little of the shesh water on the palms of his hands, holds them by the fire warming the hands. With each of the seven mantras, he should apply the water over his face and on the head.

1. This fire is the preserver of the body. May it preserve my body.
2. This fire is the giver of life. May it grant me long life.
3. This fire is the giver of brilliancy. May it grant me brilliancy.

4. Whatever gets exhausted in my body, let this fire replenish that.
5. May Savita grant me wisdom. May the goddess Saraswati grant me wisdom.
6. Let the teacher and preacher, wearing garlands, give us knowledge.

The student then touches various organs with various Mantras.

*"Om Vak Cha Ma Aapyaayataam." (touches the mouth)*

*"Om Praanascha Ma Aapyaayataam." (touches the nose)*

*"Om Chakshushcha Ma Aapyaayataam." (touches the eyes)*

*"Om Shrotrancha Ma Aapyaayataam." (touches the ears)*

*"Om Yasho Balancha Ma Aapyaayaataam." (Touches both arms)*

O Lord! May my organ of speech be sound and well developed. May my nose, eyes, ears be sound and well developed. May my arms, which are the source of fame and strength, be strong and develop properly.

The student then meditates (offers prayer) with the following Mantra. May Agni, the Self-refulgent God give me wisdom, progeny and strength, May Indra, the almighty god, bestow upon me the favour of wisdom, progeny, and properly developed organs. May Surya, the all controlling god, grant me wisdom, progeny and brilliance. O effulgent and powerful Lord, grant me effulgence, power and prominence.

Now the student walks to the north side of the Yajnakunda. Facing the east, he kneels on his knees before the Acharya.

Balakoktihi: (The student says:)

"Aadhihi Bhuhu Savitri Bho Anubroohi."

O Acharya! Please instruct me 'The Gayatri Mantra', the subject matter of which is Savitar, the sun. Please teach me.

The Acharya then places a piece of cloth on his own shoulder and on the shoulder of the student, and holding both hands of the student in his hands, teaches the Gayatri Mantra to the student in three parts.

*First part:*

The Acharya makes the student pronounce the following, word by word.:

"Om Bhurbhuvah Svah Tatsaviturvarenyam."

*Second part:*

"Om Bhurbhuvah Svah Tatsaviturvarenyam Bargo Devasya Dhimahi."

*Third part:*

"Om Bhurbhuvah Svah Tatsaviturvarenyam

Bargo Devasya Dhimahi Dhiyo Yo Nah Prachodayaat."

The Acharya then explains in short the meaning of the Gayatri Mantra.

Thereafter the student affirms vows. (The same vows as for the Sacred Thread ceremony). The student is given a girdle and a wooden staff (rod, well- made, smooth and free of any defect). For the Brahmana boy, the girdle be made of Darbha or Munja grass, for the Kshatriya boy, the girdle be made from Dhanusa grass and for the Vaisya boy, the girdle be made from Jute.

The Brahmana boy should be given a rod (stick) made of Palash or Bilva wood. The length of the rod to extend from the ground to top of the head.

The Kshatriya boy should be given a rod made from Vat or Khadir wood. The length of the rod from the ground till his eyebrow.

The Vaisya student should be given a rod made from Peepul or Gular wood. The length of the rod to reach from the ground till the tip of his nose.

In addition the student is given a deerskin to sit on, one pot or container to hold water, and two small pots or containers.

The student, holding the rod, says:

This staff (rod) that I hold, I accept it specially for the attainment of long life, knowledge of the Vedas, for (adherence to) disciplines and strength of continence.

***Father's Advice to His Son***

The father of the celibate student then gives general information regarding the life of a Brahmacharin (celibate student) and preaches the code of conduct. (Scriptural sources Gobhil Grihyasutra, Ashvalayans Grihyasutra, Paraskar Grihyasutra).

You realise that you are a Brahmachari (celibate) from today. You must always sip a little clean (pure) water and say your food prayer before taking meals.

Always keep away from evil acts and do all pious and righteous acts. You do not ever sleep in day time.

Remaining under the guidance and control of your Acharya, you will always with perseverance learn the Vedas with all their limbs and sub-limbs.

Always follow the rules of Dharma (righteousness) under your Acharya. You do not ever do anything of Adharma (unrighteous), even if such request be made by your Acharya even (to do anything of adharma).

You must abstain from anger. Always speak the truth (do not tell a lie.)

Always keep away from the eight kinds of acts of passion.

*Note:* these eight acts of passion are: 1. To think of a woman. 2. To gossip about woman. 3. To touch a woman. 4. To play with a woman. 5. To gaze at a woman. 6. To embrace a woman. 7. To be alone with a woman. 8. To cohabit with a woman.

Sleep only on the ground and not on beds with four legs.

Never be in the habit of Kaushilava (bad songs sung or played on musical instruments, dances; abominable acts, use of perfumes etc.).

Always observe rules of moderation in bathing, eating, sleeping, and keeping awake. The same applies to greed, undue indulgence, fear and grief.

Always wake up and rise from bed during the early hours of Brahmamuhurta (between 4 and 6 in the morning). Perform your daily ablutions. You must take a bath everyday. Twice every day you must do acts of communion with God, pray, meditate and practice Yogic systems.

Do not eat meat. Do not eat dry, coarse cereals. Do not drink intoxicating drinks.

Do not ride on bullocks, horses, elephants, camels etc.

You are not to stay in any village (any place inhabited by people) except in Gurukula (Gurukula is a system of boarding school within the compounds of which stay only the teachers and the students).

As a Brahmachari you do not use shoes or umbrella.

Do not play with the organ of procreation (so as to prevent the discharge of semen). By conserving the semen in the body it transforms into Ojas, opening the full potential of your mind and intellect, becoming the source of attaining knowledge of the Vedas and all their branches. Do not massage your body with oil etc. Do jot use mustard-paste (cosmetics) for the beauty of the body.

Do not eat foods that are very sour like tamarind etc., very pungent like chilies etc., very astringent like haldi, very purgative like Jamalgota, very saltish foods, or very acidic foods. Do your daily chores with care and regularity and be fully attentive to the task of learning (acquiring knowledge and wisdom).

You will always possess good character. You should never be extravagant in talk. Cultivate good behaviour and develop courtesies when meeting people, sitting in assemblies.

Keep yourself bound by the duties of wearing the girdle, keeping the wooden staff (stick) and the rules of mendicancy.

*Note:* A Brahman's child, when asking for alms from a man should address him "Bhavaan Bhikshaam Dadaat." When asking for alms from a woman, he should address "Bhavati Bhikshaam Dadaatu." The Kshatriya student to men "Bhikshaam Bhavaan Dadaatu." To women "Bhikshaam Bhavati Dadaatu." Vaisya student should address men, "Bhikshaam dadaat Bhavaan" To woman, "Bhikshaan Dadaat Bhavati."

Do not deviate from the daily performance of: your daily bath, daily prayer and meditation, Prostrate with reverence before your Acharya every morning and every evening.

These are the deeds of your daily performance. You should abstain from acts that have been prohibited.

The student then with folded hands bows (or prostrates before his father). The student addressing his father says:

"I shall certainly act according to your instructions and advice."

Thereafter the celibate student circumambulates the fire of the Yajnakunda and stands in the west of the Yajnavedi. He then asks for alms from his mother, father, brother, sister, maternal uncle, mother's sister, uncle etc., who do not hesitate in giving alms. The student hands over all the alms to the Acharya. The Acharya takes some wheat cereals from the alms and gives to the student.

The Acharya then asks for some cooked rice for offering oblations. Mixing with a little ghee, three oblations are offered with the following Mantras.

Having worshipped with truthful action and speech, God, who is wondrous, the lovely friend of the soul, May I acquire wisdom that discriminates between truth and untruth.
-Yajur Veda 32.13.

"Tatsavituvarenyam Bhargo Devasya Dhimahi Dhiyo Yo Nah Prachodayaat" Svaha, Idam Savitar Idam Na Mama.

"O creator of the universe! O All holy and worthy of adoration. May we contemplate Thy adorable Self. May Thou guide our understanding." Whatever has been uttered herein is true. The oblation offered is meant for Savitar and it is not for me.

"Om Rishibhyah Svaaha. Idam Rishibhyah Idam Na Mama."

We pay homage to Rishis (seers) who study the Vedas and understand their meanings. Whatever has been uttered herein is true. The oblation offered is for the Rishis and it is not for me.

Thereafter the Acharya offers a fourth ahuti with the Swishtakrit Homahuti Mantra "Om Yadasya Karmanah Tyariricham......"

Thereafter the Havan ceremony is brought to conclusion with the rest of the Mantras and the Purnahuti.

The student seats facing the east, addresses the Acharya:

"Amuk (mention here the name of the family) Gotrotpanno Aham Bho Bhavantam Abhivaadaye"—Gobhil Grihyasutra 2/10/25

I, born in the genealogy of...........(name of family) salute you (prostrate before you), O my teacher.

The student then prostrates before the acharya.

The Acharya says:

"Ayusmaan Vidyaavan Bhava Saumya."

(O my dear disciple!) May you be long lived and may you attain knowledge with wisdom.

After the Acharya has given his blessings to the Brahmachari, some of the food remaining from the Yajna (cooked rice, cereals, sweetmeats etc.) should be give to the Acharya, and to the student to eat.

Thereafter, all the guests are served meals prepared for this function.

Before leaving, people bless the student with the following sentence:

"O Child! May you, by the grace of God, become learned, strong in body and soul, blessed with skills, vigour and excellent health. After having attained knowledge of the Vedas and all their branches, may you come back from the Gurukula, with the desire of seeing us."

### *The Qualified Student*

The Brahmachari (celibate student), shining with knowledge, becoming fully fledged, upon completion of his studies in the Gurukula, completing the state of Brahmacharya called Purvasamudra, enters immediately into the householder's life called Uttarsamudra (gets married). He encourages all people to achieve their goals. He exerts continuously to achieve the goal of life (Dharma, Artha, Kama and Moksha). He makes the world happy with his speech of righteousness and truth.

### *Only that is the King (Qualities Needed to Lead a Nation)*

Only that is the king who by observing austerities, strict disciplines of celibacy, has become a perfectly learned man (with knowledge and wisdom), perfectly educated (in arts and sciences) and who is a symbol of good conduct, who is self controlled and can rule the country in various ways (all the various departments of government).

### *Only that is the Acharya (qualities needed to become a teacher)*

In the same manner, only that is the Acharya who by observing austerities and strict disciplines of celibacy, leading a life of continence, has become a perfectly learned man (with knowledge and wisdom), perfectly educated (in arts and sciences) and who is a symbol of good conduct. Only such a person can desire to teach a celibate student. Only such a person can become the Acharya in the real sense.

### *Education for Girls*

As the boys, completing the life of perfect Brahmachari, attaining the complete knowledge of the Vedas and all their branches, knowledge of all the sciences, and in the full bloom of youth, are now fit to wed girls, so the girls, completing the courses of all sciences with perfect disciplines of continence, in the full bloom of their youth, should wed young men.

*Note:* Women are barred from the study of the Vedas. Therefore, study of the sciences only is mentioned. Study of the Vedas is not mentioned here. The Laws of Manu, IX, 18 states: "For women no sacramental rite is performed with sacred texts, thus the law is settled; women who are destitute of strength and destitute of the knowledge of Vedic texts, are as impure as falsehood itself, that is a fixed rule."

11. *Samavartana:* Upon completion of studies, the teacher instructs the pupil. (From Taittiriya Upanishad, 1.11)

Translations by Swami Nikhilananda, Sri Ramakrishna-Vivekananda Center, New York.

Having taught the Vedas, the teacher thus instructs the pupil:

Speak the truth. Practise Dharma (religious duties; rightoousncss and ritualistic worship). Do not neglect the study of the Vedas. Having brought to the teacher the gift desired by him, (enter the householder's life and see that) the line of progeny is not cut off. Do not swerve from the truth. Do not swerve from Dharma. Do not neglect (personal) welfare. Do not neglect prosperity (refers to righteous actions by which wealth is earned). Do not neglect the study and teaching of Vedas.

Do not neglect your duties to the gods and the Manes. Treat your mother as god (Matru Devo Bhava). Treat your father as god (Pitru Devo Bhava). Treat your teacher as god (Aacharya Devo Bhava). Treat your guest as god (Atithi Devo Bhava). Whatever deeds are faultless, these are to be performed- not others. Whatever good works have been performed by us, those should be performed by you- not others.

Those Brahmins who are superior to us- you should comfort them by giving them seats. Whatever is to be given should be given with faith, not without faith- according to one's means, with modesty, with fear (of the scriptures or of sin), with sympathy.

Now, if there arises in your mind any doubt concerning conduct, you should conduct yourself in such matters as Brahmins would conduct themselves- Brahmins who are competent to judge, who (of their own accord) are devoted to good deeds, and are not urged to their performance by others, and who are not too severe, but are lovers of Dharma. Now, with regard to persons spoken against, you should conduct yourself in such a way as Brahmins would conduct themselves-Brahmins who are competent to judge, who (of their own accord) are devoted to good deeds and that are not urged to their performance by others, and who are not too severe, but are lovers of Dharma.

This is the rule. This is the teaching. This is the secret wisdom of the Vedas. This is the command of God. This you should observe. This alone should be observed.

### *Funeral-Antyeshti the Last Rites of the Dead*

The last rites of the dead body are called the Antyeshti Samskara. There is no other Samskara thereafter for this body. This Samskara is also called by the names of Naramedha, Purushmedha, Narayaga and Purusheayaga.

*From the Yajur Veda 40.15 (also Isa Upanishad).*

"Vayurnilammamritamathedam Bhasmantam Shariram

Om Krto Smara. Klibe Smara. Kritghvam Smara."

O active soul, at the time of death, remember OM, remember God for thy vitality and thy eternity, remember thy deeds. Know that soul is immaterial and immortal but the body is finally reduced to ashes. (translation by Devi Chand)

***The Procedure:*** Source Ashwalayana Grihyasutras:

1. The dead, if male, should be given bath by men and if female, should be given bath by women. Sandal-wood paste should be applied to the body. The dead body should be dressed with new clothes.

2. Ghee (clarified butter) should be in equal proportion to the weight of the dead. Well-to-do people can use more ghee but in the case of poor people, the ghee should not be less than ½ mound in weight. The poor should be assisted by a moneyed man or by the head of the Panchayat (5 man village council), or contributions from the people. Well-to-do people can add or mix with the ghee the following items.

   Kesar, Saffron—One masha in each one Seer of Ghee

   Kasturi, Musk—One Ratti in each one Seer of Ghee

   Agar Acquilaria Malaccensis—One Seer in each one mound

   Tagar Veleriana Walichli—One Seer in each one Maund

   Sandal-wood powder—One Seer in each one mound

   Camphor—As the circumstances permit
3. Well-to-do people should arrange for one maund Sandal-wood, twelve maunds of fuel wood and Samagri two times the weight of the dead body.
4. All these items should be brought to the cremation ground (crematorium).
5. If there is a permanent Kunda made in the cremation ground for the purpose of cremation, then it should be used. If not, then a new one should be made (dug out). The dimensions of the Kunda should be as follows:
   (i). Length of the Kunda should be equal to the length of a man standing with his hands stretched upwards.
   (ii). The breadth (width) should be equal to the a person sleeping with his two hands stretched outwards (more than 1 ½ yards).
   (iii). Depth should be chest high (taking into account average heights of men).
   (iv). The bottom should be one yard in breadth.
6. The Kunda should be made clean and if cow-dung is available, it should be purified by applying that.

7. Wood fuel should be arranged in the Kunda in the manner of how bricks are arranged when building a wall.
8. Ghee should be liquid (not solidified or frozen).
9. Four big size spoons should be firmly attached to the end of long sticks so that oblations can be offered into the blazing fire burning inside the Kunda. Four men at a time should offer ahutis (oblations). The size of each spoon should be big enough to hold ghee that is not less than half chhatak and should not be so big that it holds more than one chhatak of ghee.
10. Cremation ground should be situated in the south (of village, town etc.).
11. The dead body should be laid on the fuel pyre arranged in the Kunda. The dead body should be totally covered with fuel-wood. The head of the dead should be in the north direction and the feet in the south.
12. The hair of the dead should be removed before giving bath to it.
13. First a diya (small lamp) should to be lit. Camphor (placed in the spoon) should be lit from the diya (lamp) and this should be used to set alight the pyre. Begin lighting the pyre from that end of the pyre where the head is and ending by the feet. Thus the whole pyre should be set ablaze.

Oblations should be offered in the blazing fire with the following Mantras.

"Om Agnaye Svaha/ This oblation is for Agni. Whatever is uttered herein is true.

*Om Somaaya Svaha / " " " Soma. " " " "*

*Om Lokaaya Svaha / " " " This world Loka) " "*

*Om Anumataye Svaha / " " Earth " "*

*Om swargaaya Lokaaya Svaha / " the other world (heaven)"*

***Funeral Prayer***

"Om Suryam Chakshurgacchatu Vatimaatmaa Dyaam Cha Gachchha Prithivim Cha Dharmana/Apo Va Gachchha Yadi Tatra Te Hitamoshadhishu Pratimtishtha Sharirai svaha."

O Jiva (Soul)! After thy death, (may all the components of thy body be merged into the five elements). May the power of thy sight be absorbed in the sun and thy breath be absorbed in the air (atmosphere). May thy other parts be absorbed in appropriate elements. And in accordance with the meritorious deeds thou hast performed here, may thy spirit dwell in the appropriate body.

***The Rig Veda***

From the Yajur Veda 40.15 (also Isa Upanishad).

"Vayurnilammamritamathedam Bhasmantam Shariram

Om Krto Smara. Klibe Smara. Kritghvam Smara."

(Translations by Pandit Nardev Vedalankar assisted by Mr.Sookraj Chotai, B.A., B.Ed.)

The spirit which is immortal is not made of the five elements and does not perish. This body will be reduced to ashes. Therefore, O mortal! (At the time of death) remember the almighty Om, remember God, and remember thy past deeds, as by so doing can one attain salvation.

*From the Atharva Veda:*

O effulgent God! Thou art the dispenser of justice. Thou recompense every one according to his or her deeds. Peace be to the spirit of this dead body in the westward direction. May there be peace to this spirit in the east, the north and the south and all the other directions. O Omniscient and all-illuminating God! Thou art the Creator, the Sustainer and the destroyer of this universe. May thou bestow a worthy abode to this soul.

*From the Rig Veda:*

O Jiva! By thy austerity and enlightenment, and by they good deeds, attain the bliss in heaven and join the company of thy forbears. Be free from all sins and once again may thy spirit acquire (reside in) noble body full of lustre. And once again may thou come to this world to perform noble deeds.

*From Manusmriti:*

"Everything perishes with the death of the body. It is only Dharma (righteousness) that is our real friend, which even after death remains with the spirit. Therefore do not allow the Dharma to perish, for Dhrama (when) perished brings about our (own) destruction."

*From the Bhagavad Gita 11/38:*

Thou are the primal God, the ancient Being. Thou art the final resting place of this universe. Thou art the Knower and That which is to be known and the Ultimate Goal. By Thee is the universe pervaded, O Thou of infinite form.

*From the Bhagavad Gita 2/22:*

Even as a person casts off worn-out clothes and puts on others that are new, so the embodied Self casts of worn-out bodies and enters into others that are new.

*From the Bhagavad Gita 2/20:*

It (the Self ) is never born, nor does It ever die, nor, having once been, does it again cease to be. Unborn, eternal, permanent and primeval, It is not slain when the body is slain.

*Note:* The Self is destitute of the six kinds of modification inherent in every living thing: birth, subsistence, growth, change, decay and death. The Self is altogether changeless.

*From the Bhagavad Gita 2/23:*

Weapons cannot cut It (Self or the individual Soul), fire cannot burn It, water cannot wet It, wind cannot dry (wither) It.

*Note:* Weapons can destroy an object by cutting it into parts; but the Self is without parts and is therefore indestructible. The same applies to the other methods of destruction. Only a material object consists of parts and is therefore destructible.

*From the Bhagavad Gita 2/27:*

For to that which is born, death is certain, and to that which is dead, birth is certain. Therefore you should not grieve over the unavoidable (inevitable).

*From the Bhagavad Gita 2/28:*

All beings are unmanifest in their beginning, O Arjuna, manifest in their middle state, and unmanifest again in their end. Why, then, lament (grieve) for them?

*Note:* Commentary by Swami Shivananda, Divine Life Society, Rishikesh: The physical body is a combination of the five elements. It is perceived by the physical eye only after the five elements have entered into such combination. After death the body disintegrates and the five elements return to their source. The body cannot be perceived now. Therefore, the body can be perceived only in the middle state.

*From Yajur Veda 2/54:*

May we get in future births again and again the mind, for doing virtuous deeds, for acquiring strength, for longevity, and contemplation of God for long.

The shaving of the head of the male whose near relation has died is customary and practised in many Hindu homes. It may be a voluntary custom because we have not come across reference to this practice in scriptural texts. The period of impurity (Asaucha) or pollution or defilement is generally for ten days (from the day of last rites or cremation) for near relations. The rules to be observed during the period of impurity are of two kinds- negative (passive) and positive. The negative rules require the mourners to forego the many pleasures and comforts and even the routine business of daily life, thus exhibiting the feelings of grief and sorrow. They forbid certain things such as cutting of the hair and beard; forbid the study of the Vedas (during this period), Grhya offerings etc. The positive rules have also their origin in the aggrieved feelings of the survivors. They enjoin for a period of three days, to observe continence, to sleep on the ground, to live on begged or purchased food, to eat only in the day time etc.

5

# THE EVOLUTION OF LANDED PROPERTY IN ANCIENT INDIA

## Introduction

At some time or the other during our lives we observe the practices of dana and dakshina. Dana is the traditional Indian form of charity. We are told that giving away of dana secures divine blessings for the giver. As such dana can be given to anybody but the emphasis has always been on giving dana to Brahmins. Hindu tradition has never extolled Dana to Kshatriyas, Vaishyas or Sudras.

Since ancient times kings and noblemen have organised mass feeding ceremonies, distribution of grain and utilities as dana. Such giving away of wealth without expecting anything in return except blessings, was termed Dana. On any occasions like marriage, thread ceremony, opening ceremony, rites at death etc., we ask a Brahmin priest to officiate over the ceremony and in return for his services we offer him grain, cloth, gold and nowadays even cash. This offering is termed dakshina.

### *Dana and Dakshina are given in Cash and Kind*

Traditionally dakshina was given, and had the nature of a payment in kind for services rendered by a priest. But nowadays with this offering being made also in terms of cash its nature as a payment becomes clear. When it is given in cash, it is in the denomination of eleven, twenty-one, fifty-one, one hundred and one-etc Although has the nature of a voluntary payment it is not looked upon as such and is considered to be an offering to an officiating prbst. In spite of the fine difference between the terms dana and dakshina, these terms are used interchangeably with the same connotation. But the common element in both dana and dakshina is that they are payments in cash or kind articles of use, such as, cloth, grain, utensils etc.

Dana and dakshina are never offered in terms of physical labour in the form of social work. This is where they are different from the Christian concept of charity which involves social work and provision of social services. The custom of dana has always been part of Indian society and like Yagna, its origins seem to be in the collective hunting and common sharing way of life of life of the Vedic period.

### *The Havana a Method of Distribution of the Common Tribal Wealth*

The Rig Veda mentions the incendiary wars that the different nomadic tribes fought in their search for better pastures and hunting grounds. The way of life both during peacetime and war was based on collective activity. In the tribal way of life even during peacetime the share (Havi) of every member of the tribe was distributed in a function called the Havana. Whatever was gathered, hunted or cooked was shared among all members of the tribe.

The same principle was applied to the distribution of the booty of war. Articles that were plundered after a successful military campaign such as weapons, clothing and other articles of personal consumption were distributed amongst members.

This distribution which was carried out in festive atmosphere after a successful campaign is perhaps the progenitor of our custom of offering dana especially on festival days and other auspicious occasions like the crowning of a king, royal birthdays, etc.

### *Dana Originally Connoted Distribution not Charity*

The term dana is used in Vedic literature to describe the act of distributing such wealth among members of a tribe. The original connotation of the word dana was thus not just to give but to distribute. And in the tribal way of life this distribution did not have the nature of one person giving away his wealth to another but as distribution among members of a tribe (Gana) the captured property that was under common ownership of the tribe as a whole, but for its consumption it had to be allotted to individual members.

That dana connoted only the distribution of proceeds of war is corroborated by the fact that it was not part of daily life and was held on select occasions that called for festivities. The practice of offering of dana especially on festive occasions survived the passing away of the tribal way of life of collective activity and common sharing.

But with the passage of time, the tribal way of life broke up and so did the institution of common property. With the division of labour according to different specialised occupations, war became a profession of a select body of men who constituted the army, the commander of which was the king. In India those of the warrior profession were known as Kshatriyas or Rajanyas and their chieftain was the Rajan.

The proceeds of war and later on the proceeds of tributes and taxes came into the hands of the warriors and the king. These proceeds were no longer looked upon as common property to which every member of society had an equal claim. It now came to be looked upon as Rajasva, literally meaning that which belongs to the king (Raja = king, sva = own or self). But the practice of distributing wealth accumulated in the royal treasury and in the smaller private hoards of noblemen-warriors, among the kingdom's of populace continued. Religious festivals and public events such as coronation were occasions for distributing wealth and this distribution was looked upon as dana. This practice was normally respected but it was not a compulsory or obligatory requirement. If the king followed it he was looked upon as virtuous if not then he was an evil king.

## Dana became a Transfer of Wealth

But there was no formal law that made it imperative for the king and noblemen to observe this custom. Dana, thus acquired a voluntary character which was looked upon as an act of piety. With the passage of time Dana came to be bestowed mainly upon the clergy which in India was the Brahmin caste. Dana which under the tribal set up was an instrument for equi-distribution of wealth became one of discriminatory enrichment of a section of the society. This was so as the practice of Dana gradually came to acquire the nature of transfer of wealth from the nobility to the clergy. The clergy by virtue of the psychological hold exercised on all sections of society enforced this transfer though not always successfully. There did exist some justification for this transfer as it was normally the clergy which was a repository of knowledge as under the caste system only it had the right to acquire education. It was mainly the king and the nobility who could sustain the practice of dana although the trading community (Vaishyas) also joined their ranks of donees, when mercantile activity favoured them with disposable surplus wealth. In the later ages the observance of dana was ensured by fostering ideas that giving of dana results in Punya (God's blessings). Hence, it was the holy duty of everybody to offer dana this was especially so for the King and the nobility to give dana. The episode of Karna in the Mahabharata, highlights the overwhelming importance attached to honouring the practice of dana by the nobility in ancient India. Briefly the episode is as follows:

### *The Story of Karna in the Mahabharata*

Karna was born to Kunti mother of the Pandavas before marriage. According to the mythological account he was fathered by the Sun from whom he inherited the Kavacha and Kundala which were protective organs as a part of his physical body. It was deereed that as long as he wore the Kavacha (a bony shield on the chest) and Kundala (ear rings), Karna would be immortal. Out of shame, Kunti abandoned the baby Karna by setting his cradle afloat in the Ganges river. He was found by a person from a menial Profession and was brought up as a son. Karna grew up to be a brave and expert archer whose extraordinary talent was spotted by Duryodhana the eldest of the Kaurava brothers. The wily Duryodhana enrolled Karna into the ranks of the Kaurava army in spite of Karna being looked upon as a member of a menial caste for which he was contemptuously referred to as Sutaputra (low born).

Karna's prowess as an archer was superior to that of Arjuna of the Pandavas, who himself was an accomplished archer. During the Mahabharata war between Pandavas and Kauravas, Karna and Ariuna were to confront each other. The outcome of their encounter was a foregone conclusion. When Kunti came to know that Karna was also her son, she rushed to Karna and begged him not to fight his brother Arjuna in what would be a fratricidal war. But Karna was unmoved in his determination to stand by his master, Duryodhana during the war.

Lord Srikrishna who acted as adviser to the Pandavas knew the inevitability of Karna's victory against Arjuna and to preclude this possibility he decided to deprive Karna of his protective Kavacha and Kundala in a way that Karna could not refuse. Srikrishna took upon the guise of a Sadhu and went to Karna before the inception of the battle and demanded that Karna offer him dana. Considering the giving of dana to a Brahmin before setting off for battle to be an auspicious deed, the innocuous Karna told the lord in guise to ask for anything he wanted and consider it to have been granted. Horrified as he might have been when the lord in guise demanded the Kavacha and Kundala.

But Karna refused to go back on his word and gave away his impregnable armour to the malevolent Sadhu. Thus unprotected he proceeded to the battle and the lack of his armour along with the misfortune of a ruptured chariot wheel became the reason for his undoing. Karna preferred death rather than the stigma of dishonour that would have attached to him had he refused to carry out his word and offered whatever the malevolent lord in the guise of a Sadhu had demanded. This anecdote illustrates the moral grip on the psyche that has insured the existence of dana over the ages till today.

## Gotra

Gotra is one of the many considerations that exist during match making in the traditional manner. Janmakundalis (horoscopes) of the prospective bride and groom are compared to see if a match could be made.

***Gotras have to be Different while Matchmaking for a Marriage:*** While in matching Janmakundalis the consideration is for the common and symmetrical features, but surprisingly while comparing Gotras the requirement is that the bride and groom should belong to different Gotras. If their Gotras are identical a match cannot be made. Today most of us may not be aware as to what Gotra is. Its meaning is lost and it is doubtful whether even the astrologers who compare horoscopes can satisfy an inquisitive student as to the origin and meaning of Gotra and the reason why identical Gotras preclude a match in a traditional Hindu marriage.

***Gotra Originated as the Common Cowpen or Cow Shed During the Tribal Aryan Past:*** The origin of this concept of Gotra also seems to lie in a tribal ethos and is linked to the system of common ownership of property. The word Gotra literally means cowpen or cowshed and is derived from "Go" meaning cow.

With the domestication of animals, cattle became an important source of meats and milk. With the rearing of cattle, hunting as the principal source of subsistence lost its importance and the lifestyle became less nomadic as compared to the earlier days when hunting was the main activity of sustenance.

With the coming of a pastoral way of life it was possible to have individual ownership of the means of subsistence which was impossible during the days of hunting.

But the older practice of holding property in common could not die out abruptly. Even in a pastoral society the principle means of subsistence-cattle-continued to be held as common property. The members of a tribe had one object for solidarity and this was the cattle they held in common. While in a society of hunters, the prisoners of wars and other fellow travellers could either be sacrificed or absorbed into the tribe so as to increase the strength of the hunt party; the pastoral society ruled out such absorption of new members who would only be additional mouths to feed. The tribe henceforth became an endogamous clan which kept outsiders out and insiders in.

### *Sa-Gotra (Marriage Within a Gotra) was the Norm Originally*

But the endogamous clan still retained some features of the tribal way of life like common ownership of property (and promiscuity). This new solidarity that emerged from the common ownership of cattle, acquired the name Gotra from its very nature. *But then the Gotra which was the foundation of life and livelihood also became its limit.* Sexual pairing was limited to member of a Gotra. This form of pairing was termed Sagotra. Our Present day prohibition on marriage within one Gotra is a later development.

The shift from pairing within a Gotra to prohibition on marriage between two members having the same Gotra must be a result of a variety of factors.

As long as promiscuity survived, society must have been matriarchal as the mother would have been the only identifiable parent. But with the rising productivity and gradual emergence of individual holding of property, this way of life had to make way for another.

The title to the increasing hoard of wealth was held by male members of a clan due to their being the physically dominant sex. It was the efforts of the more powerful males that won for the clan the property of other clans and also enabled defense of their own property from being grabbed by other clans. With the gradual increase in productive power, the acquisition of slaves etc. The title to property also changed from being collective to individual. This change in the title to property from communal to individual must have been the result of evolution over hundreds of years. But why did this change have to prohibit the established practice of marriage within a Gotra?

The answer perhaps lies in Human Social Evolution. Primitive promiscuity as it exists among the lower animals, also existed among humans to begin with. Later on came monogamous marriage. Simultaneously, with the rise in the productive power of human beings there came about accumulation of property initially in the form of cattle. The common ownership of this object of wealth made essential marriage only within members of the clan that held the wealth so as to prevents outsiders from claiming a share of it. But while this solidarity was based on the common ownership of wealth there still existed a commonality in the title to that wealth. And this commonality was first disturbed with the removal of promiscuous matriarchy which did take place with the passage of time. In matriarchy and its earlier form, promiscuity, there existed no bar on members of a clan (Gotra) whether they be the progeny of the same mother, the father not being an identifiable parent.

But with the eclipse of matriarchy and the coming of individual ownership and monogamy, the father became an identifiable parent and strains of patriarchy appeared. The ethic of matriarchal society that allowed marriage between the progeny of one mother or between paternal cousins now came to be frowned upon as these progeny were now the sons and daughters of one (identifiable) father or of one grandfather. This encouraged marriage outside the clan (Gotra). The prohibition on marriage outside a Gotra was made irrelevant by individual ownership of property and the custom of inheritance whereby property passed from father to son. As the title to property was individual and private and the transfer of this title to property was also fixed, there was no reason why a female member of one Gotra should not be tied in wedlock with a male member of another Gotra. Thus while formerly marriage within a Gotra was the rule, later marriage outside a Gotra became one.

Today it is difficult to imagine that marriage within one Gotra between members who were the progeny of one mother or were immediate maternal cousins by virtue of having the same grandmother could have once been a solemn custom. But the later rigid injunction against marriage within a Gotra itself implies that once the practice of marrying within one Gotra must have existed.

Thus as Sagotra marriage was once the norm, there arose the need for its prohibition. Something that has never existed need not be prohibited. Hence the existence of prohibition on Sagotra marriage itself is one evidence of its existence sometime in the past. With the disappearance of a pastoral society and also the clan ownership of cattle (Gotra as 'cowpen'), the emergence of monogamy and ownership of property and later urban civilization and with it a much wider social unit of human existence, the Gotra as an institution and a consideration for matchmaking vanished and marriage outside one's Gotra became the rule. But even afterwards the custom of prohibition on marriage within a Gotra continued. Today this prohibition is still observed as a matter of ritual and custom when even the original connotation of the term Gotra is generally not known.

## The Evolution of Landed Property in Ancient India

***Ownership of Land was Common in Vedic Times:*** To begin with, as long as human beings roamed in tribal clusters from place to place, land must have naturally been looked upon as a gift of nature and thus the common property of everybody.

But when settled agriculture became the main occupation a system would have become necessary for the title to land to be allocated to different individuals. Initially, land was considered to belong to the person who first cleared it. In times of peace, this doctrine to establish the title to landed property would have seemed a logical one. In the transitory stage between nomadic hunting and gathering and the establishment of settled agriculture, there must have existed shifting agriculture. Under the nomadic lifestyle the only items owned by a tribe would have been the weapons used for hunting; and as hunting had to be undertaken collectively even the weapons would have been owned collectively.

In the very next stage of nomadic (shifting) agriculture, the pieces of land that were cleared for cultivation would also have been held under the common ownership of the tribe. Only when settled agriculture became the order of the day would the practice of individual ownership of land could have come into being.

## Vedas Prohibited Land Grants

But in an age when in the then recent past all property was under common ownership, the idea of gifting property to any person would have appeared strange.

The tradition embodied in the Shatapatha Brahmana (a Vedic text) and referred to in the Mahabharata that land must not be given away even on the plea of a sacrificial fee, reflects this attitude. The fact that land grants were being scoffed at indicates that up to the Mahabharata period (dated around 1200 BC.) the idea that land could be an object of purchase and sale had not yet been established. This attitude is in direct contrast to the regular practice of making land grants to Brahmins and noblemen, apart from land becoming an object of regular purchase and sale which was the characteristic of later times.

### *Tribal Morality Influenced the Prohibition of Land Grants*

The above attitude against Land Grants which was seen up to the time of the Mahabharata seems to typify the attitude towards land ownership in Vedic and the Post Vedic times when land was no longer held as common property of the tribe (*i.e.* the Gana), but in that scenario, individual (private) ownership of land was gradually being established. The fact that land grant also had started is established by the fact that they were frowned at in the legal literature which goes to prove the ambivalent attitude that existed towards a practice that was not prevalent before those days, but had since then begun to be observed.

The Shatapatha Brahmana and the Mahabharata are chronologically placed in the Post-Vedic period but before the rise of the big monarchical states of Koshala and Magadha. In those days the purchase, sale and grants of land was frowned at as land had been till then held till as common property and when individual ownership had finally come to be established it had been linked to the labour put into making it cultivable, as the statement in the Manusmriti (a later text) reflects.

Secondly, in those days of social stratification and the caste system of the later days of Magadhan imperialism (*i.e.* after 500 BC.) had not yet come about. In the tribal set-up of the days of the Rig Veda (*i.e.* before 1500 BC.) every male member of a tribe had to work in the collective activity of hunting. When the disintegrating tribal society of hunters, took up agriculture to be its prime occupation, land was collectively owned to begin with. Every member of the tribe seems to have had an equal right to whatever the tribe produced collectively.

Even the tribal chief did not wield the absolute powers that characterised the monarchs of later ages. That the Vedic king's authority was limited is clear from the fact that in the Atharva Veda, Indra is invoked to give the king's share (Bhaga) in the village. But in later times the king himself is stated to be the collector of his share according to the Panchavimsa Brahmana.

## Manusmriti on Rights to Land Ownership

According to an ancient India text, the Manusmriti "Land belong to him who first cleared the timber and a deer to him who first wounded it." This couplet provides a clue to the understanding of a very important doctrine of ancient Indian economics. It makes it clear that, at least to begin with the title to property of land was allied to the labour put into making it cultivable. Finally in a society where the title to property in land was linked to the labour put in to make it cultivable; land grants as well as purchase and sale of land would have seemed strange when there existed vast tracts of freely available virgin land which could be cleared and claimed by any person.

But as the Aryans society established itself on the Gangetic plains, the population gradually increased and the shortage of arable land began to be felt and frequent transfer in the ownership of land became the order of the day. Transfer of land apart from being a sign of settled agriculture also indicates a shortage of land. When virgin land is abundant the motive to transfer land or to get it transferred is naturally weak.

### *Pattern of Ownership of Land changed from Common to Individual*

The changes in the pattern of land ownership also brought about corresponding changes in the connotation of words used in day to day language. In this context it is relevant to note the gradual change in the meaning of the words Bhratru and Bhratrivya. These words occur in the Atharva Veda where they stand for brother and brotherhood. But gradually they came to mean rival and rivalry. This change in connotation shows that hostility had started manifests itself with the Vedic Kulas *i.e.* families, over the division of property, of which, land was the primary constituent in an agrarian society.

The system of landholding also gradually underwent fundamental changes. Whereas to begin with the whole tribe (Gana) held the ownership of land being cultivated, the ownership gradually narrowed down to the Vamshas or blood relations which further disintegrated to the Kulas or families.

This narrowing down of ownership must have affected the size of the individual holdings. Tribal holding upon which the entire tribe used to work, must have been much bigger in size. Its fragmentation into separate family holdings must have naturally limited its size. It must have been further limited in the subsequent period with the rise of the individual proprietary rights on land.

### *The Ashwa Medha Sacrifice was a Method for Land Grabbing*

But after the individual ownership of land had come to be established parallel to the tendency of fragmentation there was also an opposite tendency of the formation of large landed estates. As people practiced settled agriculture on individually owned land, it could be grabbed by others. The landed estates must have come into being in this way, as a result of war and the grabbing of land of one kingdom by another. The martial caste of the Kshatriyas would have been in the position of carrying out such plunder. The Ashva-Medha Yagna was another method of extending ownership to the lands under weak kings or over lands which had not come under individual proprietary ownership. Such accumulation of land in the hands of a few landlords created a class of landlords and cultivators.

### *Rise of the Big Monarchical States in the Ganges Valley*

With the formation of monarchical states and their capital cities which were the hub of mercantile activities, there emerged a class of absentee landlords who largely lived in the cities but had vast landed properties in rural areas. Such absentee landlords are mentioned in the Pali text of Buddha's time. These absentee landlords had landholdings relatively near the monarchical states of the Ganges valley. These states were mainly Koshala and Magadha. As these landlords came under the sovereignty of the kings of Koshala and Magadha their landholdings came to be integrated with the prospering mercantile economy of these kingdoms. In the Pali texts we find mention of landlord-merchants like Anathapindaka and

Kossiyagotta. The state in whose territory these landlord-merchants lived also gained in the form of increasing collection of taxes and the general prosperity.

In these monarchical states, the landlord-merchants played the role of intermediaries between the state and the actual tillers of the soil. Thus a nexus was established between the state and the landed aristocracy. But in the foothills of the Himalayan range which were outside the Gangetic monarchical states of Magadha and Koshala the landed aristocracy was not under the sovereignty of any outside king. The landlords were their own rulers and had conglomorates of oligarchies. Such oligarchies of the Mallas, Lichavvis, Koliyas, etc. are mentioned in the Pali texts.

### *The Struggle between the Tribal Oligarchies and the Monarchs*

These landholding oligarchs were different from the absentee landlords of the plains, in that they were based on their landholdings, did not have any significant mercantile contacts with the outside world and above all did not owe loyalty to any King as did their counterparts in the Gangetic Valley. These landlords were bound to one another in a tribal oligarchy which refused to yield taxes to the monarchies from the Ganges Valley nor did they acknowledge any sort of sovereignty of any outside monarch. Herein lay the seeds of the struggle between the tribal oligarchies and the monarchical states. Right from Ajatashatru who ruled Magadha in the 6th Century BC. during Buddha's time up to the Nandas of the 4th century BC. we hear of a running struggle between the tribal oligarchies of the Himalayan foothills comprising the Mallas, Lichavis, Koliyas and some other tribes with the monarchical states of Koshala and Magadha.

This struggle brought about the destruction of the independent tribal oligarchies. The victory of the monarchies over the tribal oligarchies was also the victory of a more advanced and organised economy over the closed tribal economy. But as a result of this struggle, land the primary factor of production came under state supervision. While the state did not deny the right to private property, it nevertheless adopted measures which siphoned off a large segment of the produce as revenue to be collected in the royal treasury. This further increased the strength of the monarchical states. Thus in the Ganges valley and in the Himalayan foothills, the administrative suzerainty of the Magadhan King came to be absolute. The nexus between the state and the large landholders came to be firmly established. But the regions to the south of the Ganges valley *viz.*, Madhya-desha and Dakshina-patha *i.e.* Central and Southern India, were still outside the pale of Magadhan imperialism.

### *Fableised recollections of the Aryan Migrations into South India*

From the earliest Aryan migrations into the Ganges valley in the Post Vedic period, some Aryan tribes had started trickling down into Central and Southern India. The fableised recollectlon of the Sage Agastya leading the Aryans across the Vindhyas and that of Parshurama retrieving the land of Kerala from the sea so that the Aryans could settle there indicate the migration of the Aryans to Central and Southern India. These immigrants had established pockets of settled agriculture and had mushroomed into small kingdoms. The earlier non-Aryan settlers already had their own kingdoms located in pockets of agriculture, throughout the country. But these kingdoms were relatively small and were separated from each other by dense un-reclaimed forests. Along with this population pressures were being felt in the Ganges Valley by the 4th century BC. This was the general situation when the country's first pan-Indian empire was established by Chadragupta Maurya.

### The Fall Towards Feudalism

As described above, we find that in the post-Mauryan times, the geographical spreading of farmlands over vast areas, due to which the jurisdiction of tax collection was no longer limited to the tiny isolated Janapadas as in the Mauryan times.

As long as the centralised apparatus of the Mauryan state existed it could carry out the process of revenue collection but with the collapse of the empire and the disintegration of this centralised apparatus, this task became increasingly difficult. This created the necessity for an intermediate class between the tillers of the widespread farmlands and the sovereign monarch. The extension of farmlands on a scale that seemed almost limitless in those days along with the corresponding absence of a centralised tax collecting apparatus was one of the most important reasons for the emergence of intermediaries and the rise of feudalism.

## Disappearance of the Shreni Guilds

This expansion of the physical dimensions of the agrarian economy required the large scale supply of various commodities to the countryside. The apparatus of the Arthashastra type with its heavy tolls at every Janapada frontier now became a hindrance for the essential commodity movements due to large scale trade handled by private traders and not by the state as in Mauryan times.

The absence of a central authority after the downfall of the Mauryan empire accounted for the absence of good and secure means of transport to all corners of the expanding settled territory. This became an hindrance to extensive commerce.

The only way to satisfy the village demand was for the producer-artisans to move out of the centralized Shreni guilds and spread out into the countryside. With the strengthening of this tendency, the urban based centralised production units of the Mauryan period began to disintegrate. So also did the till now cohesive Shreni guilds.

## The Rise of the Self-sufficient Village Economy

The individual producers who resulted from this falling mode of production, settled in the scattered villages throughout the countryside. In the absence of good means of communications. The village now began to get the characteristic of being itself self-sufficient closed economic unit which produced all its required commodities internally. Without any exchange or trade. While trade did exist it was a much smaller and irregular scale than it was in the Mauryan times. Thus while in Europe the coming of feudal relations in the middle ages saw the rise of craftsmen-guilds, in India the rise of feudal relations was marked by the disintegration of the Shreni guilds.

## *Rise of a Class of Hereditary Revenue Collectors-the Feudal Lords*

This shifting of economic activity was accompanied by the shifting of political power to the rising class of village feudatory revenue collectors who stood one above the other in a hierarchy in place of the salaried bureaucrats who collected revenue for the Mauryan State. In the changed circumstances the practice that was gaining ground was of appointing revenue collectors who would not be paid a salary by the king but who would be entitled to a share in the revenue collected by him. Thus the position of a revenue collector changed from being that of a salaried employee of the king to that of a petty chieftain himself. Such hereditary revenue collectors were called "Samant". They also maintained a fighting force which could be called upon by the king when needed to defend or attack other kingdoms. The Samants were the feudal nobility.

## Role of Temples in Revenue Collection

When such revenue collectors were to be appointed for the first time, the opposition of the tax paying tillers was smothered by making religious institutions like temples, Ashrams, Viharas, Chaityas, etc., perform the function of collecting revenue. Hence the practice of generous land grants to temples, ashrams. individual Brahmins, etc. Along with the right to collect revenue there was an obligation to pass on a part of the proceeds to the king who had given the land grant. Only in rare cases was the obligation to pass on part of the revenue to the donor-king was waived. Thus these temples and monasteries served both as the institutional and ideological arms for establishing this new mode of revenue collection. Thus the administrative costs of overcoming the opposition to this new revenue system was also reduced by making ecclesiastical institutions as intermediaries.

### *Brahmadeya, Devadana and Agrahara Land Grants*

These land grants were to religious institutions were called Brahmadeya, (*i.e.* donated to Brahmins) Devadana (donated to Gods) and Agrahara (Settlement-of priests) These lands donated to the temples and monasteries apart from being used as normal tenancy also carried a right vested with the temple authorities to call for unpaid labour (called Vishti) as a religious service to the temple from the tillers on the donated land. This unpaid labour, became an important method of enrichment of the intermediary revenue collectors, which the temples were, apart from having the rights of revenue collection.

### Right to Carry Arms for the Nobility 'Samants'

But the physical muscle of this method of revenue collection through intermediaries, was the right to bear arms which was given to the feudal lords and the petty local chieftains. These armed feudal lords could be called upon by the king to render military service to quell a rebellion to defend the kingdom from attack or to launch an attack on neighbouring kingdoms.

The armed retinue of every feudal revenue collector-administrator was maintained out of the revenue collected locally. Thus the local feudal lord was the paymaster of this armed soldierly, and not the king whose kingdom they might be called on to defend. This undermined the power of the king and we hear of rebellious nobles in this period. This was unthinkable during the centralized administration of Mauryan times.

Ultimately the maintenance of armed guards and the obligation to render military service became the qualification for making grants of land with revenue collection rights. These grants were made in recognition of valour displayed by the various feudal lords in the battles in which the particular kingdom was involved. The Jagirdari, Subahdari and Inamdari grants of the Muslim period which came later were also of this type. But the feudal relations were established in the Post-Maurya period, much before the coming of the Muslims.

## The King was at the Mercy of his Noblemen

But the political consequences of this type of dependence of the king on the feudal lords in military matters often turned out to be unfortunate for those kings who did not have sufficient control over their vassals and their private armies of retainers. Many a times the vassals did not pass on the revenue collected to their king, this led to a perpetual struggle between the king and the feudal lords under him. Often the feudal lords would switch loyalties from one king to another whenever circumstances favoured this.

The feudal system as a whole was characterised by the diffusion of executive authority in the hands of innumerable petty chieftains vastly reducing the absolute power of the king. Summing up of the Landholding Scenario in the Ancient Hindu (Pre-Muslim) Period To sum up we can say in the period of 2200 years from the post-Vedic Period (*i.e.* 1000C.E.) upto the establishment of Muslim rule in India (around 1200C.E.) Indian socio-economic development passed through the following three stages.

***The 1st Stage:*** In the post-Vedic age with the rise of caste divided society, to begin with, cattle and later largely land became the object of ownership. There existed large landholdings of two types-the first were the tribal oligarchies like the Mallas and Lichhavis as depicted in the Jataka stories. These oligarchies were eliminated by the pre-Mauryan monarchical states of Koshala and Magadha.

Alongwith these oligarchies in the hills, there existed on the plains within the kingdoms of Koshala and Magadha, large landed estates owned by absentee landlords. These were the second type of large land-holdings. Such absentee landlords are mentioned in the Pali text of Buddha's time. These absentee landlords had landholdings relatively near the monarchical states of the Ganges valley. As these landlords came under the sovereignty of the kings of Koshala and Magadha their landholdings came to be integrated with the prospering mercantile economy of these kingdoms.

In the Pali texts we find mention of landlord-merchants like Anathapindaka and Kossiyagotta. The state in whose territory these landlord-merchants lived also gained in the form of increasing collection of taxes and the general prosperity. In these monarchical states, the landlord-merchants played the role of intermediaries between the state and the actual tillers of the soil. Thus a nexus was established between the state and the landed aristocracy.

The corollary of these large estates of the absentee landlords were classes like the ardha-sitika share croppers. This indicates the existence of a society sharply polarised into two classes. Extensive landed estates in the Ganges Valley which were under private ownership were tilled by the labour of classes like the ardha-sitikas. Indepedent small peasantry seems to be largely absent in the civilized belt of the Ganges valley in that period.

***The 2nd Stage:*** The imperialism of the Mauryas marked the second stage which led to the extinction of the big landowners and also of the urban merchants. The object of this was to eliminate centres of potential opposition to the state, through the almost complete elimination of this intermediate class between the state and the peasantry. The Mauryan state itself assumed the role of this class which it had successfully eliminated. But after the departure of the Mauryas and alongwith them of the highly centralised multifunctional administrative apparatus, a void was left between the state power and society (of peasant cultivators).

***The 3rd Stage:*** The filling up of this void marks the beginning of the third stage. This void was filled up by the policy of giving land grant; followed by the emperors in the post-Maurya period and continued by the Gupta and Post-Gupta Kings. The titles assumed by the Gupta kings also indicate that they ruled their large empire by proxy. The Gupta kings did not call themselves Samrat as Ashoka, Maurya and Chandragupta Maurya were called. The titles of the Gupta kings like Samudragupta and Vikramaditya included Param-Eshwara (The Greatest-God), Param-Bhattaraka (The Greatest-Protector of the Brahmins), Maharaj-Dhi-Raj (King of Kings). All this indicates that the Gupta kings recognised themselves not as undisputed absolute monarchs, but as Chieftains of many other lower (and defeated) chieftains who paid tribute to the Guptas.

But now the social relationships were of a qualitatively different nature than those prevailing in the pre-Maurya period. During the Maurya period too land was granted to farmer cultivators. But what was granted was not the right of revenue collection, but the right to cultivate and pay a part of the produce to the Mauryan state in the form of tax. The land grantees of the Gupta age were not owners of the lands and the villages granted to them. They were not interested in actual cultivation of the land themselves. They were only invested with the rights of revenue collection and exacting of forced labour, etc. A part of this revenue collected they gave to their overlord-the Gupta Emperor. In this respect they were neither land-owning aristocrats, nor were they absentee landlords, they were feudal intermediaries between the state and the peasantry.

It can thus roughly be summed up that in the pre-Mauryan period the landholding class in the tribal oligarchies comprised mostly the Kshatriyas. This must have been so as the passage from a tribal to a settled agrarian society the social class that could have established, through muscle power, its ownership over property (mainly land in an agrarian society) would have been that which wielded arms. (But in the kingdoms they seem to have been mainly Vaishyas like Kossiyagotta and Anathapindika).

In the later periods *i.e.* in the Gupta and Post-Gupta Periods, the grantees must have been largely, though not necessarily individual Brahmins and temples as they constituted the class which commanded royal patronage and had a lesser tendency to rebel against the king, unlike the nobility which had a martial attitude. The temples also exercised religious influence and hence were most acceptable as revenue collectors to the God-fearing peasantry.

These land grants along with the rights of revenue collection and the free forced-labour services of nearby villagers and the generous offerings of devotees had made Hindu temples into conglomorates of vast collections of wealth in terms of gold, silver, gems, artifacts apart from acres of land and the rights of revenue collection.

## Sati (practice)

Sati (also suttee) is a Hindu funeral custom, largely defunct in Modern India, in which the dead man's widow used to immolate herself on her husband's funeral pyre.

The term is derived from the original name of a goddess, who immolated herself, unable to bear the humiliation of her (living) husband. The term may also be used to refer to the widow herself. The term *sati* is now sometimes interpreted as 'chaste woman'.

***Origin:*** Few reliable records exist of the practice before the time of the Gupta empire, approximately 400 CE. While a couple of instances of voluntary self immolation by women as well as men are mentioned in the Mahabharata and other works that may be considered at least partly historical accounts, it is known that large parts of these works are relatively late interpolations into an original story. Also, the immolation or desire of self immolation is not regarded as a custom in the Mahabharata and as such the word 'sati' as a custom never occurs in the epic as compared to other customs such as the Rajasuya yagna. Rather, the instances are viewed as an expression of extreme grief on the loss of a beloved one.

Aristobulus of Cassandreia, a Greek historian who traveled to India with the expedition of Alexander of Macedon, recorded the practice of *sati* at the city of Taxila. A later instance of voluntary co-cremation appears in an account of an Indian soldier in the army of Eumenes of Cardia, whose two wives vied to die on his funeral pyre, in 316 BCE. The Greeks believed that the practice had been instituted to discourage wives from poisoning their husbands.

Voluntary death at funerals has been described in northern India before the Gupta empire. The original practices were called *anumarana*, and were not common. They were not necessarily practices that would be understood as *sati* at present, since it was not necessarily a widow who died. Those who died could be anyone, male or female with a personal loyalty to the dead person. They included other relatives of the dead person, servants, followers or friends. Sometimes these deaths were because of vows of loyalty taken in life. Compare with later Japanese seppuku.

Widow burning, the practice as understood today, started to become more extensive after about 500 CE, and the end of the Gupta empire. The neo-Buddhists have ascribed to the decline of Buddhism in India, the rise of caste based societies, and the idea that sati was used to reinforce caste status. There are also suggestions that the practice was introduced into India by the Huna Buddhist invaders who contributed to the fall of the Gupta empire.

At about this time, instances of *sati* began to be marked by inscribed memorial stones. The earliest of these is in Sagar, Madhya Pradesh, though the largest collections are some centuries later, in Rajasthan. These stones, called *devli*, or sati-stones, became shrines where the dead woman became an object of reverence and worship. They are most common in western India.

By about the 10th century *sati*, as understood today, was known across much of the subcontinent. It continued to occur, usually at a low frequency and with regional variations, until the early 19th century.

***Practice:*** The act of *sati* was supposed to take place voluntarily, and from the existing accounts, most of them were indeed voluntary. The act may have been expected of widows in some communities. The extent to which any social pressures or expectations should be considered as compulsion has been the matter of much debate in modern times. It is frequently stated that a widow could expect little of life after her husband's death, especially if she was childless. However, there were also instances where the wish of the widow to commit *sati* was not welcomed by others, and where efforts were made to prevent the death.

Traditionally, the funeral of any dead person would usually have taken place within a day of the death. Thus a decision by a widow to die at her husband's funeral would often have to be made quickly. In some cases, such as when the husband died elsewhere, it was still possible for the widow to die by immolation, but at a later date.

The connection with the original marriage between the widow and the deceased was emphasized. Unlike other mourners, the *sati* at the funeral was often dressed in marriage robes or other finery. Her death may have been seen as a culmination of the marriage. In the preliminaries of the related act of Jauhar, both the husbands and wives have been known to dress in their marriage clothes and re-enact their wedding ritual, before going to their separate deaths.

There are accounts of many different approaches of the widow to her death. The majority have the widow seated or lying down on the funeral pyre beside her dead husband. There are also many descriptions of widows who walked or jumped into the flames after the fire had been lit, and there are descriptions of widows who lit their own funeral pyres after seating themselves on it.

Some written prescriptions to the practice exist; a recent one has been quoted at a mailing list.

***Compulsion:*** *Sati* was supposed to be voluntary, but it is agreed that in many cases it may not have been voluntary in practice. Leaving aside the matter of social pressures, there are many accounts of widows being physically forced to their deaths.

Pictorial and narrative accounts often describe the woman seated on the unlit pyre, and tied or otherwise restrained to keep her from fleeing after the fire was lit. Some accounts say that the woman was drugged. There is one description of men with long poles preventing a widow from fleeing the flames.

***Royal Funerals:*** Royal funerals sometimes have included the deaths of many wives and concubines. A number of examples of these occur in the history of Rajasthan.

***Symbolic Sati:*** There have been accounts of symbolic *sati* in some Hindu communities. A widow lies down next to her dead husband, and certain parts of both the marriage ceremony and the funeral ceremonies are enacted, but without her death.

***Jauhar:*** The practice of jauhar, known from Rajasthan and Madhya Pradesh was the collective suicide of a community. It consisted of the mass immolation of women, and sometimes also of the children, the elderly and the sick, at the same time that their fighting men died in battle. It is detailed in a separate article.

***Burials:*** In some Hindu communities, it is conventional to bury the dead. It has been known for similar widow deaths to occur in these communities, but with the widow being buried alive with the husband, in ceremonies that are otherwise largely as in the immolation.

***Prevalence:*** Records exist of *sati* across most of the subcontinent. However, there seem to have been major differences historically, in different regions, and among different communities.

***Numbers:*** There are no reliable figures for the numbers who died by *sati* across the country. A local indication of the numbers is given in the records kept by the Bengal Presidency of the British East India Company. The total figure of known occurrences for the period 1813 to 1828 is 8,135, thus giving an average of about 600 per year. Bentinck, in his 1829 report, states that 420 occurrences took place in one (unspecified) year in the 'Lower Provinces' of Bengal, Bihar and Orissa, and 44 in the 'Upper Provinces' (the upper Gangetic plain). Given a population of over 50 million at the time for the Presidency, this suggests a maximum frequency of immolation among widows of well under 1%.

***Communities:*** It is said by some authorities that the practice was more common among the higher castes, and among those who considered themselves to be rising in social status. It was little known or unknown in most of the population of India and the tribal groups. According to at least one source, it was very rare for anyone in the later Mughal empire except royal wives to be burnt.

However, it has been said elsewhere that it was unusual in higher caste women in the south (quoted from Kamat).

***Regional Variations:*** It was known in Rajasthan from the earliest (6th century) to the present. About half the known *sati* stones (about 150 in total) in India are in Rajasthan. However, the extent to which individual instances of deaths resulted in veneration (glorification) implies that was not very common.

It is known to have occurred in the south from the 9th century through the period of the Vijayanagara empire, which fought Islamist kingdoms up to the 17th century. Madhavacharya, who is probably the best known of those historical figures who justified the practice, was originally a minister of the court of this empire. The practice continued to occur after the collapse of the empire, though apparently at a fairly low frequency. A record exists of a minister of the kingdom of Mysore giving permission for a widow to commit *sati* in 1805.

In the Upper Gangetic plain, while it occurred, there is no indication that it was especially widespread. The earliest known attempt by a government to stop the practice took place here, that of Muhammad Tughlaq, in the Sultanate of Delhi in the

14th century.

In the Lower Gangetic plain, the practice may have reached a high level fairly late in history, it appears possible, based on available evidence and the existing reports of the occurrences of it, that the greatest incidence of *sati* in any region and period, in terms of total numbers, occurred in Bengal and Bihar in the late 18th and early 19th centuries. This was during the earlier period of British rule, and before the abolition. The Bengal Presidency kept records from 1813 to 1829. The frequency increased in periods of hardship and famine. Ram Mohan Roy suggested that it was more prevalent in Bengal than in the rest of the subcontinent. An unusually large number of the surviving reports for this period are from Bengal, also suggesting that it was most common there.

In modern times, *sati* has been largely confined to Rajasthan, mostly in or near Shekhawati, with a few instances in the Gangetic plain.

***Recent Incidence:*** *Sati* still occurs occasionally, mostly in rural areas. About 40 cases have occurred in India since independence in 1947, the majority in the Shekhawati region of Rajasthan. The last clearly documented case was that of Roop Kanwar. However there are claims that other more recent deaths have also been cases of *Sati.*

Roop Kanwar, a childless 18-year old widow, committed sati on 4 September 1987, some allege forcibly, dressed in her red wedding dress, in Rajasthan's Deorala village. Several thousand people were said to have been at the event. After her death, she was hailed as a 'sati mata', meaning pure mother. The event quickly produced a public outcry in urban centres, pitting a modern Indian ideology against a traditional one. A much-publicised investigation led to the arrest of a large number of people from Deorala, said to have been present in the ceremony, or participants in it. Eventually, 11 people were charged. On January 31, 2004, a special court in Jaipur acquitted all of the 11 accused in the case, observing that the prosecution had failed to prove charges that they glorified *sati*.

On 18th May 2006, Vidyawati, a 35-year-old woman allegedly committed sati by jumping into the blazing funeral pyre of her husband in Rari-Bujurg Village, Fatehpur district in the State of Uttar Pradesh.

On 21 August 2006, Janakrani, a 40-year-old woman, burnt to death on the funeral pyre of her husband Prem Narayan in Sagar district.

***Justifications and Criticisms:*** Brahmin scholars of the second millennium justified the practice, and gave reasonings as to how the scriptures could be said to justify them. Among them were Vijnanesvara, of the Chalukya court, and later Madhavacharya, theologian and minister of the court of the Vijayanagara empire, according to Shastri, who quotes their reasoning. It was lauded by them as required conduct in righteous women, and it was explained that this was considered not to be suicide (suicide was otherwise variously banned or discouraged in the scriptures). It was deemed an act of peerless piety, and was said to purge the couple of all accumulated sin, guarantee their salvation and ensure their reunion in the afterlife.

***Law Books:*** These are relatively late works. Justifications for the practice are given in the Vishnu Smriti.

> *Now the duties of a woman (are)... After the death of her husband, to preserve her chastity, or to ascend the pile after him.*
>
> *—(Vishnu Smriti, 25-14).*

There is justification also in the later work of the Brihaspati Smriti (25-11). Both this and the Vishnu Smriti date from the first millennium. The Manusmriti is often regarded as the culmination of classical Hindu law, and hence its position is important. It does not mention or sanction *sati* though it does prescribe life-long asceticism for most widows.

***Scriptures:*** Although the myth of the goddess Sati is that of a wife who dies by her own volition on a fire, this is not a case of the practice of *sati*. The goddess was not widowed, and the myth is quite unconnected with the justifications for the practice.

The Puranas have examples of women who commit *sati* and there are suggestions in them that this was considered desirable or praiseworthy: *A wife who dies in the company of her husband shall remain in heaven as many years as there are hairs on his person.* (Garuda Purana 1.107.29) According to 2.4.93 she stays with her husband in heaven during the rule of 14 Indras, *i.e.* a kalpa.

It is notable that in the Ramayana, Tara, in her grief at the death of husband Vali, wished to commit *sati*. Hanuman, Rama, and the dying Vali dissuade her and she finally does not immolate herself. Examples of the act in the puranas include the following.

In the Mahabharata, Madri, the second wife of Pandu, immolates herself. She holds herself responsible for the death of her husband, who had been cursed with death if he ever had intercourse. He died while performing the forbidden act with Madri, who blamed herself for not having rejected his advances, although she was well aware of the curse.

Passages in the Atharva Veda, including 13.3.1, offer advice to the widow on mourning and her life after widowhood, including her remarriage.

***Argument that the Rig Veda Sanctions Sati:*** It is often claimed that this most ancient text sanctions or prescribes sati. This is based on verse 10.18.7, part of the verses to be used at funerals. Whether they even describe *sati* or something else entirely, is disputed, The hymn is about funeral by burial, and not by cremation. There are differing translations of the passage. The translation below is one of those said to prescribe it.

> *Let these women, whose husbands are worthy and are living, enter the house with ghee (applied) as collyrium (to their eyes). Let these wives first step into the pyre,*

> *tearless without any affliction and well adorned.*

The text does not mention widowhood, and other translations differ in their translation of the word here rendered as 'pyre' (*yoni*, literally "seat, abode"; Griffith has "first let the dames go up to where he lieth"). In addition, the following verse, which is unambiguously about widows, then contradicts any suggestion of the woman's death; it explicitly states that the widow should return to her house.

> *Rise, come unto the world of life, O woman — come, he is lifeless by whose side thou liest. Wifehood with this thy husband was thy portion, who took thy hand and wooed thee as a lover.*

A reason given for the discrepancy in translation and interpretation of verse 10.18.7, is that one consonant in a word that meant house, *yonim agre* "formost to the *yoni*", was deliberately changed by those who wished claim scriptural justification, to a word that meant fire, *yomiagne*.

***Argument that Sati was an Act of self Defence:*** Hindu scholars such as Prabhat Varun have tried to show [26] that Sati was not part of Hindu doctrine at all, but a practice of voluntary immolation by Hindu women as a means to avoid the humiliation and stigma associated with rape. The argument is that the practice came into effect during the Islamic invasion of India, to protect their honour from Muslims who were known to commit mass rape on the women of cities that they could capture successfully. It is argued that the prevalence of sati has been exaggerated by Europeans and Muslims as a canard against Hinduism.

***Counter-arguments within Hinduism:*** No early descriptions or criticisms of the practice within Hinduism, (or in the other native religions of Buddhism or Jainism), are known before the Gupta period, as the practice was little known at that time.

Explicit criticisms later in the first millennium, included that of Medhatithi, a commentator on various theological works.

He considered it suicide, which was forbidden by the Vedas:

*One shall not die before the span of one's life is run out,*

Another critic was Bana, who wrote during the reign of Harsha. Bana condemned it both as suicide, and as a pointless and futile act. There does not seem to be any thought or suggestion among any of these critics that the act would not be voluntary.

Reform and bhakti movements within Hinduism tended to be anti-caste, favoured egalitarian societies, and in line with the tenor of these beliefs, they generally condemned the practice, sometimes explicitly. The Alvars condemned sati, in the 8th century. The Virashaiva movement in the 12th and 13th centuries, also condemned it.

In the early 19th century, Ram Mohan Roy wrote and disseminated arguments that the practice was not part of Hinduism, as part of his campaign to ban the practice.

***Non-Hindu Views and Criticisms:*** The Sikh religion explicitly proscribed the practice, by about 1500. The principal foreign early visitors to the subcontinent whose have left records of the practice, are from Western Asia, mostly Muslim, and later on, Europeans. Both groups were fascinated by the practice, and sometimes described it as horrific, but often also as an incomparable act of devotion. Ibn Battuta described an instance, but said that he collapsed or fainted and had to be carried away from the scene. European artists in the eighteenth century produced many images for their own native markets, showing the widows as heroic women, and moral exemplars.

As Islam established itself in the subcontinent, their opinion of sati changed to regarding it as a barbaric practice. The earliest known governmental effort to halt the practice were by Muslim rulers, including Muhammad Tughlaq.

Europeans also showed a change in their attitude to local customs as they became dominant local powers. The earliest Europeans to establish themselves were the Portuguese in Goa. They tried early on to override local customs and practices, including *sati*, as they attempted to Christianise territories in their control. The British entered India as a trading body, and in the earlier periods of their rule, they were largely indifferent to local practices. A campaign against *sati* was however set up by the evangelical movement in Britain, particularly by William Wilberforce, as part of a campaign to increase missionary activity in India. The practice of *sati*, and its later legal abolition by the British (along with the suppression of thuggee) went on to become one of the standard justifications for British rule. British attitudes in their later history in India are usually given in the following much repeated quote, usually ascribed to General Napier-

> *You say that it is your custom to burn widows. Very well. We also have a custom: when men burn a woman alive, we tie a rope around their necks and we hang them. Build your funeral pyre; beside it, my carpenters will build a gallows. You may follow your custom. And then we will follow ours.*

**Suppression**

***Mughal Period:*** Humayun issued a royal fiat against sati, which he later withdrew.

Akbar required that permission be granted by his officials, and these officials were instructed to delay the woman's decision for as long as possible. The reasoning was that she was less likely to chose to die once the emotions of the moment had passed. In the reign of Shah Jahan, widows with children were not allowed in any circumstances to burn. In other cases governors did not readily give permission, but could be bribed to do so. Later on in the Mughal period, pensions, gifts and rehabilitative help were offered to the potential sati to wean her away from committing the act. Children were strictly forbidden from the practice. The later Mughals continued to put obstacles in the way but the practice carried on in the areas outside their capitals.

The strongest attempts to control it were made by

Aurangzeb. In 1663, he "issued an order that in all lands under Mughal control, never again should the officials allow a woman to be burnt". In spite of such attempts however, the practice continued, especially in conditions of war and upheaval.

***Influences on Art and Culture:*** A famous fictional depiction of sati is found in *Around the World in Eighty Days* (1872). The English gentleman Phileas Fogg and his servant Passepartout are travelling India when they find a sati. They risk their lives battling the Indians and rescue the drugged princess Aouda from death.

In Tom Robbins' 1984 novel *Jitterbug Perfume*, the main character Alobar witnesses and attempts to intervene in an act of sati.

George MacDonald Fraser's character Flashman witnesses a mass sati by the wives and concubines of an Indian ruler, Jawaheer, in the Punjab in *Flashman and the Mountain of Light*, which is set during the First Sikh War. In *Flashman in the Great Game*, he questions the widowed ruler of Jhansi, Lakshmibai about why she, when her husband died, did not follow the custom; Lakshmibai's response is to ask whether Flashman thinks she is a fool. (While Fraser is normally a most meticulous researcher, whose books are quite accurate on matters of historical fact, the Sikh prohibition on sati mentioned above indicates that, in this case, he may have been in error—or that the Sikhs' prohibition did not apply at this time, or not to royalty).

Rudyard Kipling wrote a poem entitled "The Last Suttee" in 1889. In this poem, the Boondi Queen escapes her British captors (who are seeking to prevent her carrying out sati, and keep her alive) and throws herself upon her husband's burial fire, to become his foremost queen in the afterlife—"To rule in Heaven his only bride, while the others howl in Hell."

***British and other European Territories:*** By the end of the 18th century, the practice had been banned in territories held by some European powers. The Portuguese banned the practice in Goa by about 1515, though it is not believed to have been especially prevalent there. The Dutch and the French had also banned it in Chinsurah and Pondicherry. The British who by then ruled much of the subcontinent, and the Danes, who held the small territory of Shrirampur, permitted it into the 19th century.

Attempts to limit or ban the practice had been made by individual British officers in the 18th century, but without the backing of the British East India Company. The first formal British ban was in 1798, in the city of Calcutta only. The practice continued in surrounding regions. Toward the end of the 18th century, the evangelical church in Britain, and its members in India, started campaigns against *sati*. Leaders of these included William Carey and William Wilberforce, and both appeared to be motivated partly by a desire to convert Indians to Christianity. These movements put pressure on the company to ban the act, and the Bengal Presidency started collecting figures on the practice in 1813.

From about 1812, the Bengali reformer Ram Mohan Roy started his own campaign against the practice. He was motivated by the experience of seeing his own sister-in-law commit *sati*. Among his actions, he visited Calcutta cremation grounds to persuade widows not to so die, formed watch groups to do the same, and wrote and disseminated articles to show that it was not required by scripture.

On 4 December 1829, the practice was formally banned in the Bengal Presidency lands, by the then governor, Lord William Bentinck. The ban was challenged in the courts, and the matter went to the Privy Council in London, but was upheld in 1832. Other company territories also banned it shortly after. Although the original ban in Bengal was fairly uncompromising, later in the century British laws include provisions that provided mitigation for murder when "the person whose death is caused, being above the age of 18 years, suffers death or takes the risk of death with his own consent".

*Sati* remained legal in some princely states for a time after it had been abolished in lands under British control. The last such state to permit it, Jaipur, banned the practice in 1846.

***Modern Times:*** In modern India, following outcries after each instance, there have been various fresh measures passed against the practice, which now effectively make it illegal to be a bystander at an event of *sati*. The law now makes no distinction between passive observers to the act, and active promoters of the event; all are supposed to be held equally culpable. Other measures include efforts to stop the 'glorification' of the dead women. Glorification includes the erection of shrines to the dead, the encouragement of pilgrimages to the site of the pyre, and the derivation of any income from such sites and pilgrims.

Enforcement of these measures is not always consistent however. The enforcement of some measures, such as the possible stopping of worship at ancient shrines, is a matter of modern controversy.

# 6

# A STUDY IN THE RITUALS OF FESTIVALS

## Diwali

The date of Diwali is based on the Hindu calendar, which has solar sidereal years and lunar months. Although the festival is worshipped on exactly the same set of days across India, it falls in different months depending on the version of the Hindu calendar being used in the given region. This is perhaps the most well-known of the Indian festivals: it is celebrated throughout India, as well as in Indian communities throughout the diaspora. It usually takes place eighteen days after Dusshera. It is colloquially known as the "festival of lights", for the common practice is to light small oil lamps (called *diyas*) and place them around the home, in courtyards, verandahs, and gardens, as well as on roof-tops and outer walls. In urban areas, especially, candles are substituted for diyas; and among the nouveau riche, neon lights are made to substitute for candles. The celebration of the festival is invariably accompanied by the exchange of sweets and the explosion of fireworks.

As with other Indian festivals, Diwali signifies many different things to people across the country. In north India, Diwali celebrates Rama's homecoming, that is his return to Ayodhya after the defeat of Ravana and his coronation as king; in Gujarat, the festival honors Lakshmi, the goddess of wealth; and in Bengal, it is associated with the goddess Kali. Everywhere, it signifies the renewal of life, and accordingly it is common to wear new clothes on the day of the festival; similarly, it heralds the approach of winter and the beginning of the sowing season. Diwali (also called Deepavali) is a major Hindu festival. Known as the "Festival of Lights," it symbolises the victory of good over evil, and lamps are lit as a sign of celebration and hope for mankind. Celebrations focus on lights and lamps, particularly traditional diyas. Fireworks are associated with the festival in some regions of the country. Deepavali is celebrated for five consecutive days in the Hindu month of Ashwayuja. It usually occurs in October/November, and is one of the most popular and eagerly awaited festivals of India.

Hindus, Jains and Sikhs alike regard it as a celebration of life and use the occasion to strengthen family and social relationships. For Jains it is one of the most important festivals, and beginning of the Jain year. It is also a significant festival for the Sikh faith. The *Amanta* ("ending on the no-moon") version of the Hindu Calendar has been adopted as the Indian national calendar.

According to this calendar, which is prevalent in southern India and Maharashtra, Deepavali falls in the middle of the month of Ashwayuja. According to the *Purnimanta* ("ending on the full-moon") version prevalent in northern India, the 5-day celebration is spread over the last three days of the month of Ashwayuja and the first two days of the new month of Kartika. According to this calendar, the festival of Deepavali marks the new year's day of this calendar and is therefore an especially significant festival. Diwali is also known as festival of lights. Shown here is the view of Jaipur city on Diwali days. The festival marks the victory of good over evil. The Sanskrit word Deepavali means array of lights that stands for victory of brightness over darkness.

As the knowledge of Sanskrit diminished, the name was popularly modified to Diwali, especially in northern India. On the day of Diwali, many wear new clothes, share sweets and light firecrackers. The North Indian business community usually starts their financial new year on Diwali and new account books are opened on this day.

Hindus find cause to celebrate this festival for different reasons:

- As per sacred texts, according to Skandha Purana, the goddess Shakti observed 21 days of austerity starting from ashtami of shukla paksha (waxing period of moon) to get half part of the body of Lord Shiva. This vrata is known as kedhara vrata. Deepavali is the completion day of this austerity. This is the day Lord Shiva accepted Shakti into the left half of the form and appeared as Ardhanarishvara. The ardent devotees observe this 21 days vrata by making a kalasha with 21 threads on it and 21 types of offerings for 35 days. The final day is celebrated as kedhara gauri vrata.
- Diwali also celebrates the return of the Lord Rama, King of Ayodhya, his wife Sita and brother Lakshmana to Ayodhya from a war in which hc killed the demon king Ravana. It is believed that the people lit oil lamps along the way to light their path in the darkness. In North India, the festival is held on the final day of the Vikram calendar. The following day marks the beginning of the North Indian new year, and is called Annakut.
- It commemorates the killing of Narakasura, an evil demon who created havoc, by Lord Krishna's wife Sathyabhama. This happened in the Dwapara Yuga during this time of Lord Krishna's avatar. In another version, the demon was killed by Lord Krishna himself. In South India, Diwali does not coincide with the beginning of a new year as South Indians follow a different calendar, the Shalivahana calendar.
- In Bhavishyottara and Bramhavaivarta Purana, Diwali is associated with the Daitya king Bali, who is allowed to return to earth once a year.

***The Five Days of Diwali:*** Diwali is celebrated over five days in most of North India. All the days except Diwali are named using the designation in the Indian calendar. A lunar half-month is 15 days. Diwali as a new-moon day, marks the last day of a 15-day period. Diwali has emerged as one of the most famous Hindu festivals. An integral part of Diwali decorations, Rangoli is a colorful pattern drawn on the floor.

1. *Dhan-trayodashi* or *Dhan teras*: Dhan means "wealth" and Trayodashi means "13th day". Thus, as the name implies, this day falls on the 13th day of the first half of the lunar month. It is an auspicious day for shopping.
2. *Naraka Chaturdasi*: *Narak* means 'of a new era of Light and Knowledge'. *Chaturdasi* implies fourteenth day.
3. *Diwali*: the actual day of Diwali, is celebrated on the third day of the festival, when the moon completely wanes and total darkness sets in the night sky.
4. *Varsha-pratipada* or *Padwa*: Beginning of the New Year (Kartikadi Vikram). Pratipada means the first.
5. *Bhayiduj* (also Bhayyaduj, Bhaubeej or Bhayitika)—on this day, brothers and sisters meet to express their love and affection for each other.

The celebrations vary in different regions:

- In Southern India, *naraka chaturdashii* is the main day, with firecrackers at dawn.
- The main festival is on *Amavasya* evening with *Lakshmi Puja* which is followed by lighting of oil lamps around the house.

***Diwali in Sikhism:*** Every year, thousands of Sikhs and Hindus celebrate Diwali at the Golden Temple in Amritsar, India. Sikhs also celebrate Diwali to commemorate the laying of the foundation stone for the Golden Temple in 1577. It is also known as Bandi Chhorh Divas. The Mughal emperor Jahangir arrested the Sikh Guru Hargobind and imprisoned him in Gwalior. Later Jehangir relented and released the Guru. The

Guru asked that 52 rulers imprisoned with him should also be released. To the joy of the Sikhs the Guru returned to Amritsar on Diwali and it prompted the followers to celebrate the day with joy and happiness.

On Diwali the Sikhs illuminate their Gurdwaras and homesare with Deewé (earthen oil lamps) or candles. Early in the morning, Sikh pilgrims take a dip in the sacred tank while reciting Japji Sahib, and then pray at the Golden Temple. Circumambulation of the tank is done.

***Diwali in Jainism:*** Lord Mahavira, the last of the Jain Tirthankaras, attained Nirvana on this day at Pavapuri. According to Jain tradition the chief disciple of Mahavira, Ganadhar Gautam Swami also attained complete knowledge on this very day, thus making Diwali a really special occasion for the Jains to celebrate.

Diwali is first mentioned in Jain books as the date of the nirvana of Lord Mahavira. The oldest use of the word "Diwali/ Dipavali" occurs in Harivamsha-Purana written by Acharya Jinasena, composed in Shaka Samvat 705. The sample of text containing the word Diwali is below:

The way Jains celebrate Diwali is different in many respects. There is a note of asceticism in whatever the Jains do, and the celebration of Diwali is not an exception. The Jains celebrate Diwali during the month of Kartik for three days. During this period, among the Shvetambaras, devoted Jains observe fasting and chant the Uttaradhyayan Sutra, which contain the final pravachans of Lord Mahavira, and meditate upon him.

***Vira Nirvana Samvat:*** The Jain year starts with Pratipada following Diwali. Vira Nirvana Samvat 2532 starts with Diwali 2005. The Jain businessmen traditionally started their accounting year from Diwali.

***Diwali in Other Parts of the World:*** Diwali is celebrated in various parts of the world, in countries such as Britain, The Netherlands, Suriname, Canada, Guyana, Mauritius, Fiji, Japan, Indonesia, Malaysia, Myanmar, Nepal, Singapore, Sri Lanka, South Africa, Trinidad and Tobago, Thailand, United

Arab Emirates, Australia, much of Africa, and the United States. With more and more Indians now migrating to various parts of the world, the number of countries where Diwali is celebrated has been gradually increasing. While in some countries it is celebrated mainly by Indian expatriates, in others it has become part of the general local culture. In most of these countries Diwali is celebrated on the same lines as described in this article with some minor variations. Some important variations are worth mentioning.

In Malaysia, Diwali is known as "Hari Deepavali," and is celebrated during the seventh month of the Hindu solar calendar. It is a federal public holiday. In many respects it resembles the traditions followed in the Indian subcontinent.

In Nepal, Diwali is known as *Tihar* and celebrated during the October/November period. Here, though the festival is celebrated for five days, the traditions vary from those followed in India. On the first day, cows are given offerings, in appreciation of the food they have given and agricultural work they have performed. On the second day, dogs and all living animals are revered and offered special food. On the third day, celebrations follow the same pattern as in India, with lights and lamps and much social activity. On the fourth day Yama, the Lord of Death, is worshipped and appeased. On the fifth and final day, brothers and sisters meet and exchange pleasantries.

Diwali is celebrated in the Caribbean Islands as well. Especially in Trinidad and Tobago, Diwali is marked as a special occasion and celebrated with much fanfare. It is observed as a national holiday in this part of the world and some Ministers of the Government also take part in the celebrations publicly.

***Economics of Diwali:*** Diwali is an annual stimulus for the Indian economy. Indians purchase gold, gifts, decorations, crackers and household appliances during this festival. Companies offer huge discounts during the Diwali season to attract customers, which helps the economy and also helps the poor. It also helps the community in hunger since this festival shares it food. It also brings tourists to the country.

Since Diwali period also marks school holidays in most parts of India, many Bollywood movies are released during this period.

This Diwali which leads us into Truth and Light is celebrated on a nation-wide scale on Amavasya- the 15th day of the dark fortnight of the Hindu month of Ashwin (Aasho) (October / November) every year. It symbolises that age-old culture of our country which teaches us to vanquish ignorance that subdues humanity and to drive away darkness that engulfs the light of knowledge. Diwali, the festival of lights even to-day in this modern world projects the rich and glorious past of our country and teaches us to uphold the true values of life.

The word "Diwali" is the corruption of the Sanskrit word "Deepavali"—Deepa meaning light and Avali, meaning a row. It means a row of lights and indeed illumination forms its main attraction. Every home—lowly or mightly—the hut of the poor or the mansion of the rich—is alit with the orange glow of twinkling diyas-small earthen lamps—to welcome Lakshmi, Goddess of wealth and prosperity. Multi-coloured Rangoli designs, floral decorations and fireworks lend picturesness and grandeur to this festival which heralds joy, mirth and happiness in the ensuring year.

This festival is celebrated on a grand scale in almost all the regions of India and is looked upon mainly as the beginning of New Year. As such the blessings of Lakshmi, the celestial consort of Lord Vishnu are invoked with prayers. Even countries like Gkyena, Thailand, Trinidad, Siam and Malaya celebrate this festival but in their own ways. This Diwali festival, it is surmised dates back to that period when perhaps history was not written, and in its progress through centuries it lighted path of thousands to attain the ultimate good and complete ecstasy. Diwali or more aptly Deepavali is very enthusiastically celebrated for five continuous days and each day has its significance with a number of myths, legends and beliefs.

The *First day* is called *Dhanteras* or *Dhantrayodashi* which falls on the thirteenth day of the month of Ashwin. The word "Dhan" means wealth. As such this day of the five-day Diwali festival has a great importance for the rich mercantile community of Western India. Houses and Business premises are renovated and decorated. Entrances are made colourful with lovely traditional motifs of Rangoli designs to welcome the Goddess of wealth and prosperity. To indicate her long-awaited arrival, small footprints are drawn with rice flour and vermilion powder all over the houses.

Lamps are kept burning all through the nights. Believing this day to be auspicious women purchase some gold or silver or at least one or two new utensils. "Lakshmi-Puja" is performed in the evenings when tiny diyas of clay are lighted to drive away the shadows of evil spirits. "Bhajans"-devotional songs-in praise of Goddess Laxmi are sung and "Naivedya" of traditional sweets is offered to the Goddess. There is a peculiar custom in Maharashtra to lightly pound dry coriander seeds with jaggery and offer as Naivedya.

In villages cattles are adorned and worshipped by farmers as they form the main source of their income. In south cows are offered special veneration as they are supposed to be the incarnation of Goddess Lakshmi and therefore they are adorned and worshipped on this day.

A very interesting story about this day is of the sixteen year old son of King Hima. As per his horoscope he was doomed to die by a snake-bite on the fourth day of his marriage. On that particular fourth day of his marriage his young wife did not allow him to sleep. She laid all the ornaments and lots of gold and silver coins in a big heap at the entrance of her husband's boudoir and lighted innumerable lamps all over the place. And she went on telling stories and singing songs. When Yam, the god of Death arrived there in the guise of a Serpent his eyes got blinded by that dazzle of those brilliant lights and he could not enter the Prince's chamber. So he climbed on top of the heap of the ornaments and coins and sat there whole night listening to the melodious songs. In the morning he quietly went away. Thus the young wife saved her husband from the clutches of death. Since then this day of Dhanteras came to be known as the day of "YAMADEEPDAAN" and lamps are kept burning throughout the night in reverential adoration to Yam, the god of Death.

The *Second day* is called *Narka-chaturdashi* or *Choti Diwali* which falls on the fourteenth day of the month of Ashwin. The story goes that the demon king Narakasur ruler of Pragjyotishpur ( a province to the South of Nepal) after defeating Lord Indra had snatched away the magnificent earrings of Aditi, the Mother Goddess and imprisoned sixteen thousand daughters of the gods and saints in his harem. On the day previous to Narakachaturdashi, Lord Krishna killed the demon and liberated the imprisoned damsels and also recovered those precious earrings of Aditi.

As a symbol of that victory Lord Krishna smeared his forehead with the demon king's blood. Krishna returned home in the very early morning of the Narakachaturdashi day. The womenfolk massaged scented oil to his body and gave him a good bath to wash away the filth from his body. Since then the custom of taking bath before sunrise on this day has become a traditional practice specially in Maharashtra.

In South India that victory of the divine over the mundane is celebrated in a very peculiar way. People wake up before sunrise prepare blood by mixing Kumkum in oil and after breaking a bitter fruit that represents the head of the demon King that was smashed by Krishna, apply that mixture on their foreheads. Then they have an oil bath using sandalwood paste.

In Maharashtra also, traditional early baths with oil and "Uptan" (paste) of gram flour and fragrant powders are a must. All through the ritual of baths, deafening sounds of crackers and fireworks are there in order that the children enjoy bathing. Afterwards steamed vermiceli with milk and sugar or puffed rice with curd is served.

Another legend is about King Bali of the nether world mighty power had become a threat to the gods. In order to curb his powers Lord Vishnu in the guise of a Batu Waman- a small boy- visited him and begged him to give him only that much land which he could cover with his three steps. Known for his philanthropy King Bali proudly granted him his wish. That very moment that small boy transformed himself into the all-powerful Lord Vishnu. With his first step Lord Vishnu covered the entire heaven and with the second step the earth and asked Bali where to keep his third step. Bali offered his head. Putting his foot on his head Vishnu pushed him down to the underworld. At the same time for his generosity Lord Vishnu gave him the lamp of knowledge and allowed him to return to earth once a year to light millions of lamps to dispel the darkness and ignorance and spread the radiance of love and wisdom.

Diwali is a five day Hindu festival which occurs on the fifteenth day of Kartika. Diwali means "rows of lighted lamps" and the celebration is often referred to as the Festival of Lights. During this time, homes are thoroughly cleaned and windows are opened to welcome Laksmi, goddess of wealth. Candles and lamps are lit as a greeting to Laksmi. Gifts are exchanged and festive meals are prepared during Diwali. The celebration means as much to Hindus as Christmas does to Christians.

Because there are many regions in India, there are many manifestations of the Diwali festival. In at least one area, the festival begins with Dhanteras, a day set aside to worship Laksmi. In the Indian culture, wealth is not viewed as a corruptive power. Instead, a wealthy person is considered to have been rewarded for good deeds of a past life.

The *Third day* of the festival of Diwali is the most important day of *Lakshmi-puja* which is entirely devoted to the propitiation of Goddess Lakshmi. This day is also known by the name of "Chopada-puja". On this very day sun enters his second course and passes Libra which is represented by the balance or scale. Hence, this design of Libra is believed to have suggested the balancing of account books and their closing. Despite the fact that this day falls on an amavasya day it is regarded as the most auspicious.

The day of Lakshmi-Puja falls on the dark night of Amavasya. The strains of joyous sounds of bells and drums float from the temples as man is invoking Goddess Lakshmi in a wondrous holy "pouring-in" of his heart. All of a sudden that impenetrable darkness is pierced by innumerable rays of light for just a moment and the next moment a blaze of light descends down to earth from heaven as golden-footed Deep-Lakshmi alights on earth in all her celestial glory amidst chantings of Vedic hymns. A living luminance of Universal Motherhood envelopes the entire world in that blessed moment of fulfillment of a long-awaited dream of the mortal. A sublime light of knowledge dawns upon humanity and devotion of man finally conquers ignorance.

This self enlightenment is expressed through the twinkling lamps that illuminate the palaces of the wealthy as well as the lowly abodes of the poor. It is believed that on this day Lakshmi walks through the green fields and loiters through the bye-lanes and showers her blessings on man for plenty and prosperity. When the sun sets in the evening and ceremonial worship is finished all the home-made sweets are offered to the goddess as "Naivedya" and distributed as "Prasad". Feasts are arranged and gifts are exchanged on this day gaily dressed men, women and children go to temples and fairs, visit friends and relatives. Everything is gay, gold and glitter!

One of the most curious customs which characterises this festival of Diwali is the indulgence of gambling, specially on a large scale in North India. It is believed that goddess Parvati played dice with her husband, Lord Shiv on this day and she decreed that whosoever gambled on Diwali night would prosper throughout the ensuring year. This tradition of playing cards-flush and rummy with stakes on this particular day continues even to-day.

On this auspicious day Lord Shri Krishna around whom revolved the entire story of our great epic Mahabharat and the philosopher, who preached Karmayog through his Geeta to Arjun on the battlefield of Kurukshetra, discarded his body.

Bhagwan, Mahavir, the Jain prophet also attained "Nirvan" on this day.

Swami Ramtirth, the beloved "Ram Badshah" of millions of Indians was not only born on this day and took "Sanyas" but also took "Samadhi" on this day.

Swami Dayanand Saraswati, founder of Arya Samaj in 1875 in Mumbai, with his superb yogic powers greed his soul from his body and mingled with divinity on this auspicious day of Diwali.

We kindle innumerable lights on this day to immortalise the sacred memories of those great men who lived to brighten the lives of millions of their fellow beings.

One very interesting story about this Diwali day is from Kathopanishad of a small boy called Nichiketa who believed that Yam, the god of Death was as black as the dark night of amavasya. But when he met Yam in person he was puzzled seeing Yam's calm countenance and dignified stature. Yam explained to Nichiketa on this Diwali day of amavasya that by only passing through the darkness of death, man sees the light of highest wisdom and then only his soul can escape from the bondage of his mortal frame to mingle with the Supreme Power without whose will not an at ton moves in the world. And then Nichiketa realised the importance of worldly life and significance of death. Nichiketa's all doubts were set at rest and he whole-heartedly participated in Diwali celebrations.

The *Fourth day* is *Padwa* or *Varshapratipada* which marks the coronation of King Vikramaditya and Vikaram-Samvat was started from this Padwa day. Govardhan-Puja is also performed in the North on this day. As per Vishnu-Puran the people of Gokul used to celebrate a festival in honour of Lord Indira and worshipped him after the end of every monsoon season but one particular year the young Krishna stopped them from offering prayers to Lord Indra who in terrific anger sent a deluge to submerge Gokul. But Krishna saved his Gokul by lifting up the Govardhan mountain and holding it over the people as an umbrella.

Govardhan is a small hillock in Braj, near Mathura and on this day of Diwali people of Punjab, Haryana, Uttar Pradesh and Bihar build cowdung, hillocks, decorate them with flowers and then worship them.

This day is also observed as Annakoot meaning mountain of food. In temples specially in Mathura and Nathadwara, the deities are given milkbath, dressed in shining attires with ornaments of dazzling diamonds, pearls, rubies and other precious stones. After the prayers and traditional worship innumerable varieties of delicious sweets are ceremoniously raised in the form of a mountain before the deities as "Bhog" and then the devotees approach the Mountain of Food and take Prasad from it.

Goddess Lakshmi is worshipped in every Hindu household and her blessings sought for success and happiness. This day is looked upon as the most auspicious day to start any new venture. In many Hindu homes it is a custom for the wife to put the red tilak on the forehead of her husband, garland him and do his "Aarathi" with a prayer for his long life. In appreciation of all the tender care that the wife showers on him, the husband gives her a costly gift. This Gudi Padwa is symbolic of love and devotion between the wife and husband. On this day newly-married daughters with their husbands are invited for special meals and given presents. In olden days brothers went to fetch their sisters from their in-laws home for this important day.

The *Fifth and final day* of Diwali Festival is known by the name of "*Bhayya-duj*" in the Hindi-speaking belt "*Bhav-bij*" in the Marathi-speaking communities and in Nepal by the name of "*Bhai-tika*". As the legend goes Yamraj, the God of Death visited his sister Yami on this particular day. She put the auspicious tilak on his forehead, garlanded him and led him with special dishes and both of them together ate the sweets, talked and enjoyed themselves to their heart's content, while parting Yamraj gave her a special gift as a token of his love and in return Yami also gave him a lovely gift which she had made with her own hands. That day Yamraj announced that anyone who receives tilak from his sister will never be thrown. That is why this day of Bhayyaduj is also known by the name of "*Yama-dwitiya*" Since then this day is being observed as a symbol of love between sisters and brothers. It became also imperative for the brother to go to his sister's house to celebrate Bhayyaduj.

In today's world when pressing everyday problems are teaming as under all the tender words of personal relationships, the celebrating of this day has its own importance in continuing to maintain the love between brothers and sisters for it is the day of food-sharing, gift-giving and reaching out to the inner most depths of the hearts.

Diwali on the whole has always been the festival with more social than religious connotations. It is a personal, people-oriented festival when enmities are forgotten, families and friends meet, enjoy and establish a word of closeness.

As a festival of light and beauty it encourages artistic expressions through home-decorations stage-plays, elocution competitions singing and dancing programmes, making gift items and making delectable sweets thereby discovering new talents of younger people. As a result innumerable communities with varying cultures and customs mingle together to make Diwali celebrations a very happy occasion for all.

***History of Diwali:*** India is a land of festivals. Diwali, the Festival of Lights, is celebrated with fervor and gaiety. The festival is celebrated by young and old, rich and poor, throughout the country to dispel darkness and light up their lives. The festival symbolizes unity in diversity as every state celebrates it in its own special way. The celebration of the four-day festival commences on Aswayuja Bahula Chaturdasi and concludes on Kartika Shudda Vijiya.

The first day of the festival Naraka Chaturdasi marks the vanquishing of the demon Naraka by Lord Krishna and his wife Satyabhama. 'Puranas' have it that Naraka, son of Bhudevi, acquired immense power from a blessing given by Lord Brahma after a severe penance. He soon unleashed a reign of terror in the kingdom of Kamarupa, harassing celestial beings with his invincible might. Unable to bear the tyranny of the demon, the celestial beings pleaded with Lord Krishna to save them from his torture. But Naraka could not be easily killed as he had a boon that he would face death only at the hands of his mother Bhudevi. So, Krishna asks his wife Satyabhama, the reincarnation of Bhudevi, to bc his charioteer in the battle with Naraka. When Krishna feigns unconsciousness after being hit by an arrow of Naraka, Satyabhama takes the bow and aims the arrow at Naraka, killing him instantly. Later Lord Krishna reminds her of the boon she had sought as Bhudevi.

The slaying of Naraka by Sathyabhama could also be taken to interpret that parents should not hesitate to punish their children when they stray on to the wrong path. The message of Naraka Chaturdasi is that the good of the society should always prevail over one's own personal bonds. The second day is Amavasya when Lakshmi puja is performed. It is believed that on this day Goddess Lakshmi would be in her benevolent mood and fulfill the wishes of her devotees. One version says that it was on this day that Goddess Lakshmi emerged from Kshira Sagara (Ocean of Milk) when the Gods and demons were churning the sagara (ocean) for nectar (Amrit) The other version is that when Lord Vishnu in the guise of Vamana, sought three feet of land from the generous demon king Bali, the latter had to surrender his head as Vamana had conquered the earth and the sky in two strides. Lord Vishnu banishes Bali into the Pathala Loka (netherland) by keeping his third stride on Bali's head. Later, pleased by his generosity, Lord Vishnu grants him a boon and he in turn requests the Lord to guard his palace at Pathala Loka. Meanwhile, the Goddess is unable to bear the separation and her grief affects the functioning of the entire universe. Brahma and Lord Shiva offer themselves as guards and plead with Bali to relieve Vishnu. So, on the Amavasya day, Lord Vishnu returns to his abode and Goddess Lakshmi is delighted. It is believed that those who worship Goddess Lakshmi on this day would be bestowed with all the riches.

The third day is "Kartika Shudda Padyami." On this day Bali would come out of Pathala Loka and rule Bhuloka as per the boon given by Lord Vishnu. Hence, it is also known as "Bali Padyami". The fourth day is referred to as "Yama Dvitiya." On this day, sisters invite their brothers to their homes. However, in the northern part of India it is celebrated as the return of Ram along with Sita and Lakshman from his 14 years of exile after killing Ravana.

To commemorate his return to Ayodhya, his subjects illuminated the kingdom and burst crackers. For the Gujaratis, Marwaris and other business community Diwali marks the worship of Goddess Lakshmi and also the beginning of the new financial year. For Bengalis, it is the time to worship Goddess Kali or Durga. The Goddess Durga continued her "Vilaya Tandava" even after killing demon Mahishasura.

***Significance of Diwali:*** Deepavali is a festival where people from all age groups participate. They give expression to their happiness by lighting earthen 'diyas' (lamps), decorating the houses, bursting firecrackers and inviting near and dear ones to their households for partaking in a sumptuous feast. The lighting of lamps is a way of paying obeisance to god for attainment of health, wealth, knowledge, peace, valor and fame. It is one time in the whole year that children volunteer to leave their beds long before the day begins.

In fact, the traditional oil bath at 3 a.m, is the only chore that stands between them and the pre-dawn adventures. They emerge, scrubbed clean to get into their festive attire, and light up little oil lamps, candles and scented sticks(agarbathis), the wherewithal for setting alight crackers and sparklers. Who shall set off the first chain of crackers that go boom, bang and vroom? and who is the owner of the 10-minute 'banger' that steals the thunder from your little chain of needle-sized crackers? Does the boy next door have more crackers than me? Competition is stiff, and even the little girl in silk frocks and their finery are watching out for the best sparklers and flowerpots, the rockets and Vishnuchakras, which light-up the night sky like a thousand stars. Grown-ups are the soul of generosity. Festive bonhomie abounds.

Diwali is the one Hindu festival that unites the whole of India. It is traditionally known as the "festival of lights", for the common practice is to light small oil lamps (called diyas) and place them around the home, in courtyards, gardens, verandahs, on the walls built around the home and also on the roof tops. In cities, especially, candles are substituted for diyas; and among the riches, candles are made to substitute for fashionable and classy neon lights.

The celebration of the festival is customarily accompanied by the exchange of sweets and the explosion of fireworks. Diwali is an occasion for cheerfulness and togetherness. This is an occasion for young and the old, men and women, rich and poor—for everyone to celebrate. Irrespective of their religious and economic background, the festival is celebrated throughout the country to ward off the darkness and welcome light into life as light is always associated with hope for the future Diwali is celebrated 20 days after Dussera, on Amavasya—the 15th day of the dark fortnight of the Hindu month of Ashwin (Aasho) (Oct/ Nov) every year. Diwali celebrates Rama's homecoming, that is his return to Ayodhya after the defeat of Ravana and his coronation as king.

The legend related to the festival is that King Dashratha had three wives namely Kaushalaya, Keykayee and Sumitra and four sons Rama, Bharat, Laxmana and Shatrughan. Rama was the son of Queen Kaushalaya and Bharat was the son of Queen Keykayee. Keykayee wanted Bharat to be the next King of Ayodhya, while King Dasharatha wanted Rama, his eldest son to be the King. But Keykayee made full use of the two wishes King Dasharatha had promised. Keykayee asked for sending Rama to exile for the period of fourteen years and to crown Bharat as the king, though Bharat refused to accept the kingship. During that time Lord Rama fought and won fierce battle in the southern part of the Indian subcontinent, killing the king of Demons, Ravana who had forcibly taken away his wife Sita. Diwali marks his victorious return to his kingdom along with Hanuman, the Vanar who helped him in achieving success.

The legend states it took 20 days for Rama to return to his kingdom after defeating Ravana. As with other Indian festivals, Diwali signifies many different things to people across the country. In north India, Diwali celebrates Rama's homecoming from fourteen years of exile that is his return to Ayodhya after defeating Ravana and his coronation as king; in Gujarat, the festival is celebrated to honor goddess Lakshmi, the goddess of wealth; and in Bengal, it is related with the goddess Kali.

But everywhere, it is celebrated with the same sprit and signifies the renewal of life. Diwali is one of the most celebrated festivities in the Indian culture. Uniting all members of the community, young and old, rich or poor, the lighting of the lamps represents a way of paying obeisance to God for attainment of health, wealth, knowledge, peace and valoured fame People give expressions to their happiness by lighting earthen diyas and decorating the houses to welcome Lakshmi-the Goddess of wealth and prosperity, bursting fire crackers and inviting the near and dear ones to their households for partaking in the luxurious feast. The lighting of lamps is a way of paying obeisance to God for attainment of health, wealth, knowledge, peace and fame and it also signifies goodness. It is also marked as the beginning of the Hindu New Year and as a brand new beginning for all. Diwali is celebrated for five days, each day having it's own significance, rituals and myths

The Jain communities of India celebrate Diwali as a New Year's Day. Lord Mahavira, the founder of Jainism, attained his Nirvana on the day of Diwali.

Sikhs celebrate Diwali to express joy at the return of the sixth Guru to Amritsar in 1620; Emperor Jahangir had imprisoned him along with 52 Hindu kings. The Guru was granted freedom but refused to leave until the kings were also released.

Diwali is by far the most enthusiastically enjoyed festival in India. People of different nationalities, races, religions and backgrounds come together to share their joys generating a feeling of universal brotherhood and inter-religious harmony.

Diwali, literally a garland of lamps, is an apt description of this festival of lights. Tradition maintains that lamps are lit to keep alive the memory of Prince *Rama's* return to Ayodhya after conquering the tyrant *Ravana*, the ruler of Lanka, who had abducted his consort *Sita*. The heroic deeds of Rama are recounted in the Hindu epic *Ramayan* and Diwali symbolizes the victory of virtue over vice. Rama, we are told had gladly accepted an exile in the forest to keep his step-mother happy and save his father from embarassment. He is considered the epitome of a dutiful son and a responsible ruler. Another myth traces the origins of the festival to the annual 'inspection tours' of Lakshmi, the Hindu goddess of wealth and prosperity. The faithful believe that on this day Lakshmi goes around visiting her devotees and sets up residence in the house she finds best spruced up and most hospitable. Diwali is an occasion for spring cleaning, painting the walls, decorating the floor with attractive designs wrought in coloured powder or paste made with rice.

The ritual traditionally associated with Diwali is gambling. Friends get together to indulge in games of chance, dice or cards. The 'addicts' seek legitimacy for their unusual pastime by referring to the celestial game of dice played by the great lord *Shiva* with his companion *Parvati*—a scene superbly sculpted at *Kailash* temple, *Ellora*. Others rationalise that this is just to remind oneself of the fickleness of lady luck and to inculcate a sense of balance in our pursuit of material success.

The children can be seen bursting fire crackers and lighting candles or earthen lamps. This is a time of generously exchanging sweets with neighbours and friends. Puffed rice and sugar candy are the favourite fares.

## Holi

The festival of Holi is celebrated on the day after the full moon in early March every year. Originally a festival to celebrate good harvests and fertility of the land, Holi is now a symbolic commemoration of a legend from Hindu Mythology. The story centres around an arrogant king who resents his son Prahlada worshipping Lord Vishnu. He attempts to kill his son but fails each time. Finally, the king's sister Holika who is said to be immune to burning, sits with the boy in a huge fire. However, the prince Prahlada emerges unscathed, while his aunt burns to death. Holi commemorates this event from mythology, and huge bonfires are burnt on the eve of Holi as its symbolic representation.

This exuberant festival is also associated with the immortal love of Krishna and Radha, and hence, Holi is spread over 16 days in Vrindavan as well as Mathura-the two cities with which Lord Krishna shared a deep affiliation. Apart from the usual fun with coloured powder and water, Holi is marked by vibrant processions which are accompanied by folk songs, dances and a general sense of abandoned vitality. Today Holi is an excuse for Indians to shed inhibitions and caste differences for a day of spring fever and Big Fun. Teenagers spend the day flirting and misbehaving in the streets, adults extend the hand of peace, and everyone chases everyone else around, throwing brightly colored powder (gulal) and water over each other.

The festival's preamble begins on the night of the full moon. Bonfires are lit on street corners to cleanse the air of evil spirits and bad vibes, and to symbolize the destruction of the wicked Holika, for whom the festival was named. The following morning, the streets fill with people running, shouting, giggling and splashing. Marijuana-based bhang and thandai add to the uninhibited atmosphere.

Promptly at noon, the craziness comes to an end and everyone heads to either the river or the bathtub, then inside to relax the day away and partake of candies. In the afternoon an exhausted and contented silence falls over India. Although

Holi is observed all over the north, it's celebrated with special joy and zest at Mathura, Vrindavan, Nandgaon, and Barsnar. These towns once housed the divine Krishna.

Each area celebrates Holi differently; the Bhil tribesmen of western Madhya Pradesh, who've retained many of their pre-Hindu customs, celebrate Holi in a unique way. In rural Maharashtra State, where the festival is known as *Rangapanchami* it is celebrated with dancing and singing. In the towns of Rajasthan — especially Jaisalmer — the music's great, and clouds of pink, green, and turquoise powder fill the air. The grounds of Jaisalmer's Mandir Palace are turned into chaos, with dances, folk songs, and colored-powder confusion.

Holi or Holika, also called holikotsava, is an extremely popular festival observed throughout the country (India). It is especially marked by unmixed gaiety and frolics and is common to all sections of the people.

This festival is very ancient. Known originally as *'Holika'* it has been mentioned in very early religious works such as Jaimini's Purvamimamsa-sutras and Kathaka-grhya-sutras. It must have therefore existed several centuries before Christ. It was at first actually a special rite performed by married women for the happiness and well-being of their families and the full moon (Raka) was the deity worshipped by them.

There are two ways of reckoning a lunar month: *Purnimanta* and *Amanta*. In the former, the first day starts after the full moon; and in the latter, after the new moon. Though the latter reckoning is more common now, the former was very much in vogue in the earlier days.

According to this purnimanta reckoning, Phalguna purnima was the last day of the year and the new year heralding the Vasanta-ritu (with spring starting from next day). Thus the full moon festival of Holika gradually became a festival of merrymaking, announcing the commencement of the spring season. This perhaps explains the other names of this festival: Vasanta-Mahotsava and Kama-Mahotsava.

According to the stories in the Puranas and various local legends, this day is important for three reasons.

- It was on this day that Lord Siva opened his third eye and reduced Kamadeva (the god of love, Cupid or Eros) to ashes.
- It was on this day that Holika, the sister of the demon king Hiranyakasyapu, who tried to kill the child devotee Prahlad by taking him on her lap and sitting on a pyre of wood which was set ablaze. Holika was burnt to ashes while Prahlad remained unscathed!
- It was again on this day that an ogress called Dhundhi, who was troubling the children in the kingdom of Prthu (or Raghu) was made to run away for life, by the shouts and pranks of the mischievous boys. Though she had secured several boons that made her almost invincible, this-noise, shouts, abuses and pranks of boys—was a chink in her armour due to a curse of Lord Siva. The day itself came to be called 'Adada' or 'Holika' since then.

There are practically no religious observances for this day like fasting or worship. Generally a log of wood will be kept in a prominent public place on the Vasantapanchami day (Magha Sukla Panchami), almost 40 days before the Holi Festival. An image of Holika with child Prahlada in her lap is also kept on the log. Holika's image is made of combustible materials whereas Prahlada's image is made of non-combustible ones. People go on throwing twigs of trees and any combustible material they can spare, on to that log which gradually grows into a sizable heap. On the night of Phalguna Purnima, it is set alight in a simple ceremony with the Raksoghna Mantras of the Rgveda (4.4.1-15; 10.87.1-25 and so on) being sometimes chanted to ward off all evil spirits. (Coconuts and coins are thrown into this bonfire).The next morning the ashes from the bonfire are collected as prasad (consecrated material) and smeared on the limbs of the body. Singed coconuts, if any are also collected and eaten.

In some houses the image of Kamadeva is kept in the yard and a simple worship is offered. A mixture of mango blossoms and sandalwood paste is partaken as the prasad.

The day- Phalgun krsna pratipad—is observed as a day of revelry especially by throwing on one another gulal or coloured water or perfumed coloured powder. Throwing of mud or earth dust was prevalent in the earlier days also, but among the low culture groups.

Instead of the gay and frenzied celebrations that are witnessed elsewhere in the country, Bengal observes this festival in a quiet and dignified manner as Dolapurnima or Dolayatra (the festival of the swing). The festival, said to have been initiated by the king Indradyumna in Vrndavana, is spread over 3 or 5 days, starting from the sukla Chaturdasi of Phalguna. A celebration in honour of Agni and worship of Govinda (Krsna) in image on a swing are the important features. The fire kindled on the first day is to be preserved till the last day. The swing is to be rocked 21 times at the end of the festival.

The day is also celebrated as the birthday of Sri Krsna Chaitanya (A.D. 1486-1533), mostly in Bengal, as also in Puri (Orissa), Mathura and Vrndavan (in Uttar Pradesh).

*Holi* or *Phagwah* (Bhojpuri), is an annual and popular Hindu spring festival. It takes place over two days in the latter part of March or early April. As per the Hindu calendar, it falls on the Phalgun Purnima (or Pooranmashi, Full Moon). It is also called the Festival of Colours.

On the first day, a bonfire is lit at night to signify burning Holika. On the second day, known as *Dhulandi*, people go around until afternoon throwing coloured powder and water at each other, although the powder stings the eyes. A special drink called 'thandai' or bhang is also consumed sometimes, which actually contains small amounts of marijuana (*Cannabis sativa*). People invite each other to their houses for feasts and celebrations later in the evening. *Rangapanchami* occurs a few days later on a Panchami (fifth day of the full moon), marking the end of festivities involving colours.

This festival occurs at the onset of spring. This period, during which the weather changes, is prone to cause viral fever and cold. Thus, the playful throwing of the coloured powders has a medicinal significance as the coloured powders are made of Neem, Kumkum, Haldi, Bilva, and other medicinal herbs prescribed by Ayurvedic doctors.

Amongst India's innumerable festivals, Holi ranks as the most colourful. It celebrates the arrival of spring and death of demoness Holika, it is a celebration of joy and hope. Holi provides a refreshing respite from the mundane norms as people from all walks of life enjoy themselves. In a tight knit community, it also provided a good excuse for letting off some steam and settling old scores, without causing physical injury.

Holi continues to be celebrated with great vigour through out India. Countless Hindi films have brought the vibrant colours of the festival to the screen. Indians all over the world eagerly await the Festival of Colours, as bonfires are lit to banish the cold dark nights of winter and usher in warmer spring. Dhuleti, day after Holi, is the actual festival of colours, when everything in sight is covered in a riot of colours.

Twin towns of Nandagow (where Lord Krishna grew up) and Barsana (where Shri Radha grew up), near Mathura, are the epicentre of the celebrations. Lord Krishna, while growing up in Vraj, popularised the festival with his ingenious pranks. Gopies of Vraj responded with equal enthusiasm and the festivities have continued ever since. Role reversal, feminism etc. are accepted customs for the duration of the festival! Men and women of Vraj clash in a colourful display of battle of the sexes.

Celebrations start a week earlier than rest of India. Men of Nandagow raid Barsana with hopes of raising their flag over Shri Radhikaji's temple. They receive a thunderous welcome as the women of Barsana greet them with long wooden sticks. The men are soundly beaten as they attempt to rush through town to reach the relative safety of Shri Radhikaji's temple. Men are well padded as they are not allowed to retaliate. In this mock battle the men try their best not to be captured. Unlucky captives can be forcefully lead away, thrashed and dressed in female attire before being made to dance!

Rush through Barsana is far more lethal than running with the bulls in Spain, at least you don't have to marry them one day! Famous poets like Surdas, Nand-das, Kumbhan-das and others, have written beautifully as to how Lord Krishna was similarly received and forced to wear a sari, forced to wear makeup and made to dance before being released by the gopies of Vraj.

The next day, men of Barsana reciprocate by invading Nandagow. Clouds of pink and white powder mark the frenzy of activity taking place in it's narrow streets. A naturally occurring orange-red dye, Kesudo, is used to drench all participants. Today, the women of Nadagow beat the invaders from Barsana. It is a colourful site. In the interest of tourisum and safety, the state tourist board has set up excellent vantage points for the public. A large open ground, on the outskirts of the town is specially set aside for the most magnificent display of the festivities.

The next day, the temples in Vrindavan celebrate the festival with great guesto. The renowned temple of Bakai-Bihari, the beloved lord of the 15th century saint Haridas, is at the centre of the festivities. Clouds of pink and white descend upon the pilgrims, as the Lord of Vrindavan plays Holi with all his beloved visitors.

The festival moves on to other parts of Vraj. Soon enough, it is Dhulati and entire India celebrates the joys of spring as the "festival of colour".

Gulal-Kund in Vraj is a beautiful little lake, set in a delightful groves near the mountain Goverdhan, in the Mathura district. Here the festival is commemorated on a more regular basis. Pilgrims who visit the holy land of Vraj, can see the reenactments of Holi throughout the year at this lake. Local boys, acting in the Krishna-Lila drama troupes reenact the scenes of holi for the pilgrims.

Royal courts all over North India refined the festival in to an art form of its own. Rajput warriors of the Rajasthani courts used to show off their equestrian skills during the festival. Rajput men would ride their steeds through the white and pink clouds of colour, throwing colour powders on each other. Even the members of the royal families were not immune from being drenched by colour. The entire court would be drenched in saffron water and an orange-red dye of the "kasuda" flowers.

Pushti-Marga temples, spread throughout North and Western States of India, celebrate the festival in a way reminiscent of rajput courts. The Deity, and the laity, are liberally sprinkled with perfumes, saffron water, kesudo, and covered in sandalwood aswell as the white and pink powder, abil and gulal. Joyous celebration is accompanied by classical music, poetry and folk songs appropriate for the occasion. Deity's white clothes' are soon transformed into a mass of colour as gold and silver syringes spray colourful water on all participants.

The celebrations officially usher in the pleasant season of love, spring. In the Pushti-Marga temples, the festivities last for almost a month. Beginning on the day of Vasant-Panchami, the festivals last till the day after Holi. This helps prolong the season of joy.

*The weather is most pleasant and the spring flowers are in full bloom.*

*Skies are clear, days are warm and nights are pleasantly cool.*

*What more could you ask for,*

*except to be covered in the "ranga" (colour) of your beloved!*

After *dakshayAga,* shakti took the form of the daughter of the mountain king *himavAn* called *Arvati.* From the early childhood she was devoted to Lord shiva and started penance for getting married to the God Shiva. Lord Shiva was however staying as *dakshinamurthi* making the sages *sanaka, sanandana, sanatana, sanatkumara* realize the Ultimate Truth.

In the meanwhile the celestials were put to deep hardship by the demons lead by *Surapadma, simhamukha and tharaka*. This was a curse on them for attending the dakshayaga. Surapadma had the boon that none other than the son who is the power of shiva could kill him. As Lord shiva was teaching the path of Bliss to the sages and Parvati doing penance, the celestials were desparate for the solution which is the son of Lord Shiva. Out of the desperation, they lost the sense of what they were doing and sent forcibly the *kama* (cupid) to induce lust in God for Arvati.

Kama, whose arrows never failed elsewhere, was sure that he was getting into trouble. However out of pressure from the celestials (devas) he went to the abode of Lord Shiva and shot an arrow that would kindle lust on the God. kama has been vested with the power by Lord Shiva to induce lust in all creatures—lives in order to maintain the reproduction as a system, so he was successful. Will that logic work on the One Who is beyond all these principles, the One Who has no pleasure out of external things? The arrow of kama failed to induce lust in God. As the Lord opened slightly the third-eye, kama who shot the arrow was burnt down to a heap of ash. Unperturbed the Lord continued the explanation to the sages!

This incident of burning off kama is called *kamadahana* or Holi. The posture of God burning kAma is called *kama dahana murthi* and is one of the 25 *maheshvara murthis*.

As the lust was won over by the Eternal Bliss of Lord Shiva the kamadahana or Holi festival is celebrated as an event associating with the Bliss of God. The Holi bonfire is in commemoration of this event. The ash of kama's body settled over the Lord shiva. (The kama dahana murthi dhyana shloa states, *bhasma uddhulita vigraham*). So following kamadahana during Holi, people put the powders on themselves and others remembering this victory over lust. To this day, people offer sandalwood paste to Kamadeva to relieve from his stinging burns and mango blossoms that he loved on Holi.

The celebration of Holi is very ancient in its origin. And by its very origin, it celebrates an ultimate triumph of the 'good' over the 'evil'. While, a feast of colors associated with the Holi, is the face of this celebration, the original reason of celebrating Holi, lies in its soul. And this gives us the 'why' of this ancient festival.

Literally "Holi" signifies "burning" in Indian language. But, how it came to be associated with 'burning', is a story. The reference is found only in ancinet Indian mythology. And It is the legend of Hiranyakashipu, to whom the celebration of Holi is associated.

Way back in the pre-Christian era, there lived a demon king named Hiranyakashipu in ancient India. He wanted to avenge the death of his younger brother. The brother, also a demon, had been killed by Lord Vishnu, one of the supreme trio, monitoring the life and death in the universe, (according to the Hindu belief). To take on Vishnu, the tyrant king wanted to become the king of the heaven, earth and the underworld. He performed severe penance and prayer for many years to gain enough power. Finally he was granted a boon. Powered by the boon, Hiranyakshipu thought he had become invincible. Arrogant, he ordered all in his kingdom to worship him, instead of God. The demon king, however, had a very young son, named Prahalad.

He was an ardent devotee of Vishnu. Despite his father's order, Prahalad continued to pray to Vishnu. So the demon king wanted to kill his son. He asked the favor of his sister Holika who, because of a boon, was immune to fire.

They planned that Prahalad would be burned to death. A pyre was lit up and Holika sat on it, clutching Prahalad. Yet, at the end Prahalad emerged unscathed by the fire, And Holika, the demon, was burned to ashes. The earnest devotion and complete submission to Lord Vishnu saved young Prahlad. Thus was the triumph of Prahlad, the representative of good spirits. And the defeat of Holika, the representative of evil. Later, even the demon king Hiranyakashipu was killed by Lord

Vishnu. But that is quite a different story. It is from Holika, that the Holi originated.

This legend is relived even today on the Holi-eve when the pyre is relit in the form of bonfires. Even today, people celebrate this occasion. Huge bonfires are lit up every year on the eve of the full moon night of the Holi to burn the spirit of the evils. Hence the story associated with the soul of the celebration.

According to the Hindu belief, Krishna was a reincarnation of lord Vishnu himself.

It was Krishna, or, Krishn, the king of the ancient city of Dwarka, who popularised the tradition of Holi. The origin of the colorful and frolicking tone of Holi lies in the boyhood of Krishna. It all came up as part of his pranks, he used to play with his boyhood mates of Gokul and Vrindavan. Situated in north India, these are the places where he spent his childhood.

It was at this time of year, Krishna used to play pranks by drenching the village girls, with water and colors. At first it offended the girls. But they were so fond of this mischievous boy that soon their anger melted away.

For other boys to join in, making it a popular sport in the village. Later, as Krishna grew up, the play assumed a new dimension. It added more colors to Krishna's legendary love life. The legend of Krishna's courtship with Radha, and playing pranks with the 'Gopi's. The girls in the 'dairy' village of Gokul were mostly milkmaids, and, hence locally known as the Gopis. The same tradition has transpired through the ages, turning it into a community festival of the masses. As time kept flowing, the culture spread roots to other regions of the country. The Holi play of Krishna is documented in hundreds of ancient paintings, murals, sculptures and scriptures found across the subcontinent.

The purana continues that later the celestials realized their foolishness in trying to alter the course of God by force and smartness. They begged to God for pardon and pleaded to revive kAma. They further begged that the Lord accept Arvati as the consort and put an end to their sufferings from the demons. The highly benevalent Lord accepted their prayers and married Arvati. On the day of wedding revived kama but made him invisible except for the eyes of his wife rati, making him *ananga*. This day of Arvati parameshvara wedding is the *kalyana vratam* also known as *panguni uttaram* kamadahana festival is celebrated in the month of *masi* (mid Feb to mid Mar) on the full moon day.

Holi is spread out over two days (it used to be five, and in some places it is longer). The entire holiday is associated with a *loosening of social restrictions* normally associated with caste, sex, status and age. Holi thus bridges social gaps and brings people together: employees and employers, men and women, rich and poor, young and old. Holi is also characterized by the *loosening of social norms* governing polite behavior and the resulting general atmosphere of licentious merrymaking and ribald language and behavior. A common saying heard during Holi is *bura na mano, Holi hai* ("don't feel offended, it's Holi").

On the evening of the first day of Holi, a *public bonfire* is held, commemorating the burning of Holika. Traditionally, Hindu boys spend the weeks prior to Holi combing the neighborhood for any waste wood they can find for the bonfire. The fire is lit sometime between 10 p.m. and midnight (at the rising of the moon), not generally in an orderly fashion. Everyone gathers in the street for the event, and the air rings with shouts, catcalls, curses and general mayhem.

The central ritual of Holi is the throwing and applying of *colored water and powders* on friends and family, which gives the holiday its common name "Festival of Colors." This ritual is said to be based on the above story of Krishna and Radha as well as on Krishna's playful splashing of the maids with water, but most of all it celebrates the coming of spring with all its beautiful colors and vibrant life.

In Bengal, Holi features the *Dolayatra* (Swing Festival), in which images of the gods are placed on specially decorated platforms and devotees take turns swinging them. In the meantime, women dance around and sing special songs as men spray colored water at them.

***Holi—Legends and Myths:*** Interesting legends of Holi that are most commonly cited revolve around the soul bond of Lord Krishna and Radha, Prahlad, the child-devotee of Lord Vishnu, Kamdeva, the Indian Cupid-God and Dhundhi, the immortal ogress. All these legends focus on different aspects of Holi that can be attributed to them. The romantic fervor of Holi festival is derived from the love pranks of Radha and Krishna while the story of Kamdeva gives a clue to celebrate this festival to welcome the Spring. The story of Prahlad encompasses the religious nature of the festival and the origin of Holi while the tale of Dhundhi gives a reason to use rude words and play pranks to the young boys of the village.

There was a mighty demon king named Hirnakashyipu who had won all the three worlds of heaven, earth and hell and had thus, become very proud. He assumed that he could defeat even Lord Vishnu with his valor. He went to the extent that he had enforced a law that everybody would worship him instead of gods and deities. However, his little son Prahlad refused to accept his commands and continued to worship Lord Vishnu with complete devotion. Infuriated by this defiance of his son, he ordered his soldiers to throw him down a hill. Praying fervently and having full faith in Lord Vishnu, Prahlad did not retract from his word. True to his faith, Lord Vishnu rescued him at the last moment.

Flustered by this news, Hirnakashyipu invoked the help of his sister Holika, who had a boon that she could walk through the fire unharmed to do away with his son. The wicked aunt agreed to the evil desires of his brother and entered the fire with her nephew Prahlad. However, the brother and sister had forgot that Holika could only enter the fire alone or she would perish. Thus, blessed by Lord Vishnu, the child Prahlad remained unharmed but Holika got burnt and died instantly. Holi is thus celebrated to commemorate the death of the evil aunt, after whom the festival is named, and the new life granted to Prahlad for his devotion and faith. To this day, cow dung is hurled into the fire and obscenities are shouted at the Holi fire at some places to insult Holika.

***Invincible Dhundhi:*** During the reign of Prithu, there was a terrible ogress called Dhundhi, who loved to devour innocent children. She had performed severe penances and had won several boons from the deities that made her almost invincible. However, due to a curse of Lord Shiva, she was not so immune to the pranks and abuses of young boys as she was to weapons and arrows. One day, the courageous boys of the village decided to get rid of her forever and chase her away from the village forever. They got intoxicated on bhaang and drunk and then followed Dhundhi to the limits of the village, beating drums, making loud noise, shouting obscenities and hurling insults at her and continued doing this until she left the village for good. This is the reason that even today young boys are allowed to indulge themselves in rowdiness, using rude words and intoxication on Holi.

***Love Play of Radha Krishna:*** Lord Krishna has often been portrayed as a naughty prankster in his childhood and a lover-boy in his youth. His beloved Radha and the cowherd girls 'Gopis' in general loved him even more for his pranks and eve teasing. The Holi of Braj is famous all over India for its intimate connection with the divine deities and their love plays. It is said that when Krishna was a young boy, he asked the reason for his dark color while Radha was so fair. His mother Yashoda playfully suggested that he should smear color on Radha's face too and change her complexion to any color he wanted. Captivated by the idea, Krishna proceeded to do so and thus, introduced the play of colors on Holi.

Even today, Holi is one of the most important festival of Braj, where the men of Nandgaon and women of Barsana play 'latthmar Holi' in the remembrance of the playful throw of colors by Krishna on 'Gopis' and their resistance. The trace of eroticism and romance pervades Holi as depicted in the love plays of Krishna and Radha. In Mathura, Vrindavan, Gokul and Barsana, Holi is a two-week long festival featuring play of colors, folk songs called 'Hori', folk dances such as Raas-Lila, staging the various aspects of Radha and Krishna's love. The world's balance soon crumbled in his absence and Sati took rebirth as Goddess Parvati to try and win Lord Shiva's heart and wake him up from his trance. She tried all ways to get the attention of Shiva. When she had exhausted all her feminine ways, she invoked the help of Kamadava, the Indian cupid-god, who agreed to help her in the cause of the world despite the risks involved. He shot his love-arrow on Shiva's heart. Disturbed in his trance, Lord Shiva opened his third eye that fired anger and instantly incinerated Kamadeva.

It is said that it was on the day of Holi that Kamadeva had sacrificed himself for the good of all beings. Later, when Lord Shiva realized his mistake, he granted Kamadeva immortality in invisible form. To this day, people offer sandalwood paste to Kamadeva to relieve from his stinging burns and mango blossoms that he loved on Holi.

***Sacrifice of Kamadeva:*** According to Hindu mythology, the world is looked after the Trinity of Gods—Lord Brahma, the creator; Lord Vishnu, the nurturer; and Lord Shiva, the destroyer. According to a legend, Goddess Sati, the daughter of Daksha Prajapati, one of the first sons of Lord Brahma, married Lord Shiva against the wishes of her father. Thus, Daksha did not invite her and her husband to a grand yagya arranged by him. When Sati came to know about the event in her father's house, she thought it to be a slip of mind and proceeded to participate in the event despite the warnings of her husband. But once she reached there, she realized her fault and was infuriated by the insult of her husband. As a penance for her disobedience, she entered the fire. When Lord Shiva came to know of her sudden demise, he was furious. Even after he controlled his anger, he started a severe meditation and renounced all work.

Holi or Holikotsava is a festival that occurs around March and is celebrated over two days. On the evening of the first day bonfires are lit, normally in a public place. On the second day people throw coloured powder and water at each other. The first day is Holi proper, the second day is called Dhuleti or

Rangapanchami (Ranga-colour, Panchami=fifth day). Rangapanchami was originally the fifth day as the festival was earlier spread over five days and so it was called Rangapanchami because in earlier times it was celebrated till the fifth day of the fortnight.

***Holi Centers Around a Bonfire:*** Holi is one of the few festivals that has yet to acquire the character of being a religious and private festival along with being a public occasion for rejoicing which all festivals are. Holi is almost totally a public festival and as such there is hardly any Holi celebrations inside private homes in the sense in which is understood. Holi is not only a purely public festival in the manner of its celebration but also in the manner in which people prepare for it.

Weeks before the arrival of Holi, gangs comb the neighborhood and collect all waste-wood, old wooden furniture etc. which they can lay their hands upon. After weeks of preparation judiciously combined with activities that come close to pillaging, assorted pieces of wood are piled up to be lit on the evening of the festival day. (These days with Cable TV, the interest of the boys in urban India seems to be waning in the pre-Holi preparations).

***Sexual License during Holi:*** The lighting takes place late in the night between 10 p.m. and 12 p.m. Very rarely is this ceremony conducted in an orderly manner. Except when the ceremony is taking place in a temple, gesticulation, howling, catcalls and trading of abuses is a part of Holi.

All this is obviously reminiscent of attitudes originating in a backward cultural environment. But even against this background, the aspect that stands out is the sexual license that the mobs exercise. A display of loose morals, a morbid rejoicing with contempt for all laws and norms of behaviour that are considered civilized by present-day standards—what does this reflect?

How is it that even those sections of society that are educated and cultured allow themselves to bo carried away by the wild outburst associated with this festival? Why is it that this has been the nature of Holi for centuries together?

These questions sound quite provocative to an average Indian mind. To answer them we need to look beyond what is visible and evident as there is more to it than meets the eye during Holi celebrations. As already mentioned, Holi does not have much of a private or individual character, it is almost entirely a public festival. But does it at least have any religious significance? A hard look proves otherwise. Holi is not dedicated to any deity from the Hindu pantheon, as are other festivals like, Mahashivaratri, Ramanavami, Krishnastami, etc. And although mythology does involve Shiva and Madana (the God of love) with Holi, the religious significance is not immanent as in the case of other festivals. It is for this reason that very few religious rites are associated with Holi and almost none of them are generally observed.

Festivals displaying features similar to Holi can be found in many modern societies. Carnival and Guy Fawkes Day are two instances. The Guy Fawkes Day which is observed in Britain on the 5th of November commemorates the discovery of Gunpowder and is celebrated with fireworks and bonfires.

The Carnival which is another instance of a similar festival is celebrated in Portugal and Spain. Carnival is an occasion for revelry. Carnival that is celebrated before the beginning of Lent—the beginning of the austerity period that goes up to Good Friday and Easter. The term carnival being close to terms like carnal (meaning sensual or bodily), carnage, carnivore, carnivorous is itself quite suggestive of the origin of carnival in a less civilized environment. Recently in India the Roman Catholic Church of Goa has refused to extend religious sanction to carnival, but this has not succeeded in abating the tide of public enthusiasm. This is one instance of how a popular festival which owes it origin to a life-style (existing or extinct) can continue in face of withdrawal of religious sanction..

The on-goings during Holi celebrations closely resemble life in a nomadic tribal society especially in the wintry regions. The festival revolves around a bonfire. It is observed in the winter. These two aspects are eloquent as to the festival's social origin. Fire, we know was one of the earliest tool used to ward off the freezing cold of the long winters in the northern hemisphere. Even today among the poorest sections of society, the lighting of fire made of waste-wood is the cheapest and affordable form of keeping oneself warm during the long wintry nights.

Although no offence is meant, we cannot help saying that the tradition of mobocracy and sexual license reflects in a telling manner an attitude typical of tribal people living in a harsh environment in a society where the institution of monogamous marriage had not developed fully.

But such elements in a festival are not specific to India. Festivals displaying features similar to Holi can be found in many modern societies. Carnival and Guy Fawkes Day are two instances. The Guy Fawkes Day which is observed in Britain on the 5th of November commemorates the discovery of Gunpowder and is celebrated with fireworks and bonfires.

The Carnival which is another instance of a similar festival is celebrated in Portugal and Spain. Carnival is an occasion for revelry. Carnival that is celebrated before the beginning of Lent—the beginning of the austerity period that goes up to Good Friday and Easter. The term carnival being close to terms like carnal (meaning sensual or bodily), carnage, carnivore, carnivorous is itself quite suggestive of the origin of carnival in a less civilized environment. Recently in India the Roman Catholic Church of Goa has refused to extend religious sanction to carnival, but this has not succeeded in abating the tide of public enthusiasm. This is one instance of how a popular festival which owes it origin to a life-style (existing or extinct) can continue in face of withdrawal of religious sanction.

***The Burning of Kamadeva Madana:*** For that matter, a formal religious sanction does exist in the case of most festivals. For instance, it is said that Holi commemorates an event in lord Shiva's life. In mythology Shiva is portrayed as having a meditative but violent temperament. For hours together he is said to meditate in his icy abode atop mount Kailas in the

Himalayas. Solitude and serenity are essential for him. Looking at Shiva's abnormal trait, Madana, the God of love decided to see for himself if Shiva was, in fact, above normal passions. To do this he took on the form of a beautiful nymph and tried to disturb Shiva's meditation by singing and dancing in front of him. Unfortunately for Madana, he succeeded in disturbing Shiva's meditation, and when Shiva opened his eyes and recognised the beautiful nymph as Madana in disguise, he was furious. In a fit of rage he opened his third eye located on his forehead, that could emit fire and reduced the guileful Madana to ashes. Holi we are told is observed in memory of this event.

***Holi: The Lordly Way:*** But the most famous Holi has to be that of Barsana, (a small town in the Northern Indian state of Uttar Pradesh) the house of adolescent Krishna's love, Radha. Romance is not quite what comes to mind when you see men from Nandgaon (Krishna's home) being beaten up with sticks from Radha's village, after they have been provoked by the colorful language.

Celebrations start a week earlier than the rest of India. Men of Nandagaon raid Barsana with hopes of raising their flag over Shri Radhikaji's temple. They receive a thunderous welcome as the village women greet them with long wooden sticks. The men are soundly beaten as they attempt to rush through the town and reach the relative safety of Shri Radhikaji's temple. Men are well padded with foam, since they are not allowed to retaliate. In this mock battle, the men try their best not to be captured. Unlucky captives can be forcefully lead away, thrashed and dressed in female attire before being made to dance!

Poets like Surdas, Nand-das, Kumbhan-das and others have recounted tales of Krishna being captured and forced to wear a sari, makeup and then dance before being released by the gopis of Vraj.

The next day, men of Barsana reciprocate by invading Nandagaon. Clouds of pink and white powder mark the frenzy of activity taking place in its narrow streets. The women of Nadagaon beat the invaders from Barsana. There are even vantage points for tourists who choose to look on. A large open ground, on the outskirts of the town, is specially set aside for the most magnificent display of the festivities.

The next day, the temples in Vrindavan (close to Mathura) celebrate the festival. The temple of Bakai-Bihari, the beloved lord of the 15th century saint Haridas, is at the center of the festivities. Clouds of pink and white descend upon the pilgrims, as the Lord of Vrindavan plays Holi with all his visitors.

The festival moves on to other parts of Vraj. Gulal-Kund in Vraj is a beautiful little lake, set in delightful groves near the mountain Goverdhan, in the Mathura district. Here, the festival is commemorated on a more regular basis. Pilgrims, who visit the Holy Land of Vraj, can see the reenactments of Holi throughout the year.

Local boys, acting in the Krishna-Lila drama troupes, reenact the scenes of Holi for the pilgrims. The next day onwards it's business as usual in both God's houses and men's. And spring can be a hard taskmaster. One returns to the business of living with fun to last a year.

*Holi* festival of India. The *Holi* Festival is known as the "Festival of Color" and is a celebration of Lord Krishna and God's Creations. The colorful festival of *Holi*, literally means 'burning', is celebrated on the full moon day in the month of Phalguna and heralds the onset of spring season. *Holi* is the time when people from all castes and social strata come together forgetting all past differences and grievances.

Originally the festival was primarily for the Sudras who were otherwise not allowed to participate in festivals. This is specially significant in the rural areas where in many places, there still exists a clear demarcation between each caste and community.

In ancient India too, this festival was celebrated as a day when people forgot caste and gender differences and were allowed many liberties, otherwise forbidden. In fact Holi bears close resemblance to the important ancient festival called Vasantotsava.

In Bengal, Holi is called Dol Yatra, or the swing festival. Idols of Radha and Krishna are placed on swings and devotees take turns to swing them. Women dance around the swing and sing devotional songs, as men spray colored water at them. In Manipur too, Holi is extremely interesting. It is a six-day festival here, commencing on the full moon day of Phalguna. The traditional and centuries-old Yaosang festival of Manipur amalgamated with Holi in the18th century with the introduction of Vaishnavism. The entire theme of the festival is woven into the worship of Krishna and Chaitanya Mahaprabhu, also known as Lord Gauranga.

Thabal Chongba, a popular Manipuri folk dance, is associated with this festival. The literal meaning of Thabal is 'moonlight' and Chongba means 'dance', thus 'dancing in the moonlight'. Traditionally conservative Manipuri parents did not allow their daughters to go out and meet any young men without their consent. Thabal Chongba therefore provided the only chance for girls to meet and talk to the boys. In earlier times, this dance was performed in the moonlight accompanied by folk songs. The only musical instrument used was a dholakor drum. It is performed in every locality on all the six days of the festival. Instead of a fire, a hut is built and then set ablaze. The next day, boys go in groups to play gulal with the girls. And in return for playing with them, the girls extract money from the boys.

Another significant feature of the festival in Manipur is the groups of devotees from different areas who gather at the Shree Govindaji Temple in Imphal. Dressed in the traditional white and yellow turbans, they sing songs in praise of Krishna and Chaitanya Mahaprabhu, play gulal and dance in front of the temple. On Halangkar, the last day of the festival, hundreds of devotees gather at the temple as usual and march together towards the Vijay Govindaji Temple about 3 km west of Imphal where various cultural activities are performed. This brings to an end the Yaosang festival

***Holi or Holika:*** Holi or Holika, also called holikotsava, is an extremely popular festival observed throughout the country

(India). It is especially marked by unmixed gaiety and frolics and is common to all sections of the people.

This festival is very ancient. Known originally as 'Holika' it has been mentioned in very early religious works such as Jaimini's Purvamimamsa-sutras and Kathaka-grhya-sutras. It must have therefore existed several centuries before Christ. It was at first actually a special rite performed by married women for the happiness and well-being of their families and the full moon (Raka) was the deity worshipped by them.

There are two ways of reckoning a lunar month: purnimanta and amanta. In the former, the first day starts after the full moon; and in the latter, after the new moon. Though the latter reckoning is more common now, the former was very much in vogue in the earlier days. According to this purnimanta reckoning, Phalguna purnima was the last day of the year and the new year heralding the Vasanta-ritu (with spring starting from next day).

Thus the full moon festival of Holika gradually became a festival of merrymaking, announcing the commencement of the spring season. This perhaps explains the other names of this festival: Vasanta-Mahotsava and Kama-Mahotsava.

According to the stories in the Puranas and various local legends, this day is important for three reasons:

1. It was on this day that Lord Siva opened his third eye and reduced Kamadeva (the god of love, Cupid or Eros) to ashes.
2. It was on this day that Holika, the sister of the demon king Hiranyakasyapu, who tried to kill the child devotee Prahlad by taking him on her lap and sitting on a pyre of wood which was set ablaze. Holika was burnt to ashes while Prahlad remained unscathed!
3. It was again on this day that an ogress called Dhundhi, who was troubling the children in the kingdom of Prthu (or Raghu) was made to run away for life, by the shouts and pranks of the mischievous boys. Though she had secured several boons that made her almost invincible,

this – noise, shouts, abuses and pranks of boys – was a chink in her armour due to a curse of Lord Siva. The day itself came to be called 'Adada' or 'Holika' since then.

Festivals like Holi have their own spiritual value. Apart from the various amusements, they create faith in God if properly observed. Hindu festivals always have a spiritual significance. They wean man away from sensual pleasures and take him gradually to the spiritual path and divine communion. People perform *havan* and offer to the gods the new grains that are harvested.

On such holy occasions there should be worship of God, Satsangs, and Kirtan of the Lord's Names, not merely the sprinkling of coloured water and lighting of bonfires. These functions are to be considered most sacred and spent in devotional prayers, visiting holy places, bathing in sacred waters, and Satsang with great souls. Abundant charity should be done to the poor. Then only can Holi be said to have been properly celebrated. Devotees of the Lord should remember His delightful pastimes on such happy occasions.

All great Hindu festivals have religious, social and hygienic elements in them. Holi is no exception. Every season has a festival of its own. Holi is the great spring festival of India. Being an agricultural country, India's two big festivals come during the harvest time when the barns and granaries of our farmers are full and they have reason to enjoy the fruits of their hard labour. The harvest season is a festive season all over the world.

Man wants relaxation and change after hard work. He needs to be cheered when he is depressed on account of work and anxieties. Festivals like Holi supply him with the real food and tonic to restore his cheer and peace of mind.

The religious element in the Holi festival consists of worship of Sri Krishna. In some places it is also called the Dol Yatra. The word *dol* literally means "a swing". An image of Sri Krishna as a babe is placed in a little swing-cradle and decorated with flowers and painted with coloured powders. The pure, innocent frolics of little Krishna with the merry milkmaids—the Gopis of Brindavan—are commemorated. Devotees chant the Name of Sri Krishna and sing Holi-songs relating to the frolics of little Krishna with the Gopis.

The social element during Holi is the uniting or "embracing" of the great and the small, of the rich and the poor. It is also the uniting of equals. The festival teaches us to "let the dead bury the dead". We should forget the outgoing year's ill-feelings and begin the new year with feelings of love, sympathy, co-operation and equality with all. We should try to feel this oneness or unity with the Self also.

Holi also means "sacrifice". Burn all the impurities of the mind, such as egoism, vanity and lust, through the fire of devotion and knowledge. Ignite cosmic love, mercy, generosity, selflessness, truthfulness and purity through the fire of Yogic practice. This is the real spirit of Holi. Rise from the mire of stupidity and absurdity and dive deep into the ocean of divinity.

The call of Holi is to always keep ablaze the light of God-love shining in your heart. Inner illumination is the real Holi. The spring season is the manifestation of the Lord, according to the *Bhagavad Gita.* Holi is said there to be His heart.

If you're in any of the northern states of India around the time of the full moon in late February/early March be prepared to come under heavy fire from hordes of dye-totin' revellers.

The festival of Holi is a riotious celebration of the coming of spring and, in that infectious flowers-are-a'bloomin' and sun-is-a'shinin' kind of way, sweeps everything before it. More than any other festival, Holi brings out the flagrant, gaudy India—the land of hennaed hands, maharanis and silk saris, tikas and bindis, sparkling bangles, fluttering prayer flags, burnished temples, and bejewelled mausoleums.

There are several different myths surrounding the festival of Holi—the version you get depends on where you are. Down in the southern regions, particularly around Kerala, legend has it that Kamdev-the-love-God, forgetting all those boyhood admonitions about not pointing sharp missiles at people ('it's all fun and games until someone gets their eye poked out'), aimed an arrow at Lord Shiv's third eye.

For this silly adolescent act he was not just grounded but, hyper-punitively, burnt to the ground. His wife pleaded for his return, a wish that was only half-granted when Lord Shiv sent him back but sent him back ever-'anang' (without human form). Hence the lamentations sung during Holi.

Another more lurid and gothic story has she-demons suckling children to death and attempting to take the life of Krishna in the same manner. The fires on the eve of Holi somehow represent the death of the she-devil, Putana, and the triumph of spring life over deathly winter. Then there's the Hiranyakashyap-Prahlad myth, a kind of Luke Skywalker-Darth Vader Yoda-less tale of fathers and sons, good and evil, and the triumph of abstract faith over physical limitations.

In this version Holika, the sister of Hiranyakashyap, was sent to kill Prahlad, the good son, who refused the blandishments of the Dark Side by continuing to worship Lord Vishnu over his father who had installed himself as a god. For this sin, Holika carried him into a crematorium, but she was hoisted on her own petard when she was burnt by the very fires that were meant for Prahlad. Holika's firey nature is remembered in the bonfires that are burnt each Holi eve.

While the legend has all the elements of a classic tragedy, the festival itself is a day of uninhibited exuberance and joy, fuelled by spring's arrival and the timely consumption of marijuana-based bhang and thandai.

Gangs of revellers roam the streets armed with packets of gulal (dye) and coloured water bombs and, from early in the day, it's on for young and old. The coloured wars rage all morning but promptly at midday a general cease-fire is observed and the streets turn eerily quiet as people flock to bathtubs and rivers for a hose down.

The afternoon is spent eating candy and reliving the glories of battle. Originally the colours were extracted from a flower that blossoms only during the festival but these days ammunition is usually bought at the local markets. The row upon row of luscious gulal- mountains of tumeric yellow, saffron orange, indigo blue, deep turquoise and the entire spectrum in between—will have you itching to join in.

Tourists and foreigners should be warned that they are not immune to the kamikaze water-bomb raids and there's not much point in getting upset over being the target. Better to drag out an old wash-n-wear from the back pack or something that could do with a bit of a dye-job, get your own gulal ammunition and fight fire with fire.

# 7

# THE STUDY OF INDIAN CASTES

## Introduction

The Hindus have Varna System. It is not at all caste-equivalent. It simply indicates a social division based on Gunas There exists all over the world one sort of division or the other in a society, which is so inevitable for social growth and prosperity. Each individual is possessed of a particular ability by nature. One may well perform a physical labour, another may be more of a thinker and some may be artistic some inclined to technology, music. Medicine, trade, industry or any other material or spiritual activity. The Lord speaking on action and inaction in Geeta (IV-13) says,'the four Varnas have been created by Him according to differentiation of Gunas and Karmas.' These Varnas are 1-Brahman; 2-Kshatriya; 3-Vaishya; and 4-Sudra.

Varna means different shades of texture or colour. They represent mental temper. There are three Gunas—Sattva, Rajas and Tamas. Sattva is white, Rajas red and Tamas black. These in combination of various proportions constitute the group or class of people all over the world with temperamental differences. The above classification is based on this assumption. In continuation, Veda Vyasa says in the same couplet, 'by the differentiation of the mental quality and physical action of the people.' It is clear that the type of ones action, the quality of ego, the colour of knowledge, the texture of ones understanding, the temper of fortitude and the brilliance of ones happiness defines ones Varna. Not by birth a man becomes Brahman but by cultivating noble thoughts and good intentions of service alone, one can ever aspire to Brahman hood.

The Brahman is generally Sattvik. Sama and Dama are his valuable assets. He is serene and self-controlled and is possessed of the quality of austerity. (Tapas) He has purity, uprightness and forbearance. He has a will to acquire knowledge (Jnan), Vigyan (Wisdom) and faith.

The Kshatriya is a warrior class, powerful of physique and might. They are possessed of more of Rajas Guna with base of Sattva. They have a duty to protect the Dharma and the people. They are bold, alert and full of fortitude, generosity. discipline and modesty along with masterly behaviour mingled with Ishvar Bhava (Love of God).

The Vaishya class is a trader class and prefers business of all kinds. It is possessed of Raj Guna mixed with Tamas. They deal with wealth and gold and strive for material prosperity of the self as well as of the people in general. The Sudras are working class people, artisans and craftsmen. They are physically strong and hard working. They are possessed of Tamas with a base of Rajas. Really speaking, Sudra class is indispensable to society as they are like a spiral chord on which rests the social structure.

Thus it is clear that the whole Varna System stood on the basis of Gunas and karmas of the individual. It has nothing to do with birth. To quote Mahabharata, the serpent god asked Yudhisthir to tell him the virtues of the caste. He says that those Brahmans who were fond of personal pleasures, prone to violence, had forsaken their duties and were red limbo, fell into the category of Kshatriya. Those Brahmans who derived their livelihood from kine, who were yellow and sub-divided by agriculture and who neglected to practice their duties, fell into the category of Vaishyas.

Those Brahmans who were addicted to mischief and falsehood and were covetous, lived by all kinds of works and fell from purity and were black went to the condition of Sudra.

As a conclusion, the serpent god says that the man in which the marks of a Sudra are not found is no Sudra, whereas while a Brahman who acts so is not a Brahman and may be called a Sudra. It is clear that the world being the projection of Brahma is therefore Brahma-roopa and these castes came up later as a creation of man in society. Therefore it stands for modification and change according to times.

## The Confusion

Today people have mistaken Varnas for caste and treat them as identical. Varnas are God created and caste is not. Varnas are conditioned with one's actions and desires based on Gunas. The caste is man made. It is simply a social institution and can easily be changed and modified according to changing needs of society. Caste-by-birth was never the original intent nor it ever was the basis upon which the Varnas were constituted, Sutra says that a person should be engaged only in a field of activity that he is capable of doing.

Today we have miserably failed to understand what a Brahman is. Generally we believe that one is born by birth in a certain class. This belief has keenly been protected and propagated by the vested interests. It also served the policy of divide and rule of the foreign rulers and served an easy prey to conversions. The confusion has been repeatedly tried to be removed by the saints. Vajra Suchikopanishad clearly states that one can not be a Brahman either by its being, birth, physical equipment of body and colour or by wisdom and knowledge nor by religious action even.

Hindus believe in rebirth and countless yonis of births. So the very idea of being born in one birth as Brahman is unscientific. Even the physical body structure does not make one a Brahman. The body is made of matter and matter acts uniformly in every clime and time. Every one is so born and there can not be any difference. The ill-found belief that a Brahman is fair, Kshatriya black, Vaishya yellow and Sudra dark black is entirely baseless. Even the cremation and last rites are the same for all of us. The possession of super brain and knowledge is also not the monopoly of Brahman alone. Vishvamitra, the warrior was a talented seer and was not a Brahman. So were many saints, and even Kabir, Dadu, Nabhadas. Raiyadas, the Alvars and the Saivites, etc. We have also to remember that even a wise man goes astray and loses the right path.

Vajra Suchikopanishad states clearly that a Brahman is one who lives and moves in Brahma. He remains above the pair of opposites. He is unmoved in joy and sorrow, pain and pleasure, pride and prejudice, and has conquered desires and is free from ego-sense. The one so equipped is indeed a Brahman.

***The Cause of Confusion:*** It is indeed disheartening that a system based on very sound principles has come to result in such an evil. It is annoying to note that the basic principles of Varna system were distorted beyond any controlled limit in due course of time. During the foreign rule, the caste System that stood firm like a rock in support and defense of our religion and culture lost its metal, when the spirit of exclusiveness was perpetuated by a group of vested interests who gained political and economic mileage over their fellow beings. It soon degenerated into an instrument of oppression and intolerance. It threw away all norms of human behaviour and fellowship and distanced man from man with a clear cut division of population even in small village's. This degeneration is man-made and is a social evil. It is the weakness of Hindu society. All other religious groups suffer such evils. Unfortunate it is that others blame the Hindu religion for this whereas they do not blame their religions likewise on such grounds; rather they call it social weakness.

The whole confusion is caused by the differences among the Brahman class. During Vedic era, there were Brahmans who did all the sacrificial rituals for their own sake. Some others did for others on payment. These Brahmans were looked down as inferior. Gradually the prosperity brought their group in position of advantage and these ritualistic Brahmans imagined Brahma in their own way, They wrote, 'From mouth of Brahman came out the wise priest Brahman, the warrior Kshatriya was born of his hands, the Vaishyas from the thighs and the Sudra from legs.' (Rig Veda 10-90-12) Dr R.B. Sharma, an authority on Rig Veda in his book 'Bharatiya Navajagaran Aur Europe' says that it is an interpellation of a later period. He says that a study of Rig Veda would reveal that the word 'Kavi' (Poet, Composer) was used in deep reverence and the word Brahman does not find a similar mention. Many Devas have been addressed as Kavi and even as Brahman, but no one as Brahman even once, as these people have been associated with rituals and economy away from the Kavis. They did all that for the sake of more and more remuneration.

Dr Sharma says that the word Sudra comes only once in the mantra and it is here in this mantra that the word Vaishya used only once has been repeated. The word Brahman has found expression many times but not in the sense of a Varna. More over the word "Kshatriya" is not used in that mantra. The word used is Rajanya and that too only once. It is clear that there was no mention of four Varnas in most of the Rig Vedic period. No one can imagine a Brahman without a Sudra and a Vaishya. Even in the later Vedic period the word Kshatriya was not prevalent. Rajanya was used as much as the Sudra and Vaishya were used. Scholars conclude that the Sukta is an interpellation. and an after thought. Max Muller and Colebrook both agree that from the point of view of style and language, this mantra is totally different and of a later period. (Sanskrit Ke Char Adhyaya).

Needham in 'Science and Civilization Vol II' points at the penetrating cultural influence of Indian thoughts on Iran. We notice philosophical similarities between Rig Veda and Avesta. It was not accidental. In the third and fourth century, the Indian religious sects had deeply entered into Iranian religious life and had created a great impact. The Greek work 'Mangeeste' and the works of Iran were influenced by the concept of four Varnas. They divided the human body into four parts. The Purohit was the head; the warrior was the hand, the agriculturist stomach and the handyman or the artisan the leg. (Nava Jagaran

Aur Europe p358). In pahelvi, the word used for Varna is Peshak. These Peshaks (occupation) were Astronan (Brahman), Auteshteran (Rajanya), Vastryoshan (Vaishya) and Hutukhsan (Sudra). These Hutukhsan were artisans and not sevaks or servants. Dasas were called servants. Sudras stood apart from them. Gradually with the decline of prosperity and urban life, the Sudras were dragged into as servants. This form of thought was prevalent in the 3rd century It can easily be concluded that there was no division on the line of casts by birth. We can not also say how the Sudras came to be known as untouchables.

A lot of confusion prevails in reference to Manusmriti, Law of Conduct, and a judicial theory written about 200 BC. Manusmriti in (1-5-118) speaks about the liberality in Kalyuga and says, 'He, the most resplendent one, assigned separate duties and occupation to those who sprang from his mouth, arms, thighs and feet.'

To Brahman, he assigned teaching and study of Vedas, Sacrificing for their own benefits and for others, giving and accepting of alms. To Kshatriyas, he commanded to protect the people, to study the Vedas, and abstain from sensual pleasures. The Vaishyas were to trend cattle, bestow gifts study Vedas and lend money and cultivate land. He asked the Sudras to do meek service to the above three classes.

It is a rule of conduct and not a religious canon or word of scripture. Manu says that the rule is transcendent law and belongs to social institution of Kalyuga. In the Vedic era, people firmly believed that all are born from the Supreme. Sruti says that the fisherman, gamblers and all such people are divine. There is only one class as there is only one God. Manu says that all men are born unregenerate (Sudra) by their physical birth. They become Dwija (regenerate) by the second birth. Manusmriti (Ix-14-48) says that,' One becomes a Brahman by his deeds, not by his family or birth. even a Chandal is a Brahman, if he is of pure character.' Was not Vashista born of a prostitute? Vyasa was born of a fisher woman and; Parashars from Chandals. It is therefore clear that conduct counts and not the birth. The caste can not stand on birth at all.

## The Intent of Varna System

The various stratification of Varna system was meant to settle the Hindu life and regulate the society for a united action. Every society in the world has some form of groups that works for the common cause of social progress and general prosperity. In the various spheres of life, cultural, spiritual, religious, economic, political and social, medical, science and technology and even unskilled workers, there are groups united differently to work for the social cause of all the people.

In Hinduism, this division is called Varna System. Each Varna has its social purpose, its own code, norms of behaviour and keeps its independent identity. Still each part remains an integral part of the whole. The whole is always present in the part and the part is ever a part of the whole. This is the spirit behind the creation of Varna System.

The four Varnas represented the people of wisdom, of action, of compassion and loving feelings, and of service to people. It was not intended to be hereditary and connected with birth. and therefore free interchange and intermixing was liberally permitted.

It is indeed unfortunate that the Varna System came to be connected with the Caste System. We can not know how and why and when it so happened. It grew up with a sort of spiritual monopoly of a certain group bent upon its material prosperity. It established the class of Brahman by birth to safeguard their posterity. It is they who created and developed the ideas of inferiority and superiority among the people.

This led to discrimination and distinction between various groups of occupations and the degradation of society began and reached so low as there came out people such as untouchables and pariahs. Thus the Varna turned Caste System brought about social degradation and downfall dividing people as low and high and the lowest. The Varna System, so sound and healthy and perfect came to such a pitiable state. It needs a reconstitution at this stage.

***Conclusion:*** India is a developing nation. It has a responsibility to safeguard the rights of people as enshrined in the Constitution, irrespective of considerations of caste, creed, colour or sex. It is the need of the day that the Hindu scriptures be thrown open to all people of caste and sex so that they may have right understanding of their faith It may lead to the fall of the man-made Caste System like a sand hill. When the boundaries of the world are vanishing and there is open mixing of people and ideas, there has to be a ready flow of crossovers among the people as in the past. The watertight compartments only stink. The Hindu society has to be wellknit for the good of the world.

It is a fact that the Buddhists discarded the Vedas to preach against Caste System; Kabir followed the same path of denouncing the Hindu scriptures while opposing the Casts System. A proper understanding of scriptures can remove the ignorance and illusion. Gandhi and Aurobindo favoured Varna System though opposed Caste System. Swami Dayananda with authority on Vedas declared that Vedas do not mention about Caste System and opposed caste system tooth and nail while defending the scriptures. There is nothing in the scriptures to justify the caste division, only the Varna System exists as an integral part of the whole society. It is not the Caste System at all.

There are people in large majority who realise that the most oppressed people today called as Sudra were really a great adherent of Hinduism. In the Buddhist dominated era, they did not change their religion though the call was in their favour. During the terror rule of Islam for conversion, they did not convert and suffered from the rulers as well as from their own people who called them by many abusive names such as Sudra, Chamar. Bhangi. Harijan. Achuta or untouchables and even today remain bracketed in schedule caste and schedule tribes. They had opportunity to convert and be saved from humiliations and insults but they preferred to stay as Hindus and suffer as Hindus.

It is high time we get rid of such abuses and grant same and equal rights to these religious heroes as are enjoyed by the others in the Hindu society. Are they not a part of the whole and is the whole an invalid one? No, we have to restore their dignity as in the Vedic days. We have to treat them as a part of either Brahman class or as Kshatriya class to which they really belong. The ancestors of Raiyadas were Chanvar Kshatriyas and so are others. Restore them to their past glory and while doing so do not forget to undo what we have done by granting them the prevalent privileges intact for their growth without any restriction. We have to do it. No one else can do it. Do it now and here for unity of Hindu life and religion as we have a duty to rescue the present world from terror, chaos. disbelief and confusion. It is only the Hindu philosophy of unity in Diversity that can bring relief to the confused masses of humanity today.

## A Study of Indian Caste

A Graver intellectual confusion than that caused by the non-translation of the word Caste there has seldom been. The assumed impossibility of finding an equivalent for the idea in English has led to the belief that there is something mysterious and unprecedented in the institution. People become bewildered as to whether it is a religious or a social obligation. Every one demands of the reformer a conflict with it. The whole question grows obscure and irritating.

Yet all this time we have had an exact synonym for the word, and the parallel is the closer since our word connotes the same debatable borderland between morals and good taste. Caste ought to stand translated as honour. With Oriental quaintness, it is true, India has given a certain rigidity to this idea, but her analysis of the thing itself is as profound as it is acute.

Our conduct is commonly governed far more by social habit than by considerations of right and wrong. When the tide of the ethical struggle has once set in over some matter, we may regard ourselves as already half-lost. Why are my friend's open letters absolutely safe in my presence, though I am longing for the information they convey? Why can money given for one purpose not be used for another, when all the canons of common sense and expediency urge that it should? Who will confess to an effort in speaking the truth at any cost whatever? Why, when I am annoyed, do I not express myself in the language of Billingsgate? To each of which questions one would reply, somewhat haughtily, that the point was one of honour, or, that such happened to be the custom of one's class.

Yet if we examine into the sanction which honour can invoke there is nothing beyond a rare exercise of the power of ostracism. The Church excommunicates, the law imprisons, but society merely "cuts" the offender in the street. Yet which of these three inflicts the deepest wound? It is as true of London as of Benaras that caste-law is the last and finest that controls a man. For it comes into operation at that precise point where tribunals fail. It takes cognisance of offences for which no judge could inflict penalties. It raises standards and demands virtues that every man will interpret according to the stringency of his pride, and yet that no one can feel himself to have wholly fulfilled.

And it does all this without once permitting the sensation of merit. Having done all, one remains an unprofitable servant. For no one would count the punctual discharge of debts (all debts are debts of honour), the hauteur that brooks no stain upon the name, and the self-respect that builds the whole ethical code upon itself, as religious observances. These things were due, we say, to our birth or blood, or position before men. It is true that their non-fulfillment would leave a stain upon the conscience, and it is also true that the attempt to work out the obligations of honour must be the immediate test of the sincerity of one who proposes to lead a life of greater devotion and earnestness than common. Still, caste is not the same thing as personal piety and perhaps for this reason complete renunciation of its claims and benefits is essential in India to the monastic life.

There is another point about our Western conception of noblesse oblige. Few as the persons may be who could formulate their sentiment; the fact pervades the whole of the social area. Each class has its own honour. If honourable employers feel compelled to think of the comfort of their workers, honourable servants feel equally compelled to keep their lips shut on their masters' affairs, and either responds to an appeal in the name of his ideal. The priest may find the honour of his profession in conflict with that of the detective, but all the world will uphold the faithfulness of both. The efficient realisation of his ideals by the schoolmaster will involve an occasional pardon, even of a grave offence, if he conceives forgiveness to be the best formative influence which at the moment he can command. The very same effort in the merchant will require a distribution of punishment that is rigorous and just, since order, integrity, and unfailing promptitude—not the development of human character—are his ends. Thus every man, in every critical act of his life, calls silently for the judgment of his peers and refuses all other.

The weaknesses of caste everywhere are manifold. For society, like the individual, is always apt to insist upon the tithing of mint and rue, and to neglect the weightier matters of the law. But it is not usually the martyr who marks its worst failure. He is the white dove cast forth by crows, that is, a member of a higher tried by consensus of the lower castes. We have here a case of government usurping the functions of society, much as if the headmaster should exercise authority in a dispute among boys.

For it is essential to the very idea of honour that every caste should be autonomous. The true failure of caste occurs whenever it establishes such an ascendancy of social opinion over the individual's conscience that his power of advance is impeded and he becomes less of a man, or less really beneficent socially, by remaining more of a gentleman—a state of things which is not uncommon among ourselves. For we may postulate that all ideals are helpful only in so far as they subserve a man's manhood and freedom, and destructive the instant they render him less able to express his own inmost will. It is he; therefore, who ought to have been a martyr and chose ease who is the true caste victim, not the hero of an auto-da-fe.

That this is a real danger we all know. What Protestant has never exalted the creed of his sect over freedom of thought? What Catholic has never put comfort above spirituality? What politician has not preferred party above principle? What student of science has never been prejudiced against new truth? And if we look without, where do we not see the mere breaker of conventionality treated as outside brotherhood? Where do we not find persons conforming to usages that displease them, merely because they would be inconvenient to dispute?

A certain sweeping justification of such facts may be urged, inasmuch as there are circumstances under which the cohesion of the group is well worth the sacrifice of the liberty of a few individuals. And the habitual outrage of custom without reason is perhaps rightly held to be as anti-social as any felony. In the last resort, however, social pressure must be held in bounds, for nothing should interfere with a man's right to try himself, or sap the roots of his independence. And society is a vague and irresponsible magistrate, with so little illumination as to his own purposes and tendencies that he frequently mistakes the pioneers of his march for deserters and orders the stoning of prophets, whose sepulchers and monuments will be erected by his children.

The question of the inner trend or intention of the social movement must form the law in whose name all doubtful cases are tried. And, while it is never easy to determine the point accurately for one's own people, in the case of the Hindu race the supreme purpose of their past evolution is quite apparent. Even a cursory reading of the Laws of Manu displays Indian society as united in a great cooperation for the preservation of the ancient race-treasure of Sanskrit literature.

The feeling must have grown up when the Vedas alone required conserving, and the families entrusted with various portions were encouraged to become in all ways dependent on the community, that every energy might be devoted to the task in hand. This is the real meaning of prostration at the feet of Brahmans, of the great merit acquired by feeding them, and of the terror of the crime of killing one. It is not the man; it is race-culture that is destroyed by such an act.

As ages went on and the Upanishads and other things were added to the store, that which was hitherto memorised became entrusted to writing. The Vedas became Scriptures—and now the method, of psychology, of astronomy, of mathematics, made themselves felt as integral parts of the Aryan treasure, in common with Sanskrit literature. This widened the conception of culture without liberalising the social bearings of the question, and the Brahman caste continued to be recognised as the natural guardians of all learning, the old religious compositions being still regarded as the type.

If we ask how it happened that the Aryan folk became so early conscious of their responsibility in the matter of Sanskrit letters, there can be only one answer. They found themselves in the presence of other and unlearned races. This point brings us to the question of the origin of strongly differentiated castes in general. In its nature caste is, as we have seen, honour; that is to say, an ideal sentiment by whose means society spontaneously protects itself from some danger against which it is otherwise defenceless. For instance, life in Texas having been for many years dependent on the possession of horses, and safeguards against the horse-thief being few and difficult, he came to be the object of unprecedented social abhorrence. Horse-stealing was the last crime a lost soul would stoop to.

In a similar way, as some think, may have grown up the Indian feeling about cow-killing. If the cattle, in time of stress, were killed for food, agriculture would be unable to take a new start, and so a people accustomed to eat beef grasped the situation perhaps, and renounced the practice. But since these two sentiments pervade whole nations, they are not exactly what we are accustomed to think of as caste, inasmuch as in the latter there is a distinct gradation of rank connected with the sentiment. In the term "blackleg" applied by trade unionists to competing forms of labour, we have an instance of the kind we want. Here we have an occupational group giving birth immediately to the ideal which is necessary to its safety.

Throughout the worlds of love, of war, and of work, indeed, honour is an instinct of the very greatest potency. How few men, after all, desert to an enemy as spies! How strong is the feeling of class-obligation amongst servants and working men! This element is very evident in the Indian industrial castes, which are often simply hereditary trade-unions. No Englishman is so powerful, nor is any Hindu so hungry, that one man could be bribed to take up the trade of another. Nothing would induce the dairyman, for instance, to take charge of a horse, or a laundryman to assist the household.

But the very strongest, and perhaps also ugliest, of all possible roots of caste is the sense of race, the caste of blood. We have an instance of this in the animosity that divides white men from negroes in the United States, and we have other instances, less talked of, all up and down our vast British possessions. There is probably no other emotion so inhuman which receives such universal sympathy as this.

For it is fundamentally the physical instinct of a vigorous type to protect itself from fusion. And both sides participate in the revulsion. Here we have the secret of rigid caste, for the only rigid caste is hereditary, and of hereditary caste the essential characteristic is the refusal of intermarriage.

Granting, then, what could not well be denied, that the Aryan forefathers found themselves in India face to face with inferior and aboriginal races, what may we gather, from the nature of the caste system today, to have been the elements of the problem, as they more or less clearly perceived it?

Those elements we may infer to have been four in number:

1. They desired above all things to preserve the honour of their daughters from marriage with lower and savage peoples. Exclusion from marriage with any but one's own caste became the rigorous rule, the penalty fell on the father and the family that permitted a woman to go unguarded on this head. To this day, if a son marry

beneath caste he degrades himself; but if a daughter be wrongly given, the whole family becomes out-casted.

2. They seem to have desired to preserve the aboriginal races, on the one hand from extermination, and on the other from slavery of the person two solutions which seemed later the only alternatives to Aryan persons in a similar position! Those aborigines, therefore, who became dependent on the Aryan population, had their definite place assigned them in the scale of labour, and their occupations were secured to them by the contempt of the superior race.

   We must not forget, in the apparent harshness of this convention, its large factor of hygienic caution. The aborigines were often carrion-eaters, and always uncleanly in comparison with their neighbours. It was natural enough, therefore, that there should be a refusal to drink the same water, and so on.

   On the other hand, it is one of the mistakes of caste everywhere, that it institutionalises and perpetuates an inequality which might have been minimised. But we must not forget, in the case of the Indian system, the two greater evils which were avoided altogether.

3. The Aryans realised very clearly that it was not only their race but also their civilization that must be maintained in its purity. The word Aryan implies one acquainted with the processes of agriculture, an earer of the ground, to use an Elizabethan word—accustomed therefore to a fixed and industrialised mode of living, evidently in contrast to others who were not.

   Fire and the processes of cooking and eating food are easily distinguished as the core of the Personal life and establishment in a climate where habits can at any time be made so simple as in India. It is these that can never be dispensed with, though they may be arranged for to-night in a palace, and tomorrow in the jungle under a tree.

In view, then, of the necessity of safeguarding the system of manners grew up the restrictions against eating with those of lower caste, or allowing them to touch the food and wants of their betters. The fact that the Aryan could eat food cooked by Aryan hands alone implied that the strictest preliminaries of bathing had been complied with.

By a continuous crystallisation, all caste laws—from being the enunciation of broad canons of refinement as between Aryan and non-Aryan—came to be the regular caste-barriers between one class and another of the same race. In this way they lost their invidious character.

It is undeniable that this caste of the kitchen, so wittily named "don't touchism" by a modern Hindu leader, lends itself to abuse and becomes an instrument of petty persecution more readily than the intermarriage laws. Some of the saddest instances of caste-failure have occurred here. Nevertheless, the original intention remains clear and true, and is by no means completely obscured, even with the lapse of ages.

4. It was, however, in their perception of the fourth element of the problem that the early Aryans triumphantly solved the riddle of Humanity. They seem to have seen clearly that amongst the aborigines of India themselves were many degrees of social development already existent, and that these must be preserved and encouraged to progress.

From such a comprehension of the situation sprang the long and still growing graduation of non-Aryan castes, some of which have established themselves in the course of ages within the Aryan pale. Marriage, for instance, is an elabourate and expensive social function in the highest classes.

But as we descend it becomes easier, till amongst the Baghdis, Bauris, and other aboriginal castes, almost any connection is ratified by the recognition of women and children. This is a point in which Eastern scores over Western development; for in Europe the Church has caused to be reckoned as immoral what might, with more philosophy, have been treated as the lingering customs of sub-organised race-strata.

As is the nature of caste, mere social prestige constitutes a perpetual stimulus and invitation to rise, which means in this case to increase the number of daily baths and the cleanliness of cooking, and to restrict to purer and finer kinds the materials used for food, approximating continually toward the Brahman standard. For is it not true that noblesse oblige? This fact it is that makes Hinduism always the vigorous living banyan, driving civilization deeper and wider as it grows, and not the fossilised antiquity superficial observers have supposed.

Such, then, is the historic picture of the rise of caste. The society thus originated fell into four main groups:

(1) Priests and learned men—the Brahmans;

(2) The royal and military caste;

(3) Professional men and merchants—the middle-class or bourgeoisie, as we say in Europe; and

(4) The working people, or sudras, in all their divisions.

(Of the second group only the Rajput branch remains now stable. For the military caste, finding itself leaderless under the Maurya dynasty, is said to have become literary, and is certainly now absorbed in the bourgeoisie.)

This functional grouping, however, is traversed in all directions nowadays by the lines of caste. In the mountains it is no uncommon thing to find the Brahman acting as a labourer, impressed as a coolie, or working as a farmer, and in the cities he belongs largely to the professional ranks. Many of India's most learned and active sons, on the other hand, belong to the third and even fourth divisions. And the new castes, which are of constant growth, are less easy than the old to classify. Every new community means a new caste in India. Thus we have the Mohammedan, the Christian, and the modern reform castes—of all of which one peculiarity is non-belief in the caste principle!—as well as others. And who shall determine, for instance, to which of the four main grades Islamism, with its inclusion of peasant, citizen, and prince, belongs?

The fact is, if a man's mode of life be acceptable to his own caste-fellows, the rest of Indian society has no quarrel with it. And this autonomy of castes it is which is the real essential for social flexibility and fundamental equality. As bearing on this point, few utterances have ever been so misquoted as the great dictum of Buddha, that "he who attains to God is the true Brahman." For this is misquoted whenever it is made to imply that the Brahman holds in any sense a monopoly in religion. No possible statement could be more foreign to the genius of Hinduism. When we read that shortest and greatest of India's gospels, the "Bhagavad Gita" (a poem composed by Brahmans, preserved by Brahmans, and distributed through the length and breadth of the country, always by Brahmans), we find ourselves in the presence of the most comprehensive mind that ever contemplated Hindu life.

The compassion of Buddha, perhaps, looms greater across the centuries, but in dealing with social problems his very tenderness and spiritual fire make him second to Krishna, who was always calm, broad, and consistently national in his outlook. We must accept the Gita as an authoritative pronouncement on Hindu society. And the Gita rings with the constantly reiterated implication that "he who attains to God is the true man," while it interprets all life and responsibility as a means to this end. Thus, "Better one's own duty, though imperfect, than the duty of another well discharged. Better death in one's own duty; the duty of another brings on danger." We have to remember, too, that the Gita is made up of the very best of the Vedas and Upanishads, and was specially written for the benefit of women and the working classes, who, as destitute of classical learning, had little chance of studying these great scriptures.

But its contents were to depend upon Brahman effort for promulgation. Another witness to the fact that spirituality has always been regarded in India as the common human possession lies in the Hindu word for religion itself—dharma, or the manness of man. This is very striking. The whole weight, of the conception is shifted away from creed, much more from caste or race, to that which is universal and permanent in each and every human being. And, last of all, we may remember that the greatest historical teachers of Hinduism—Rama, Krishna, and Buddha, besides many of the Upanishadic period—were men of the second, or military, caste.

No, the Brahman was never in any sense the privileged monopolist of religion: he was a common channel of religious lore, because his actual function was Sanskrit culture, and Sanskrit happens to be the vehicle of the most perfect religious thought that the world ever produced, but "realisation" itself has always been recognised as a very different matter from this, and, Brahman or non-Brahman, has been accepted wherever it appeared. The advantage that the priestly caste did undoubtedly enjoy, however, lay in the fact that in their case the etiquette of rank led directly to the highest inspiration, as the scholar's life, even in its routine, will be nearest to that of the saint.

One peculiarity of the place of the religious life in the Indian system is that it is an inclusive term for all forms of higher individuation. Theoretically, to the Hindu mind, all genius is inspiration, the perception of unity; and the mathematics of Euclid or the sculpture of Michael Angelo would be as authentic an expression of the religious consciousness as the sainthood of Francis. Only the result of this method of interpretation is that sainthood takes precedence of all others as the commonest form of greatness. Scientific research, as in the astronomy of Bhashkar Acharya and the psychology of Patanjali, has not had sufficient opportunity of securing defined and independent scope. And literature has been yoked to the car of mythology as much as the art of medieval Italy.

Nevertheless, India is too well acquainted with genius to forget that the caste of the spirit is beyond human limitation, often beyond recognition. It is held that the best lower men can do for that brotherhood which asserts itself in the consciousness of greatness is to give it freedom. Hence a man can always be released from social obligations if he desire to live the life of ideas, of the soul. Only, it is held that if he will not fulfil the law, neither shall he add to the burdens of the community. So he who claims to be one of the great spiritual beyond-castes must renounce family and property, relying upon the charity of men for his daily bread, and knowing well that for any work of scholarship—such as the observatories at Benaras and Jeypore—a Hindu government at least would provide him ample means. It is only as long as one avails oneself of the benefits of the social structure that it is held not unreasonable to require conformity to its usages. This renunciation is Sannyas, the Indian form of monasticism, and Sannyas, theories to the contrary notwithstanding, has always been open to all castes. Indeed, it is held that when the responsibilities of life are over, a man's duty is to leave the world and spend the remainder of his days in that state; and in some parts of Northern India one meets with "Tyagi Mehtars," or monastics who were by birth the lowest of the low.

Theoretically, the monk is caste-fellow of the whole world, prepared to eat with any one; and where, by sheer dint of spirituality and self-discipline, such a feeling is realised; every Hindu in India considers the broken bread of this lover of mankind as sacramental food. It is usual, too, to eat from the hands of holy men without inquiry as to their standing when in the world. One of the most interesting points in all this to a Western mind is the difference implied and established between the caste of priests or chaplains on the one hand, and the fact of spiritual realisation, outside all caste, on the other. Nothing in the Indian thought about life can be more striking than this.

The family chaplain in Bengal may be the official teacher, but every man and woman discards his authority silently the instant they find some soul (in the world or out of it; it may be husband or child, or the holy man living in his garden; usually it is an ascetic), with a quickening spiritual touch upon their own. He or she then becomes the guru, or teacher, and this relationship is made the central fact of life.

The appearance of this new teacher, when he is powerful enough to be an important social phenomenon, is the historic origin of almost all new castes. The Sikh nation was formed in this way by a succession of gurus. Chaitanya welcomed all castes to Vaishnavism and made it possible for them to rise thereby. The scavengers, too low to venture to claim either Hinduism or Islamism as their own, were raised in consideration and self-respect by Guru Nanak and Lal Begi Mehtar—the last a saint of their own degree.

The preacher arises and proclaims the new idea. He gathers about him men of all classes: the educated won to the service of his thought, the ignorant swept in by the radiance of his personality. Amongst his disciples distinctions of caste break down. The whole group is stamped with his character and prestige. Eventually, if it contain a preponderance of Brahman elements, it may take rank with the best, carrying certain individuals up with it. But if it be composed chiefly of the scum of society, it will remain little considered; and yet, in the strength of its religious and intellectual significance may certainly claim to have progressed beyond its original point.

Such is likely to be the fate of the present Christian converts. Those who are recruited from the lowest pariahs may acquire a certain prestige from their new faith and take a better place in the social scale, consequently, in centuries to come. At the same time we must not forget that forty or fifty years ago, conversions were made that undoubtedly involved great sacrifices, and the descendants of these Christians may lose rather than gain in the long run.

Taking the history of Hinduism as a whole, we observe a great systole and diastole of caste, the Buddhist and the present Christian periods ranking as well-marked eras of fusion, while the intervening centuries are characterised by progressive definition, broken every now and then by a wave of reform which thought itself a movement towards caste abolition, but ended simply in the formation of a new group. For this is the fact in which all would-be reformations in India find at once their opportunity and their limit. It may now be taken as proved that in order to affect caste widely the agitator would need to aim deeper than the external phenomena, at underlying spiritual impulses.

If this theory of caste be valid, then, we find that the word signifies not so much mere rank in society as the standard of honour which is associated with rank. And as the private's conduct may be governed as much as his officer's by enlightened self-respect, we have seen that honour is something which applies to the whole of society equally. Even Tennyson, it will be remembered, pictures the country youth as outvaunting Lady Clara Vere de Vere in her pride of birth. The word caste, therefore, is by no means that antithesis of democracy which has been so commonly assumed.

Neither, amongst a people familiar with the process of self-organisation, would it prove any barrier to efficient cooperation. For the one essential to this power is an established habit of ignoring all points of mutual difference not germane to the matter in hand. What we call good-breeding, or what India calls caste, ought to make this easier. For any group of men met together for a common purpose find their individual rights secured to them in this way, and are free, by age-long acceptance, from any suspicion of another's desire to interfere with them. This is a basis of strength and not of weakness; so that it seems, if Indian men and women are not at present capable of combined action to any great degree, it is a matter of their own neglect of the habit, and not a necessary consequence of their institutions. We need not too readily accept the statement of such weakness, either, as infallible. My own observation has been that the Hindu people are capable enough of vigorous cooperation along the lines natural to them, those of the undivided family, the village community, and others. That inability which Europeans would show to face these tests, they may be expected to display before ours

To be absolutely just, however, we must admit that the observance of caste law has entailed many foolish and irritating losses upon society during the last fifty years. We have seen that there are definite reasons, not wanting in cogency, why a man of good birth should not eat in all companies, or of food cooked by hands supposed less cleanly. Such rules, however, cannot be kept by those who, for any reason, cross the seas to Europe. This fact, more than any other detail, makes it a matter of out-casting to take the journey and persecutions have sometimes ensued which are shocking to contemplate. A man may care little about the loss of station for his own sake, but the shoe pinches when he finds himself unable to make worthy marriages for his daughters; hence he will often submit to a heavy fine in order to buy back his position.

This rouses the cupidity of ignorant and conventional persons who happen to have authority with the stay-at-home community, and such are apt to be unscrupulous in bringing about the ruin or recantation of any who resist their power. This is a series of events which does occur occasionally; but it need not be supposed that every Europe-returning Hindu who is kept at arm's length is a martyr. There is an element of distrust for the moral results of a visit to the West in the situation; and this is not altogether unreasonable. It is chiefly with regard to possibilities of political, practical, or technical education that caste deterrence is to be regretted, and it is obvious that as communities progress in the power of estimating modern conditions, they must recognise the suicidal nature of such an attitude.

Yet it is curious to note here how caste may become thus a very real instrument of equality, for the power of the individual to advance is by this means kept strictly in ratio to the thinking of the society in which he lives. This fact is characteristic. The good of caste, of race, of family stands first and only second that of the individual man or woman in India. To take another plane. Let a man of the lower castes become wealthy, and he is compelled to educate men of his own rank to marry his daughters. Thus the group to which he owes birth, vigour, and development receives from him again the benefits of his life's work. This is the exact opposite of the European device, where the upper class absorbs money, talent, and beauty from the lower, while that is continually recruited by the failures from above. The fact that every human force is polar in its moral activity needs little demonstration in the case of social pride. Every day we see this working on the one hand for the highest idealism, on the other for revolting egotism. Social exclusiveness may be condoned, it may even robbed of its sting but, especially when coupled with personal exultation, it can never be made anything but vulgar-looking to the disinterested outsider. It is not to be supposed that Indian caste forms any exception to this rule of double effect. Nevertheless, it is well to understand the conditions of the sentiment, perceiving how inevitably this very thing repeats itself wherever two physically-distinguishable races are found side by side.

And it cannot be denied that great benefits as well as great evils have accrued from caste. It is an institution that makes Hindu society the most eclectic with regard to ideas in the world. In India all religions have taken refuge the Parsi before the tide of Muslim conquest; the Christians of Syria; the Jews. And they have received more than shelter—they have had the hospitality of a world that had nothing to fear from the foreigner who came in the name of freedom of conscience. Caste made this possible, for in one sense it is the social formulation of defence minus all elements of aggression. Again, surely it is something that in a country conquered for a thousand years the doorkeeper of a viceroy's palace would feel his race too good to share a cup of water with the ruler of all India. We do not easily measure the moral strength that is here involved, for the habit of guarding the treasure of his birth for an unborn posterity feeds a deep, undying faith in destiny in the Hindu heart. "Today here, tomorrow gone," says the most ignorant sotto voce as he looks at the foreigner, and the unspoken refrain of his thought is, "I and mine abide for ever." Caste is race-continuity; it is the historic sense; it is the dignity of tradition and of purpose for the future.

It is even more: it is the familiarity of a whole people in all its grades with the one supreme human motive—the notion of noblesse oblige. For though it is true that all men are influenced by this principle, it is also probably true that only the privileged are very conscious of the fact. Is caste, then, simply a burden, to be thrown off lightly, as a thing irksome and of little moment? And yet, if India is ever to regain national efficiency, this old device of the forefathers must be modified in the process,—exactly how, the Indian people themselves can alone determine. For India today has lost national efficiency. This fact there is no gainsaying. Her needs now are not what they were yesterday.

The Brahmans lose distinctiveness in these days of cheap printing and widespread literacy. But this only means that the country requires multiplied methods of self-expression as the goal and summit of her national endeavour. She wants a greater flexibility, perhaps, a readier power of self-adjustment than she has ever had. But it ought to come in an influx of consciousness of those great spiritual tides on whose surface all questions of caste and non-caste can be lifted into new and higher inter-relations. Chief among all her needs is that of a passionate drawing together amongst her people themselves. The cry of home, of country, of place is yet to be heard by the soul of every Indian man and woman in Hindustan and following hard upon it must sound the overtones of labour and of race.

□□□